THE MACARTHUR
NEW TESTAMENT
COMMENTARY

COLOSSIANS
& PHILEMON

John MacArthur Jr.

MOODY PRESS/CHICAGO

© 1992 by
THE MOODY BIBLE INSTITUTE
OF CHICAGO

Unless noted otherwise, all Scripture quotations in this book are from *The New American Standard Bible,* © 1960, 1962, 1963, 1968, 1971, 1972, 1973, 1975, and 1977 by The Lockman Foundation, and are used by permission.

ISBN: 0-8024-0761-7

3 5 7 9 10 8 6 4

Printed in the United States of America .

*To Clayton Erb, who stands beside me,
leading our congregation in glorious music and
worship, thus richly preparing their hearts
for the preaching of the Word.*

Contents

Preface

It continues to be a rewarding divine communion for me to preach expositionally through the New Testament. My goal is always to have deep fellowship with the Lord in the understanding of His Word, and out of that experience to explain to His people what a passage means. In the words of Nehemiah 8:8, I strive "to give the sense" of it so they may truly hear God speak and, in so doing, may respond to Him.

Obviously, God's people need to understand Him, which demands knowing His Word of truth (2 Tim. 2:15) and allowing that Word to dwell in us richly (Col. 3:16). The dominant thrust of my ministry, therefore, is to help make God's living Word alive to His people. It is a refreshing adventure.

This New Testament commentary series reflects this objective of explaining and applying Scripture. Some commentaries are primarily linguistic, others are mostly theological, and some are mainly homiletical. This one is basically explanatory, or expository. It is not linguistically technical, but deals with linguistics when this seems helpful to proper interpretation. It is not theologically expansive, but focuses on the major doctrines in each text and on how they relate to the whole of Scripture. It is not primarily homiletical, though each unit of thought is generally treated as one chapter, with a clear outline and logical flow of thought. Most truths are illustrated and applied with other Scripture. After establishing the context of a passage, I have tried to follow closely the writer's development and reasoning.

My prayer is that each reader will fully understand what the Holy Spirit is saying through this part of His Word, so that His revelation may lodge in the minds of believers and bring greater obedience and faithfulness—to the glory of our great God.

Introduction
to Colossians

From whatever angle one views our age, Colossians is up to date. Although written nearly 2,000 years ago, its timeless message speaks to the dilemmas facing us today. To the problems and crises of our age, it presents Jesus Christ as the answer.

Ours is an age of science. Ninety-five percent of all the scientists who have ever lived are alive today. The past century has seen a tremendous increase in knowledge in all areas of science and technology, from microbiology to astrophysics. Millions of pages of scientific and technological literature are published yearly. Even specialists find it difficult to keep up with the flood of discoveries in their fields.

The rapidly advancing pace of scientific discovery leads to the question of how God relates to the universe. Is He a part of the created universe, or its Creator? Did the universe evolve, or was it created? Colossians answers those questions. Colossians 1:16 says, "For by Him all things were created, both in the heavens and on earth, visible and invisible, whether thrones or dominions or rulers or authorities—all things have been created by Him and for Him."

This is also an age of ecumenism. Many people are seeking to unify the world's religions. Some seek a unity of political and social action, others a unity based on common experience. Efforts are being made to unite not only Protestants and Catholics, but also such diverse religions as Islam, Hinduism, and Buddhism. Such a religious amalgamation would be a body without a head. There can be no unity apart from truth.

Colossians gives us God's perspective on the push for a one-world church. It tells us there is but one true church, whose head is Christ: "He [Christ] is also head of the body, the church" (1:18). True unity can exist only among the members of Christ's Body.

Rebellion against all forms of authority also marks our age. Absolutes are denied. Truth, especially religious, is viewed as relative. All religious traditions are assumed to be of equal value. To claim that one religion is exclusively true is regarded as the height of intolerance and bigotry. In such a religious climate, Jesus becomes merely another wise man. He is nothing more than a great moral teacher, on a par with Moses, Muhammad, Confucius, and the Buddha.

Colossians gives us Jesus' true identity. Far from being just another religious leader, He is "the image of the invisible God, the firstborn of all creation" (1:15); the One in whom "all the fulness of Deity dwells in bodily form" (2:9). As God in human flesh, Jesus' word is authoritatively, absolutely, and exclusively true.

Ours is also an age of pragmatism. The question people ask about a religion or philosophy is not whether it is true, but if it works. They want to know if it will make a difference in their lives. People therefore ask pragmatic questions about Christianity. Can Christ really change lives? Can He give peace, joy, and happiness? Does knowing Christ give meaning, hope, and purpose to life? Colossians answers those questions:

•"He has now reconciled you in His fleshly body through death, in order to present you before Him holy and blameless and beyond reproach" (1:22). Christ makes sinners holy and blameless in God's sight. He changes lives.

•"As you therefore have received Christ Jesus the Lord, so walk in Him, having been firmly rooted and now being built up in Him and established in your faith, just as you were instructed, and overflowing with gratitude" (2:6-7). Knowing Christ gives stability to our lives, causing us to be thankful.

•"In Him you have been made complete" (2:10). Christ fulfills all our needs, so that we lack nothing.

•"For you have died and your life is hidden with Christ in God" (3:3). Knowing Christ so radically transforms us that our old life is dead.

This also is an age marked by frustrated relationships. People long for meaningful relationships, yet most find those longings unfulfilled. Many people do not know how to relate to their spouses, their children, or the people they work with.

Colossians speaks clearly to this issue. Chapters 3 and 4 tell us how husbands and wives, parents and children, and employers and employees can have positive relationships. To the lonely, alienated people of our day, Colossians brings a message of hope.

Finally, ours is an eschatological age. The threats of war and environmental disaster hang over our generation like twin swords of Damocles. People fear that the end of the world could be near. Books with such ominous titles as *The Biological Time Bomb, Future Shock, The Doomsday Book*, and *The Population Bomb* warn of impending doom.

Colossians has something to say about our destiny: "When Christ, who is our life, is revealed, then you also will be revealed with Him in glory" (3:4). The present age will not end in a nuclear or environmental disaster, but with the return of Christ in all His glory.

AUTHOR

From apostolic times until the rise of liberal higher criticism in the nineteenth century, the church accepted the Pauline authorship of Colossians. The arguments for rejecting the authenticity of Colossians are unconvincing. They cannot stand in the face of the internal and external testimony to Paul's authorship.

The external testimony to Colossians' authenticity is impressive. Such leaders of the early church as Eusebius, Origen, Clement of Alexandria, Tertullian, and Irenaeus all attest to its Pauline authorship. There is no evidence that anyone doubted Colossians' authenticity before the nineteenth century.

Further evidence that Paul wrote this epistle comes from its close ties to the epistle to Philemon. Both epistles mention Timothy's name in the greeting. Aristarchus, Mark, Epaphras, Luke, and Demas, Paul's other companions, also appear in both epistles. Both letters contain a message for Archippus. Onesimus, the slave who is the subject of Philemon, appears in Colossians. Both Colossians and Philemon find Paul in prison.

The evidence shows that Colossians and Philemon were written by the same author at about the same time. And since the Pauline authorship of Philemon is almost universally accepted, that provides powerful evidence that he wrote Colossians as well.

DATE AND PLACE OF WRITING

The two issues of the epistle's date and its place of writing are closely related. The date assigned for the writing depends on where Paul was imprisoned when he wrote Colossians. (Colossians, Philippians, Ephesians, and Philemon are known as the prison epistles.) Three possibilities have been suggested for the site of that imprisonment: Caesarea, Ephesus, and Rome.

That Paul was in prison in Caesarea was first proposed early in the nineteenth century. It fails to account for the facts of Paul's imprisonment as recorded in the prison epistles. In Colossians 4:2-4, he speaks of the opportunity he had to proclaim the gospel (cf. Eph. 6:18-20; Phil. 1:14-18). In Caesarea, however, Paul was kept under close guard (cf. Acts 23:35), and such opportunities would have been severely restricted. In Rome, Paul stayed for at least part of the time in his own rented house (Acts 28:30) and had the freedom to entertain visitors (Acts 28:23-31). He had hopes for a favorable verdict (Phil. 1:25; 2:24) that would have released him to visit Colossae (Philem. 22). But in Caesarea, Paul's only hope for release lay in either bribing Felix (Acts 24:26), or agreeing to Festus's request that he be tried in Jerusalem (Acts 25:9). Paul, of course, rejected both alternatives. In addition, Paul expected the decision in his case, whatever it was, to be final (Phil. 1:20-23; 2:17, 23). Since Paul, as a Roman citizen, had the option to appeal to Caesar, no final decision in his case could be made at Caesarea (or Ephesus). And Paul did in fact appeal to Caesar from Caesarea (Acts 25:11). Those considerations appear to rule out Caesarea as the place of the writing of the prison epistles.

A more popular alternative is that Paul was imprisoned in Ephesus, during his third missionary journey, when he wrote the prison epistles. That view, however, also faces serious difficulties. The most obvious problem is that Acts does not mention an imprisonment at Ephesus. Luke devotes one entire chapter (19) to an account of Paul's ministry at Ephesus. It is inconceivable that he would fail to mention it if Paul had been imprisoned. Whereas Luke was with Paul when Colossians was written (Col. 4:14), he does not appear to have been with him at Ephesus. Acts 19 is not in one of the "we" sections of Acts—those where Luke traveled with Paul. Finally Onesimus, the runaway slave led to Christ by Paul during his imprisonment, would more likely have fled to Rome than Ephesus. Rome was more than a thousand miles from his master at Colossae, whereas Ephesus was barely one hundred. Rome was also much larger than Ephesus, and it would have been easier for Onesimus to have lost himself in the crowds there. Rome was known as a haven for runaway slaves.

In light of the above, there is no convincing reason for rejecting the traditional view that Paul wrote the prison epistles from Rome.

THE CITY OF COLOSSAE

Colossae was located in the region of Phrygia, in the Roman province of Asia, in what is now part of Turkey. With nearby Laodicea and Hierapolis, it was part of a triad of cities in the Lycus Valley, about one hundred miles east of Ephesus. Colossae was located on the Lycus River, not far from its junction with the Maeander River. At Colossae the Lycus Valley narrowed to a width of about two miles, and Mount Cadmus, some eight thousand feet high, towered over the city.

Colossae was already a great city when the Persian king Xerxes (the Ahasuerus of the book of Esther) marched through it in 481 B.C. It was situated at the junction of the main trade routes running east from Ephesus and north to Pergamos. In Roman times, however, the road to Pergamos was rerouted through Laodicea, bypassing Colossae. That, coupled with the rise of Laodicea and Hierapolis, led to the decline in importance of Colossae. In Paul's day it was a small city, overshadowed by its more prosperous neighbors. Largely abandoned by the eighth century, Colossae was destroyed in the twelfth century. Archaeologists have found the remains of the acropolis, theater, and church. The site is currently unoccupied.

The area was prone to earthquakes. Colossae, Laodicea, and Hierapolis were devastated by one about A.D. 60, though they were quickly rebuilt. In its heyday, Colossae was an important center of the wool industry. Sheep grazed on the fertile pasture lands surrounding the town, and dyes were made from the nearby chalk deposits.

The population of Colossae was predominantly Gentile (cf. 2:13), but there was a sizeable Jewish community. Antiochus the Great (223-187 B.C.) transported Jewish settlers to the region. Other Jews were drawn by the trade in wool and other business ventures. Still others came for the mineral baths at nearby Hierapolis. Because Colossae had a mixed Gentile and Jewish population, it is not surprising that the heresy threatening the Colossian church contained Jewish and pagan elements.

THE CHURCH AT COLOSSAE

Luke tells us that during Paul's three-year stay in Ephesus on his third missionary journey, "all who lived in Asia heard the word of the Lord." It was at this time that the churches in Laodicea, Hierapolis, and

Colossae got their start. The man who founded them was not Paul, since he included the Laodiceans and Colossians among those who had never seen him in person (2:1). Nor does the book of Acts mention Paul's founding a church at Colossae, or even visiting there. The man God used to found the church at Colossae was Epaphras. In Colossians 1:5-7 we learn that the Colossians had heard the gospel from him. Epaphras was a native of Colossae (4:12) who was probably converted to Christ while visiting Ephesus during Paul's stay there. He then returned to his city and began the church.

THE COLOSSIAN HERESY

Despite the diligent labors of Epaphras, the Colossian church was in jeopardy. A serious heresy had arisen, and Epaphras was so concerned that he made the one thousand to thirteen hundred-mile trip to Rome to visit Paul in prison. The Colossian church had not yet been infected by that heresy, and Paul writes to warn them against its dangers. Colossians is thus a preventative letter.

As was previously mentioned, the city of Colossae included a mixture of Jews and Gentiles. It is not surprising, then, to learn that the heresy threatening them contained elements of paganism and Judaism.

The pagan culture in which the Colossian church existed worshiped many gods. Isis, Serapis, Helios, Demeter, and Artemis were among those worshiped in Colossae during Roman times. Many of the Colossian believers no doubt found the pull of the old way of life strong. The first danger facing the church was a relapse into paganism.

Paul warned them against that danger and exhorted them to continue in the faith: "If indeed you continue in the faith firmly established and steadfast, and not moved away from the hope of the gospel that you have heard" (1:23). "As you therefore have received Christ Jesus the Lord, so walk in Him" (2:6). "Set your mind on the things above, not on the things that are on earth" (3:2).

The world and the flesh exerted a strong pull on the Colossians. Yet an even greater threat came from Satan, the source of all false teaching. Therefore, the main thrust of Paul's letter is to counteract the influence of false doctrine.

Some have seen in the Colossian heresy elements of what in the second century became Gnosticism. Others have noted similarities with the teachings of the Essene sect of Judaism. The Colossian heresy, however, cannot be identified with any particular historical system. It contained two basic elements—false Greek philosophy, and Judaistic legalism and ceremonialism.

FALSE PHILOSOPHY

The Greeks loved knowledge and prided themselves on the sophistication of their philosophical systems. They scorned the gospel message as too simplistic (cf. 1 Cor. 1:22-23). To them Jesus Christ alone was not adequate; salvation involved Christ plus knowledge. They claimed visions they had supposedly seen as the basis for their superior knowledge (cf. 2:18). They believed those alleged visions gave them deeper insights than other people into the divine mysteries. Paul says of such mystics that their minds were inflated without cause (2:18). This claim to superior knowledge reached its full flowering in the second century in the dangerous heresy known as *Gnosticism.* The name comes from the Greek word for knowledge, *gnōsis.* Although the Colossian heresy was not Gnosticism, it included some similar concepts.

According to the Colossian heresy, God was good but matter was evil. Because the good God could not have created evil matter, they postulated a descending series of emanations from the divine being. It was one of the lesser emanations, far removed from God, that created matter.

In such a scheme, Jesus was simply one of the higher emanations. He was one of the good emanations, or angels, in contrast to the bad emanations, or demons. Those demons formed a barrier between man and God. Only through superior knowledge, coupled with help from the good emanations, could one break through. Thus, angels were objects of worship (2:18) because their help was essential for salvation.

The Colossian heretics denied the humanity of Christ. Since matter was viewed as evil, it was inconceivable that a good emanation could take up a human body. To combat that teaching, Paul stresses that Jesus did become a man: "He has now reconciled you in His fleshly body through death" (1:22).

The Colossian teaching also denied the deity of Christ. Since God, being good, was the very antithesis of evil matter, God could never become man. Yet speaking of Christ, Paul says, "In Him all the fulness of Deity dwells in bodily form" (2:9).

The Colossian heresy also denied the sufficiency of Christ for salvation. Paul attacks that false teaching repeatedly. He wrote of his desire to "present every man complete in Christ" (1:28). It is in Christ that "all the treasures of wisdom and knowledge are hidden" (2:3). "All the fulness of Deity dwells in Christ in bodily form" (2:9). Paul sums up Christ's sufficiency by stating that "in Him you have been made complete" (2:10).

Judaistic Legalism

The Colossian heretics also embraced elements of Jewish ceremonialism. They taught that circumcision was necessary for salvation. Like the doctrine that superior knowledge was necessary for salvation, such a teaching denied the sufficiency of Christ. It added works to salvation, which Paul rejected saying, "In [Christ] you were also circumcised with a circumcision made without hands, in the removal of the body of the flesh by the circumcision of Christ" (2:11; cf. 3:11).

The errorists also advocated asceticism, with its rigid self denial and harsh treatment of the body. Paul asks, "If you have died with Christ to the elementary principles of the world, why, as if you were living in the world, do you submit yourself to decrees, such as, 'Do not handle, do not taste, do not touch!' (which all refer to things destined to perish with the using)—in accordance with the commandments and teachings of men?" (2:20-22). He derided such teaching as "matters which have, to be sure, the appearance of wisdom in self-made religion and self-abasement and severe treatment of the body, but are of no value against fleshly indulgence" (2:23). Asceticism plays no part in salvation.

Still another aspect of the Colossian heresy was an emphasis on keeping the Jewish dietary laws and observing holy days, such as the Sabbath, festivals, and the new moon. Paul tells the Colossians not to be intimidated. Such ceremonialism was not necessary for salvation. "Therefore let no one act as your judge in regard to food or drink or in respect to a festival or a new moon or a Sabbath day" (2:16). Those things, Paul argues, were but a shadow of things to come. The reality is found in Christ (2:17).

The heresy threatening the Colossian church was thus a strange mixture of Greek philosophy and Jewish legalism. Although such a mixture seems highly unusual, there is a precedent. One of the major sects of first-century Judaism was the Essenes. Like the Colossian errorists, they were strict ascetics. They believed that matter was evil and spirit was good, thus sharing that incipient Gnostic trait with the Colossian errorists. They were rigid legalists, even surpassing the Pharisees in that regard. The Jewish historian Josephus, who was at one time a member of the Essenes, mentions their worship of angels. They were also strict vegetarians.

Although the evidence is not sufficient to equate the Colossian errorists with the Essenes, there are definite parallels. At least the existence of the Essenes demonstrates that a mixture of Greek philosophy and Jewish legalism like that of Colossae was possible. And inasmuch as both groups denied the sufficiency of Christ, the answer to both is the same: Christ *is* sufficient.

The Theme of Colossians

Although the Colossian heresy contained many diverse elements, at its core was a denial of the sufficiency of Christ for salvation. Not surprisingly, the sufficiency of Christ becomes the theme of Colossians. The errorists sought God; in Christ "the fulness of Deity was manifest" (2:9). They sought the superior knowledge necessary for salvation; in Christ are hidden "all the treasures of wisdom and knowledge" (2:3). They worshiped angels, thinking angelic beings could help them attain salvation; Paul wrote that believers are complete in Christ (2:10). They practiced asceticism, and observed Jewish holy days; those things are but the shadow, whereas the substance is Christ (2:17).

The theme of the book can be summed up in the words of Colossians 3:11: "Christ is all and in all." He is God (2:9); Creator (1:16); Savior (1:20; 2:13-14); and Head of the church (1:18). It was Paul's desire in writing Colossians that we would realize that Christ has "come to have first place in everything" (1:18).

Outline

I. Personal (1:1-14)
   A. Greetings (1:1-2)
   B. Thanksgiving (1:3-8)
   C. Prayer on behalf of the church (1:9-14)
II. Doctrinal (1:15–2:23)
   A. The Person and work of Christ (1:15-23)
   B. The ministry of Paul (1:24–2:7)
   C. The sufficiency of Christ versus worldly philosophies (2:8-23)
III. Practical (chaps. 3-4)
   A. Living the risen life (3:1-9)
   B. Putting on the new man (3:9-17)
   C. Managing the Christian household (3:18–4:1)
   D. Conducting one's speech (4:2-6)
   E. Imparting greetings and farewells (4:7-17)

The Gospel Truth

1

Paul, an apostle of Jesus Christ by the will of God, and Timothy our brother, to the saints and faithful brethren in Christ who are at Colossae: Grace to you and peace from God our Father. We give thanks to God, the Father of our Lord Jesus Christ, praying always for you, since we heard of your faith in Christ Jesus and the love which you have for all the saints; because of the hope laid up for you in heaven, of which you previously heard in the word of truth, the gospel, which has come to you, just as in all the world also it is constantly bearing fruit and increasing, even as it has been doing in you also since the day you heard of it and understood the grace of God in truth; just as you learned it from Epaphras, our beloved fellow bond-servant, who is a faithful servant of Christ on our behalf, and he also informed us of your love in the Spirit. (1:1-8)

Scripture describes the gospel with several phrases. Acts 20:24 calls it "the gospel of the grace of God." Romans 1:9 designates it "the gospel of His Son," and 1 Corinthians 9:12 "the gospel of Christ." Romans 15:16 refers to it as "the gospel of God," 2 Corinthians 4:4 characterizes it as "the gospel of the glory of Christ," Ephesians 6:15 as "the gospel of peace," and Revelation 14:6 as the "eternal gospel."

The gospel is also described as the "word of truth" (Col. 1:5), or the "message of truth" (Eph. 1:13). Those descriptions have given rise to our common expression "the gospel truth." People use that phrase when they want to stress their sincerity, so that what they say will be believed.

Although people often use that expression flippantly, there is a real gospel truth. **Gospel** (v. 5) is the Greek word *euangelion*, from which we derive the English word *evangelize.* It literally means, "good news." It was used often in classical Greek to speak of the report of victory brought back from a battle. The gospel is the good news of Jesus' victory over Satan, sin, and death. It is also the good news that we, too, can triumph eternally over those enemies through Him.

First Corinthians 15:1-4 succinctly summarizes the historical content of the gospel: "Now I make known to you, brethren, the gospel which I preached to you, which also you received, in which also you stand, by which also you are saved, if you hold fast the word which I preached to you, unless you believed in vain. For I delivered to you as of first importance what I also received, that Christ died for our sins according to the Scriptures, and that He was buried, and that He was raised on the third day according to the Scriptures." The gospel is the good news that Jesus Christ died to provide complete forgiveness of sins and rose again that those who believe might live forever.

Such glorious, thrilling truth compels Christians to respond in several basic ways, all of which are noted by descriptive phrases using *gospel.* First, we should proclaim the good news, following the example of Jesus (Matt. 4:23), the apostles, prophets, evangelists, teachers, and believers of all ages.

Second, we are to defend its veracity. Paul described himself as one "appointed for the defense of the gospel" (Phil. 1:16). Peter told his readers to "make a defense to everyone who asks you to give an account for the hope that is in you" (1 Pet. 3:15).

Third, we are to work hard for the advance of the gospel. Paul admonishes the Philippians to "[strive] together for the faith of the gospel" (Phil. 1:27). The gospel demands of us discipline and strenuous effort.

Fourth, we are to pursue the fellowship we share with others who have believed the gospel. Devotion to the fellowship of the gospel characterized the early church (Acts 2:42). Paul often expressed his gratitude for those who had received the gospel (cf. Phil. 1:3-5).

Fifth, we must be ready to suffer for the sake of the gospel. Paul exhorted Timothy, "Do not be ashamed of the testimony of our Lord, or of me His prisoner; but join with me in suffering for the gospel" (2 Tim. 1:8).

Sixth, we are to make sure that our lives do not hinder the gospel. Paul told the Corinthians that he would waive his right to be paid for his ministry rather than cheapen the message of the gospel (1 Cor. 9:12).

Seventh, we must never be ashamed of the gospel. Paul said, "For I am not ashamed of the gospel, for it is the power of God for salvation to everyone who believes, to the Jew first and also to the Greek" (Rom. 1:16).

Finally, we are to realize the gospel carries with it divine empowerment. Paul wrote to the Thessalonians, "Our gospel did not come to you in word only, but also in power and in the Holy Spirit" (1 Thess. 1:5). The power of the gospel does not come from our cleverness or persuasiveness, but from the Holy Spirit.

This wonderful gospel is the reason for Paul's thanksgiving expressed in Colossians 1:3-8. Rejoicing at the report of their faith brought to him by Epaphras, the founder of the church at Colossae, he characteristically expresses thanks that the Colossians heard the gospel, and that it bore fruit in their lives.

Following the salutation in verses 1 and 2, Paul's words in verses 3-8 suggest seven aspects of the gospel: it is received by faith, results in love, rests in hope, reaches the world, reproduces fruit, is rooted in grace, and is reported by people. Before considering those aspects, let's take a brief look at the familiar terms of Paul's opening greeting that we find in his other epistles.

The Salutation

Paul, an apostle of Jesus Christ by the will of God, and Timothy our brother, to the saints and faithful brethren in Christ who are at Colossae: Grace to you and peace from God our Father. (1:1-2)

Following the practice of correspondence in the ancient world, Paul begins the letter with his name. Paul was the most important and influential person in history since our Lord Jesus Christ. His personality was the remarkable combination of a brilliant mind, an indomitable will, and a tender heart. Of Jewish ancestry, a "Hebrew of Hebrews" (Phil. 3:5), he was a Pharisee (Phil. 3:5). Paul was educated under Gamaliel (Acts 22:3), one of the leading rabbis of that time. He was also by birth a Roman citizen (Acts 22:28) and exposed to Greek culture in his home city of Tarsus. Such a background rendered him uniquely qualified to communicate the gospel in the Greco-Roman world. It was largely his efforts that transformed Christianity from a small Palestinian sect to a religion with adherents throughout the Roman Empire. The church would be blessed to have record of even one letter from such a man, let alone the thirteen found in the New Testament.

Lest anyone doubt his authority, Paul describes himself as **an apostle of Jesus Christ.** He is not simply a messenger, but an official representative of the One who sent him. What he writes in this letter is not merely his opinion, but God's authoritative Word.

Nor did he become an apostle through his own efforts. Neither was he nominated for the position by any human organization. Paul was an apostle **by the will of God.** God, having chosen him long before, brought His sovereign choice to realization with that most striking of conversions on the Damascus Road (Acts 9:1-9). It climaxed in his being set apart for missionary service by the Holy Spirit (Acts 13:2).

Paul, as was his custom, mentions a colaborer who was with him when he wrote: **Timothy our brother.** (Timothy is also included in the introductions to 2 Corinthians, Philippians, 1 and 2 Thessalonians, and Philemon, being noted as the companion of Paul.) Such a reference does not indicate coauthorship of those epistles. Peter is certainly clear that the epistles bearing Paul's name were written by Paul (2 Pet. 3:15-16).

Paul had a unique and special confidence in and love for Timothy. Timothy had ministered to him for many years, ever since they first met on Paul's second missionary journey (Acts 19:22). Although Paul was now a prisoner, faithful Timothy was still with him. Perhaps no passage expresses Paul's feelings about his young friend more clearly than Philippians 2:19-22: "I hope in the Lord Jesus to send Timothy to you shortly, so that I also may be encouraged when I learn of your condition. For I have no one else of kindred spirit who will genuinely be concerned for your welfare. For they all seek after their own interests, not those of Christ Jesus. But you know of his proven worth that he served with me in the furtherance of the gospel like a child serving his father."

Despite his many strengths, Timothy had a delicate constitution and was frequently sick (1 Tim. 5:23). He even had an experience in Ephesus when he was timid, hesitant, perhaps ashamed and disloyal to his gift and duty, and was in need of encouragement and strength (cf. 2 Tim. 1:5-14). Still, no one served Paul as faithfully in the spread of the gospel (Phil. 2:22). He was Paul's true child in the faith (1 Cor. 4:17). It was to Timothy that Paul wrote his final letter (2 Timothy) and passed the mantle of leadership (2 Tim. 4).

Paul addresses his readers as the **saints and faithful brethren . . . who are at Colossae. Saints and faithful brethren** are not two distinct groups; the terms are equivalent. **And** [*kai*] could be translated, "even." *Hagios*, which translates **saints**, refers to separation, in this case being separated from sin and set apart to God. **Faithful** notes the very source of that separation—saving faith. Believing saints are the only true saints. **Grace to you and peace** was the greeting Paul used to open all thirteen of his letters. Inasmuch as God is the source of both, Paul says those two blessings derive from our great God and Father.

THE GOSPEL TRUTH IS RECEIVED BY FAITH

We give thanks to God, the Father of our Lord Jesus Christ, praying always for you, since we heard of your faith in Christ Jesus (1:3-4a)

Though he admires their true and continuing saving faith, which had separated them from sin to God, Paul certainly does not begin by flattering the Colossians. He gives **thanks to God, the Father of our Lord Jesus Christ.** Paul recognizes that God is the One who is owed thanks, because salvation in all its parts is a gift from Him (Eph. 2:8-9). **Always** should be considered in relation to the preceding phrase, **we give thanks to God,** not to **praying . . . for you.** Paul was not always praying for the Colossians. Rather, whenever he was praying for them, he always expressed his thanks to God.

Paul is thankful to God for their faith in Christ Jesus. The Colossians are not like those who distort the gospel (Gal. 1:7), or do not obey it (1 Pet. 4:17). Such people will face the terrifying experience of seeing "the Lord Jesus . . . revealed from heaven with His mighty angels in flaming fire, dealing out retribution to those who do not know God and to those who do not obey the gospel of our Lord Jesus. And these will pay the penalty of eternal destruction, away from the presence of the Lord and from the glory of His power" (2 Thess. 1:7-9). The Colossians are holy brothers in Christ, who have put faith in the Lord of the gospel.

FAITH'S DEFINITION

Pistis (**faith**) means to be persuaded that something is true and to trust in it. Far more than mere intellectual assent, it involves obedience. *Pistis* comes from the root word *peithō* ("obey"). The concept of obedience is equated with belief throughout the New Testament (cf. John 3:36; Acts 6:7; Rom. 15:18; 2 Thess. 1:8; Heb. 5:9; 1 Pet. 4:17). The Bible also speaks of the obedience of faith (Acts 6:7; Rom. 1:5; 16:26).

Biblical faith is not a "leap in the dark." It is based on fact and grounded in evidence. It is defined in Hebrews 11:1 as "the assurance of things hoped for, the conviction of things not seen." Faith gives assurance and certainty about unseen realities.

I often have occasion to drive on roads I have never driven on before. I do not know what is around the next bend; the road could end at a cliff with a 500-foot drop. Nor do I know personally the people who built the road. However, I know enough about how highways are built to have confidence in the road. Likewise, I sometimes will eat at a restaurant I have never been to before. I trust the food is all right because I have confidence in the inspection and preparation procedures.

We trust that highways and restaurants are safe based on the evidence. And that is precisely the case with our faith in God. It is supported by convincing evidence, both from Scripture and from the testimony of those Christians who have gone before us.

Saving faith is carefully defined in Scripture and needs to be understood because there is a dead, non-saving faith that provides false security (James 2:14-26). True saving faith contains repentance and obedience as its elements.

Repentance is an initial element of saving faith, but it cannot be dismissed as simply another word for believing. The Greek word for "repentance" is *metanoia*, from *meta*, "after," and *noeō*, "to understand." Literally it means "afterthought" or "change of mind," but biblically its meaning does not stop there. As *metanoia* is used in the New Testament, it always speaks of a change of purpose, and specifically a turning from sin. More specifically, repentance calls for a repudiation of the old life and a turning to God for salvation (1 Thess. 1:9). The repentance in saving faith involves three elements: a turning to God, a turning from evil, and an intent to serve God. No change of mind can be called true repentance without all three. Repentance is not merely being ashamed or sorry over sin, although genuine repentance always involves an element of remorse. It is a redirection of the human will, a purposeful decision to forsake all unrighteousness and pursue righteousness instead. And God has to grant it (Acts 11:18; 2 Tim. 2:25). In fact, God grants the whole of saving faith: "By grace you have been saved through *faith*; and that not of yourselves, it *is the gift of God*; not as a result of works, that no one should boast" (Eph. 2:8-9, italics added; cf. Phil. 1:29).

Although it is true that "he who believes has eternal life" (John 6:47), Jesus also said, "No one can come to Me unless the Father who sent Me draws him" (John 6:44). God effectually calls sinners to Christ and grants them the capability to exercise saving faith (cf. Matt. 16:17).

The faith that God grants is permanent. In all who receive it, faith will endure. Such passages as Habakkuk 2:4, Romans 1:17, Galatians 3:11, Philippians 1:6, and Hebrews 10:38 teach that genuine saving faith can never vanish.

Like repentance, obedience is also encompassed within the bounds of saving faith. The faith that saves involves more than mere intellectual assent and emotional conviction. It also includes the resolution of the will to obey God's commands and laws.

Obedience is the hallmark of the true believer. "When a man obeys God he gives the only possible evidence that in his heart he believes God" (W. E. Vine, *An Expository Dictionary of New Testament Words*, [Old Tappan, N.J.: Revell, 1966], 3:124). Such obedience will of necessity be incomplete, since the flesh ever rears its ugly head (cf. Rom. 7:14-25). If not the perfection of the believer's life, however, it most certainly will be the direction.

Faith, then, must never be severed from good works. Martin Luther summed up the biblical view of the link between saving faith and good works in these words: "Good works do not make a man good, but a good man does good works" (cited in Tim Dowley, ed., *Eerdmans Handbook to the History of Christianity* [Grand Rapids: Eerdmans, 1987], p. 362).

FAITH'S OBJECT

Any definition of faith is also incomplete without a consideration of its object. In contrast to the contentless faith so prevalent in our culture, saving faith has as its object Christ Jesus. The relationship of faith to Jesus Christ is expressed in the New Testament by various Greek prepositions. Acts 16:31 uses the preposition *epi*, which suggests resting on a foundation. In Acts 20:21, *eis* is used, with the meaning of "to find a dwelling place in," "to go into," "to abide in," or "to find a home." Here **in** translates *en* and has the connotation of coming to a place of security and anchor. With Christ as its object, our faith is as secure as a house on a solid foundation, or a boat safely at anchor.

Charles Spurgeon illustrated the importance of faith's object by telling of two men in a boat. Caught in severe rapids, they were being swept toward a waterfall. Some men on shore tried to save them by throwing them a rope. One man caught hold of it and was pulled to safety on the shore. The other, in the panic of the moment, grabbed hold of a seemingly more substantial log that was floating by. That man was carried downstream, over the rapids, and was never seen again. Faith, represented by the rope linked to the shore, connects us to Jesus Christ and safety. Good works apart from true faith, represented in the story by the log, leads only to ruin.

THE GOSPEL TRUTH RESULTS IN LOVE

and the love which you have for all the saints; (1:4b)

Genuine faith does not exist in a vacuum but will inevitably result in a changed life. One of the visible and strong fruits of true saving faith is love for fellow believers (cf. John 13:34-35). The apostle John emphasizes that truth repeatedly in his first epistle:

> The one who says he is in the light and yet hates his brother is in the darkness until now. The one who loves his brother abides in the light and there is no cause for stumbling in him. But the one who hates his brother is in the darkness and walks in the darkness, and does not know where he is going because the darkness has blinded his eyes. (2:9-11)

> By this the children of God and the children of the devil are obvious: anyone who does not practice righteousness is not of God, nor the one who does not love his brother. (3:10)

> We know that we have passed out of death into life, because we love the brethren. He who does not love abides in death. Everyone who hates his brother is a murderer; and you know that no murderer has eternal life abiding in him. (3:14-15)

> If someone says, "I love God," and hates his brother, he is a liar; for the one who does not love his brother whom he has seen, cannot love God whom he has not seen. (4:20)

A true child of God will love fellow believers. Faith in Christ purges us of our selfishness and affinity for sinners and gives us a new attraction to the people of God. Our love for fellow Christians is a reflection of His love for us. It is also obedience to His command to "love one another, even as I have loved you" (John 13:34).

Paul gives thanks that the Colossians love all the saints. Their love was nonselective. Apparently there were no divisive cliques at Colossae, such as those that fractured the Corinthian church. Christ's love not only drew the Colossians to Himself, but also to each other.

That does not mean we are to feel the same emotional attachment toward everyone. True biblical love is so much more than an emotion; it is sacrificial service to others because they have need. We show godly love to someone when we sacrifice ourselves to meet that person's needs.

True godly love is illustrated in John 13. Verse 1 tells us that Jesus "having loved His own who were in the world, He loved them to the end." He then showed what that love meant by washing the disciples' feet (vv. 4-5). God does not expect us to feel sentimental toward each other all the time. He does expect us to serve one another (Gal. 5:13).

There are two sides to the Christian life, both of which are crucial: faith and love. Genuine belief in the truth and experiential love for other believers characterizes every true believer. We are saved by faith; we are saved to love. True saving faith is more than a conviction of the mind. It transforms the heart to love.

THE GOSPEL TRUTH RESTS IN HOPE

because of the hope laid up for you in heaven, of which you previously heard in the word of truth, the gospel, (1:5)

Hope is one component of the great triad of Christian virtues, along with faith and love. "But now abide faith, hope, love, these three; but the greatest of these is love" (1 Cor. 13:13; cf. 1 Thess. 1:3; 5:8). Paul is thankful not only for the Colossians' faith and love, but also for their hope. Faith and hope are inseparably linked. We believe, and so we hope.

Paul describes that hope as laid up for you in heaven. *Apokeimai* (**laid up**) means "in store," or "reserved." Peter speaks of "an inheritance which is imperishable and undefiled and will not fade away, reserved in heaven for you" (1 Pet. 1:4). The writer of Hebrews speaks of "laying hold of the hope set before us. This hope we have as an anchor of the soul, a hope both sure and steadfast and one which enters within the veil" (Heb. 6:18-19). Hope is the Christian's anchor chain, connecting him inseparably to God's throne.

God established our hope by making us His sons. The Colossians became sons of God by believing the message they previously heard in the word of truth, the gospel. First John 3:1 says, "See how great a love the Father has bestowed upon us, that we should be called children of God." He will fulfill our hope by making us like His Son: "Beloved, now we are children of God, and it has not appeared as yet what we shall be. We know that, when He appears, we shall be like Him, because we shall see Him just as He is" (v. 2).

One result of our hope is a willingness to sacrifice the present on the altar of the future. That runs contrary to human nature. Young children, for example, have a difficult time waiting for something they want. My father warned me repeatedly while I was growing up not to sacrifice the future on the altar of the immediate. The world wants what it wants now.

The Christian has a different perspective. He is willing to forsake the present glory, comfort, and satisfaction of this present world for the future glory that is his in Christ. In contrast to the "buy now—pay later" attitude prevalent in the world, the Christian is willing to pay now and receive it later. What makes Christians willing to make such sacrifices? Hope, based on faith that the future holds something far better than the present. Paul writes in Romans 8:18, "I consider that the sufferings of this present time are not worthy to be compared with the glory that is to be revealed to us."

Moses serves as an example of one who willingly sacrificed the present because of the promise of his future hope. Hebrews 11:24-27 gives us his story: "By faith Moses, when he had grown up, refused to be called the son of Pharaoh's daughter; choosing rather to endure ill-treatment with the people of God, than to enjoy the passing pleasures of sin; considering the reproach of Christ greater riches than the treasures of Egypt; for he was looking to the reward. By faith he left Egypt, not fearing the wrath of the king; for he endured, as seeing Him who is unseen."

As the adopted son of Pharaoh's daughter, Moses had access to all the wealth and power of Pharaoh's court. Yet, he turned his back on it and identified with God's suffering, poor, humbled people. Moses refused to seize the moment and enjoy the temporal pleasures of sin. He sacrificed his present prospects for a future hope. He took his stand with the oppressed Israelites, an act that led to his killing an Egyptian overseer and eventual flight from Egypt. He forfeited earthly power and glory and instead wound up herding sheep in the desert for his father-in-law to be, Jethro.

What made Moses willing to make such sacrifices? "He was looking to the reward" (Heb. 11:26). Why was he willing to turn his back on the riches and power that were his in Egypt? "He endured, as seeing Him who is unseen" (Heb. 11:27). Moses knew that though he suffered loss in the present, God would richly reward him in the future.

Like Moses, believers look for a hope that is in heaven. We live in the light of eternity, knowing that our citizenship is in heaven (Phil. 3:20). We serve the Lord, making sacrifices here to lay up treasure in heaven. Like Paul, we set aside our prerogatives, obeying God's will and disciplining ourselves to win an incorruptible crown (cf. 2 Tim. 4:8). Like Jim Elliot, missionary and martyr to the Auca Indians, we must realize that "he is no fool who gives what he cannot keep to gain what he cannot lose" (cited in Elisabeth Elliot, *Shadow of the Almighty* [San Francisco: Harper & Row, 1979], p. 108).

THE GOSPEL TRUTH REACHES THE WORLD

which has come to you, just as in all the world (1:6*a*)

The gospel is also universal; it **has come to you, just as in all the world.** Christianity was not just another of the local sects of the Roman Empire. It was not merely one more cult like the others at Colossae. It was and is the good news for the whole world. The gospel transcends ethnic, geographic, cultural, and political boundaries.

This universality of the gospel is repeatedly emphasized in Scripture:

> And this gospel of the kingdom shall be preached in the whole world for a witness to all the nations, and then the end shall come. (Matt. 24:14)

> Again therefore Jesus spoke to them, saying, "I am the light of the world; he who follows Me shall not walk in the darkness, but shall have the light of life." (John 8:12)

> First, I thank my God through Jesus Christ for you all, because your faith is being proclaimed throughout the whole world. . . . For I am not ashamed of the gospel, for it is the power of God for salvation to everyone who believes, to the Jew first and also to the Greek. (Rom. 1:8, 16)

> But I say, surely they have never heard, have they? Indeed they have; "Their voice has gone out into all the earth, and their words to the ends of the world." (Rom. 10:18)

> For the word of the Lord has sounded forth from you, not only in Macedonia and Achaia, but also in every place your faith toward God has gone forth, so that we have no need to say anything. (1 Thess. 1:8)

> After these things I looked, and behold, a great multitude, which no one could count, from every nation and all tribes and peoples and tongues, standing before the throne and before the Lamb, clothed in white robes, and palm branches were in their hands; and they cry out with a loud voice, saying, "Salvation to our God who sits on the throne, and to the Lamb." (Rev. 7:9-10)

The diffusion of the gospel throughout the Roman Empire foreshadowed its spread throughout the world. It is a message of hope for all people in all cultures. The true church, the Body of Christ, is made up of people from all over the world (cf. Rev. 4:9-11).

THE GOSPEL TRUTH REPRODUCES FRUIT

it is constantly bearing fruit and increasing, even as it has been doing in you also since the day you heard of it (1:6*b*)

The gospel is not merely a stagnant system of ethics; it is a living, moving, and growing reality. It bears fruit and spreads. Hebrews 4:12 says, "The word of God is living and active." When the gospel enters a divinely prepared heart, it results in fruit (Matt. 13:3-8). It possesses a divine energy that causes it to spread like a mustard seed growing into a tree (Matt. 13:31-32). Peter says it brings spiritual growth (1 Pet. 2:2).

The gospel has both an individual and a universal aspect. It is both bearing fruit and increasing. Paul tells the Colossians he is thankful the gospel had done both among them **since the day you** [the Colossians] **heard of it.** He is grateful they believed the gospel message when Epaphras shared it with them.

The gospel produces fruit both in the internal transformation of individuals, and also in the external growth of the church. The two concepts are interrelated. The spiritual growth of individuals will lead to new converts being won to Christ. That was the pattern of the early church. Acts 9:31 tells us that "the church throughout all Judea and Galilee and Samaria enjoyed peace, being built up . . . going on in the fear of the Lord and in the comfort of the Holy Spirit," and as a result, "it continued to increase." First Thessalonians 1:6 speaks of the spiritual growth of the Thessalonians as they imitated Paul and the Lord. As a result, "the word of the Lord has sounded forth from you, not only in Macedonia and Achaia, but also in every place your faith toward God has gone forth, so that we have no need to say anything" (v. 8).

The living gospel is the power that transforms lives. As it does so, the witness of those transformed lives produces fruit, including new converts. So as the gospel produces fruit in individual lives, its influence spreads.

THE GOSPEL TRUTH IS ROOTED IN GRACE

and understood the grace of God in truth. (1:6*c*)

Grace is the very heart of the gospel. It is God's freely giving us the forgiveness of sin and eternal life, which we do not deserve and cannot earn. Christianity contrasts sharply with other religions, which assume man can save himself by his good works. Nothing is more clearly taught in Scripture than the truth that "by grace you have been saved through faith; and that not of yourselves, it is the gift of God; not as a result of works, that no one should boast" (Eph. 2:8-9).

After hearing Peter's account of the conversion of Cornelius, the rest of the apostles exclaimed, "Well then, God has granted to the Gentiles also the repentance that leads to life" (Acts 11:18). Lydia was saved after "the Lord opened her heart to respond to the things spoken by Paul" (Acts 16:14). Paul told the Thessalonians he was thankful "because God has chosen [them] from the beginning for salvation through sanctification by the Spirit and faith in the truth" (2 Thess. 2:13). He wrote to Titus that "the grace of God has appeared, bringing salvation to all men, instructing us to deny ungodliness and worldly desires and to live sensibly, righteously and godly in the present age" (Titus 2:11-12). Salvation is a gracious act on God's part (see also Acts 15:11; 18:27; Rom. 3:24; 4:1-8).

Paul describes saving grace as **the grace of God in truth.** The phrase **in truth** carries the sense of genuineness. It is truly **the grace of God** in contrast to all other claimants to the true gospel. God is freely, sovereignly merciful and forgiving. We can do nothing to cause our own salvation; God saves us freely by His grace. The hymn "Jesus Paid It All" expresses that thought in these familiar words:

> For nothing good have I
> Whereby Thy grace to claim.
> I'll wash my garments white
> In the blood of Calv'ry's Lamb.
>
> Jesus paid it all,
> All to Him I owe;
> Sin had left a crimson stain
> He washed it white as snow.

THE GOSPEL TRUTH IS REPORTED BY PEOPLE

just as you learned it from Epaphras, our beloved fellow bond-servant, who is a faithful servant of Christ on our behalf, and he also informed us of your love in the Spirit. (1:7-8)

Although salvation is solely by God's grace, He uses humans as channels of that grace. Jesus told the disciples in Acts 1:8 that they, in the power of the Holy Spirit, were to be His witnesses. First Corinthians 1:21 speaks of those who believed through hearing the message preached. But perhaps no passage states this truth as forcefully as Romans 10:14: "How then shall they call upon Him in whom they have not believed? And how shall they believe in Him whom they have not heard? And how shall they hear without a preacher?"

As noted in the introduction, Epaphras brought the good news of God's grace to the Colossian church. They learned it from him. Paul often referred to himself as a *doulos* (**bond-servant**) of Christ (Rom. 1:1; Phil. 1:1; Gal. 1:10; Titus 1:1). By referring to Epaphras as his **fellow bond-servant** (*sundoulos*), and calling him a faithful servant of Christ on our behalf, Paul connects Epaphras's ministry with his own. Epaphras was Paul's representative at Colossae, backed by his authority and that of the Lord Jesus. While Paul was imprisoned, unable to go to the Colossians, Epaphras ministered to them on Paul's behalf. He also informed Paul of the Colossians' **love in the Spirit**, a report that no doubt brought great joy to Paul's heart. Paul was thankful for the gospel, and for the Colossians' reception of it.

God gives us the wonderful privilege and sobering responsibility of being His agents in proclaiming the gospel of His grace. May we be faithful to share with others the gospel that has meant so much to us.

Paul Prays for the Colossians —part 1

2

For this reason also, since the day we heard of it, we have not ceased to pray for you and to ask that you may be filled with the knowledge of His will in all spiritual wisdom and understanding, so that you may walk in a manner worthy of the Lord, to please Him in all respects, bearing fruit in every good work and increasing in the knowledge of God; strengthened with all power, according to His glorious might, for the attaining of all steadfastness and patience; (1:9-11)

Even without the benefit of sophisticated scientific equipment or technology, every Christian can minister directly to the spiritual well-being of other believers without seeing or speaking to them. We can play a role in their spiritual growth, and even secure God's blessings for them. The amazing means is prayer.

The ministry of an apostle consisted primarily of teaching the Word and prayer (Acts 6:4). While Paul obviously gives rich instruction to the Colossians, he also shares something of his prayers for them. Verses 9-14 are a sample of Paul's ministry of prayer on their behalf. His passionate words contain two elements: petition (vv. 9-11), and praise (vv. 12-14).

Paul acknowledged the important role the prayers of others played in his ministry: "You also joining in helping us through your prayers, that thanks may be given by many persons on our behalf for the favor bestowed upon us through the prayers of many" (2 Cor. 1:11); "I know that this shall turn out for my deliverance through your prayers and the provision of the Spirit of Jesus Christ" (Phil. 1:19); "prepare me a lodging; for I hope that through your prayers I shall be given to you" (Philem. 22).

It is no surprise, then, that the New Testament exhorts us to pray for one another. We read in Ephesians 6:18, "With all prayer and petition pray at all times in the Spirit, and with this in view, be on the alert with all perseverance and petition for all the saints." Paul writes in 1 Timothy 2:1, "I urge that entreaties and prayers, petitions and thanksgivings, be made on behalf of all men." The writer of Hebrews asked of his readers, "Pray for us, for we are sure that we have a good conscience, desiring to conduct ourselves honorably in all things" (13:18).

The Bible is replete with examples of God's people praying for each other:

- Job prayed for his friends (Job 42:10).
- Moses prayed for Aaron (Deut. 9:20) and Miriam (Num. 12:13).
- Samuel prayed for Israel (1 Sam. 7:5, 9).
- David prayed for Israel (2 Sam. 24:17) and Solomon (1 Chron. 29:18-19).
- Hezekiah prayed for Judah (2 Kings 19:14-19).
- Isaiah prayed for the people of God (Isa. 63:15–64:12).
- Daniel prayed for Israel (Dan. 9:3-19).
- Ezekiel prayed for Israel (Ezek. 9:8).
- Nehemiah prayed for Judah (Neh. 1:4-11).
- Jesus prayed for His disciples (John 17:9-24).
- The Jerusalem church prayed for Peter's release from prison (Acts 12:5).
- Paul prayed for Christians (e.g., Rom. 1:9-10; Eph. 1:16-19).
- Epaphras prayed for the Colossians (Col. 4:12).

Because prayer is so important, Paul starts his letter by sharing the nature of his prayers for the Colossians before he begins to teach them. Two elements compose the content of his prayer: petition (vv. 9-11) and praise (vv. 12-14).

The Petition

For this reason also, since the day we heard of it, we have not ceased to pray for you and to ask that you may be filled with the knowledge of His will in all spiritual wisdom and understanding, (1:9)

For this reason refers to the favorable report Paul had received from Epaphras (v. 8). Since the day Paul heard that report, he had been praying for the Colossians. It may seem unnecessary to pray for those who are doing well. Much of our prayer time focuses on those who are struggling, facing difficulties, or fallen into sin or physical distress. Paul, however, knew that the knowledge that others are progressing in the faith should never lead us to stop praying for them. Rather, it should encourage prayer for their greater progress. The enemy may reserve his strongest opposition for those who have the most potential for expanding God's cause in the world.

Such unceasing or recurring prayer (1 Thess. 5:17) demands first of all an attitude of God-consciousness. That does not mean to be constantly in the act of verbal prayer, but to view everything in life in relation to God. For example, if we meet someone, we immediately consider where they stand with God. If we hear of something bad happening, we react by praying for God to act in the situation because we know He cares. If we hear of something good that has happened, we respond with immediate praise to God for it because we know He is glorified. When Paul looked around his world, everything he saw prompted him to prayer in some way. When he thought of or heard about one of his beloved churches, it moved him toward communion with God.

Nehemiah is an example of one who prayed without ceasing. After King Artaxerxes demanded the reason for his sadness, Nehemiah told him of the destruction of Jerusalem. Asked by the king for his request, he prayed a quick, brief prayer before replying (Neh. 2:4). In the midst of a stressful situation, Nehemiah was conscious of God's character and purposes.

A second aspect of unceasing prayer is people-consciousness. We cannot effectively pray for people unless we are aware of their needs. Paul exhorted the Colossians to keep alert in prayer (4:2), while to the Ephesians he wrote, "With all prayer and petition pray at all times in the Spirit, and with this in view, be on the alert with all perseverance and petition for all the saints" (Eph. 6:18).

The two elements of praying without ceasing came together in Paul's prayer life. His love for God led him to seek unbroken communion with Him. His love for people drove him to unceasing prayer on their behalf. The prayers of Paul recorded in his letters are a precious legacy. They reveal his heart and are models for us to emulate. This text records the first of those prayers.

Paul's petition is that the Colossians **be filled with the knowledge of His will.** *Plēroō* (**filled**) means to be completely filled, or totally controlled. The disciples' hearts were filled with sorrow when Jesus told them of His departure (John 16:6). Luke 5:26 tells us the crowd was filled with fear after Jesus healed the paralytic. The scribes and Pharisees were filled with rage after Jesus healed on the Sabbath (Luke 6:11). The disciples were filled with the Holy Spirit (Acts 4:31), while Stephen was full of faith (Acts 6:5). In each case they were totally under the control of what filled them.

Paul wants the Colossians to be totally controlled by **knowledge.** *Epignōsis* (**knowledge**) consists of the normal Greek word for *knowledge* (*gnōsis*) with an added preposition (*epi*), which intensifies the meaning. The knowledge Paul wants the Colossians to have is a deep and thorough knowledge.

Knowledge is a central theme in Paul's writings. He said of the Corinthians, "In everything you were enriched in Him, in all speech and all knowledge" (1 Cor. 1:5). He prayed that "the God of our Lord Jesus Christ, the Father of glory" would give the Ephesians "a spirit of wisdom and of revelation in the knowledge of Him" (Eph. 1:17). To the Philippians he wrote, "This I pray, that your love may abound still more and more in real knowledge and all discernment" (Phil. 1:9). In Colossians 2:3 we learn that all the treasures of wisdom and knowledge are hidden in Christ. Our new self "is being renewed to a true knowledge" (Col. 3:10). As those verses indicate, true biblical knowledge is not speculative but issues in obedience.

The denial of absolutes, particularly in the area of morals, characterizes our society. Without a source of authority to provide absolute standards, virtually anything goes. What moral values are enforced are often arbitrary, based merely on human opinion. But for the Christian the authoritative Word of God provides absolutes. Those absolutes are the basis upon which all truth about God and all standards of faith and conduct are set. Because knowledge of those absolutes is the basis for correct behavior and ultimate judgment, it is crucial that Christians know God's revealed truth. Ignorance is not bliss, nor can anyone please God on the basis of principles they do not know.

So the Bible views knowledge of doctrinal absolutes as foundational to godly living. Most of Paul's letters begin by laying a doctrinal foundation before giving practical exhortations. For example, Paul gives eleven chapters of doctrine in Romans before turning to godly living in chapter 12. Galatians 1-4 are doctrinal, chapters 5 and 6 practical. The first three chapters of Ephesians detail our position in Christ, while the last three urge us to live accordingly. Philippians and Colossians also conform to the same pattern of doctrine preceding practical exhortations. Godly living is directly linked in Scripture to knowledge of doctrinal truth.

The Bible warns of the danger of a lack of knowledge. Proverbs 19:2 says that "it is not good for a person to be without knowledge." It was for lack of knowledge that Israel went into exile (Isa. 5:13), and God says in Hosea 4:6, "My people are destroyed for lack of knowledge." First Corinthians 14:20 warns us, "Do not be children in your thinking; yet in evil be babes, but in your thinking be mature." Ephesians 4:13-14 tells us that lack of knowledge produces "children tossed here and there by waves, and carried about by every wind of doctrine, by the trickery of men, by craftiness in deceitful scheming." Verse 18 describes unbelievers as "being darkened in their understanding, excluded from the life of God, because of the ignorance that is in them."

How does a person obtain knowledge? First, he must desire it. In John 7:17 Jesus says, "If any man is willing to do His will, he shall know of the teaching, whether it is of God, or whether I speak from Myself." That thought is echoed in Hosea 6:3, "Let us know, let us press on to know the Lord." Second, he must depend on the Holy Spirit. It is through Him that we know the things God has revealed to us (cf. 1 Cor. 2:10-12). Finally, he must study the Scriptures, for they make the believer "adequate, equipped for every good work" (2 Tim. 3:16-17). Perhaps the most graphic text related to the pursuit of divine truth is Job 28.

Paul prays that the knowledge we have would be of His will. God's will is not a secret; He has revealed it in His Word. For example, it is God's desire that a person be saved (1 Tim. 2:4; 2 Pet. 3:9). Once a person is saved, it is God's will that he be filled with the Spirit. Ephesians 5:17-18 says, "Do not be foolish, but understand what the will of the Lord is. And do not get drunk with wine, for that is dissipation, but be filled with the Spirit." Furthermore, sanctification is God's will: "For this is the will of God, your sanctification" (1 Thess. 4:3). God also wills that the believer be submissive to the government. Peter writes, "Submit yourselves for the Lord's sake to every human institution . . . for such is the will of God" (1 Pet. 2:13, 15). Suffering may also be God's will for the believer: "Let those also who suffer according to the will of God entrust their souls to a faithful Creator in doing what is right" (1 Pet. 4:19). Finally, giving thanks is God's will. Paul writes, "In everything give thanks; for this is God's will for you in Christ Jesus" (1 Thess. 5:17).

Having the knowledge of God's Word control our minds is the key to righteous living. What controls your thoughts will control your behavior. Self-control is a result of mind-control, which is dependent on knowledge. Knowledge of God's Word will lead to **all spiritual wis-**

dom and understanding. Though the terms **wisdom** and **understanding** may be synonymous, *sophia* (**wisdom**) may be the broader of the two terms. It refers to the ability to collect and concisely organize principles from Scripture. *Sunesis* (**understanding**) could be a more specialized term, referring to the application of those principles to everyday life. Both *sophia* and *sunesis* are spiritual; they deal in the non-physical realm and have the Holy Spirit as their source.

Believing, submissive Bible study leads to the knowledge of God's will. A mind saturated with such knowledge will also be able to comprehend general principles of godly behavior. With that wisdom will come understanding of how to apply those principles to the situations of life. That progression will inevitably result in godly character and practice.

THE RESULTS

so that you may walk in a manner worthy of the Lord, to please Him in all respects, bearing fruit in every good work and increasing in the knowledge of God; strengthened with all power, according to His glorious might, for the attaining of all steadfastness and patience; joyously (1:10-11)

In verses 10-11, Paul lists five purposes that are fulfilled in such spiritual knowledge.

A WORTHY WALK

so that you may walk in a manner worthy of the Lord, to please Him in all respects (1:10*a*)

Walk is used in the Bible to refer to one's pattern of daily conduct. A mind controlled by knowledge, wisdom, and understanding produces a life **worthy of the Lord.** Although it seems impossible that anyone could walk worthy of the Lord, that is the teaching of Scripture. Paul desired the Thessalonians to "walk in a manner worthy of the God who calls you into His own kingdom and glory" (1 Thess. 2:12). He exhorted the Ephesians to "walk in a manner worthy of the calling with which you have been called" (Eph. 4:1). He told the Philippians to "conduct yourselves in a manner worthy of the gospel of Christ" (Phil. 1:27).

God has not left us to our own resources for walking the worthy walk. Paul wrote to the Galatians, "I have been crucified with Christ; and it is no longer I who live, but Christ lives in me; and the life which I now live in the flesh I live by faith in the Son of God, who loved me, and delivered Himself up for me" (Gal. 2:20). Christ dwells in us in the person of the Holy Spirit. Paul prayed for the Ephesians "that He would grant you, according to the riches of His glory, to be strengthened with power through His Spirit in the inner man; so that Christ may dwell in your hearts through faith" (Eph. 3:16-17). Trying to walk worthy in our own strength is doomed to failure. Martin Luther stated that truth clearly in his hymn "A Mighty Fortress is Our God":

> Did we in our own strength confide
> Our striving would be losing,
> Were not the right Man on our side,
> The Man of God's own choosing.
> Dost ask who that may be?
> Christ Jesus, it is He.
> Lord Sabaoth His name,
> From age to age the same.
> And He must win the battle.

The New Testament describes several features of the worthy walk. We are to walk in humility (Eph. 4:1-3); in purity (Rom. 13:13, KJV); in contentedness (1 Cor. 7:17); by faith (2 Cor. 5:7); in good works (Eph. 2:10); different from the world (Eph. 4:17-32); in love (Eph. 5:2); in light (Eph. 5:8); in wisdom (Eph. 5:15); and in truth (3 John 3-4). Such a walk will please Him in all respects.

A FRUITFUL LIFE

bearing fruit in every good work (1:10*b*)

Fruitfulness also results from knowledge. Fruit is the by-product of righteousness. It is the mark of every redeemed individual. Jesus said in John 15:8, "By this is My Father glorified, that you bear much fruit, and so prove to be My disciples" (cf. vv. 2, 5-6). Paul told the Romans, "You also were made to die to the Law through the body of Christ, that you might be joined to another, to Him who was raised from the dead, that we might bear fruit for God" (Rom. 7:4).

The Bible defines **fruit** in various ways. Here Paul speaks of **bearing fruit in every good work.** Converts are referred to as fruit. Paul spoke of the household of Stephanas as the "first fruits of Achaia" (1 Cor. 16:15). He also desired some fruit among the Romans (Rom. 1:13). Hebrews 13:15 defines praise as fruit: "Through Him then, let us continually offer up a sacrifice of praise to God, that is, the fruit of lips that give thanks to His name." Giving money can also be fruit (Rom. 15:26-28). Godly living is fruit, as indicated when the writer of Hebrews tells us that God's discipline produces in us "the peaceful fruit of righteousness" (Heb. 12:11). Finally, the holy attitudes mentioned in Galatians 5:22-23 are referred to as "the fruit of the Spirit."

What produces fruit in believers' lives? First, union with Christ. Jesus said in John 15:4-5, "Abide in Me, and I in you. As the branch cannot bear fruit of itself, unless it abides in the vine, so neither can you, unless you abide in Me. I am the vine, you are the branches; he who abides in Me, and I in him, he bears much fruit; for apart from Me you can do nothing."

Second, wisdom is a necessary prerequisite for bearing fruit. "But the wisdom from above is first pure, then peaceable, gentle, reasonable, full of mercy and good fruits, unwavering, without hypocrisy" (James 3:17). Lack of fruit is directly related to lack of spiritual wisdom. Finally, diligent effort on the Christian's part is required, as Peter writes:

> Applying all diligence, in your faith supply moral excellence, and in your moral excellence, knowledge; and in your knowledge, self-control, and in your self-control, perseverance, and in your perseverance, godliness; and in your godliness, brotherly kindness, and in your brotherly kindness, love. For if these qualities are yours and are increasing, they render you neither useless nor unfruitful in the true knowledge of our Lord Jesus Christ. (2 Pet. 1:5-8)

GROWTH

increasing in the knowledge of God; (1:10*c*)

A third result of knowledge is spiritual growth. Spiritual growth is progressing **in the knowledge of God.** *Tē epignōsei* (**in the knowledge**) is an instrumental dative case. It indicates the means by which our **increasing,** or growth, takes place. The knowledge of God revealed in His Word is crucial to spiritual growth. Peter wrote, "Like newborn babes, long for the pure milk of the word, that by it you may grow in respect to salvation" (1 Pet. 2:2). As always, the Holy Spirit infuses our own efforts with God's enabling grace (2 Pet. 3:18), without which we could not grow.

The marks of spiritual growth include: first, a deeper love for God's Word. "Oh how I love Thy law! It is my meditation all the day" (Ps. 119:97).

Second, spiritual growth is reflected in a more perfect obedience.

> By this we know that we have come to know Him, if we keep His commandments. The one who says, "I have come to know Him," and does not keep His commandments, is a liar, and the truth is not in him; but whoever keeps His word, in him the love of God has truly been perfected. (1 John 2:3-5)

Third, spiritual growth will result in an enlarged faith. "We ought always to give thanks to God for you, brethren, as is only fitting, because your faith is greatly enlarged" (2 Thess. 1:3; cf. 2 Cor. 10:15).

A fourth mark of spiritual growth is a greater love: "This I pray, that your love may abound still more and more in real knowledge and discernment" (Phil. 1:9).

STRENGTH

strengthened with all power, according to His glorious might, (1:11a)

A fourth result of knowledge is spiritual strength. *Dunamoumenoi* ("strengthened") is a present participle, signifying continuous action. God is not like a booster rocket giving believers an initial boost of power and then leaving them to fly on their own. Believers are continually **strengthened with all power** throughout their Christian lives.

The measure of that power is **according to His glorious might. Glorious** is from *doxa* and refers to the manifestation of God's attributes. **Might** translates *kratos*, which refers to strength in action. It refers to God eleven out of the twelve times it is used in the New Testament. The **power** available to us is the limitless power of God Himself.

God's power is manifested in us through the ministry of the Holy Spirit. Our Lord told the disciples they would receive power after the Holy Spirit came upon them (Acts 1:8). Paul prayed for the Ephesians that they would be "strengthened with power through His Spirit in the inner man" (Eph. 3:16). To the Romans he wrote, "May the God of hope fill you with all joy and peace in believing, that you may abound in hope by the power of the Holy Spirit" (Rom. 15:13). That power is available to the believer who is filled with the knowledge of God's Word.

ENDURANCE

for the attaining of all steadfastness and patience; joyously (1:11*b*)

Paul gives one last result of true spiritual knowledge: joyous endurance of trials. Knowledge of God's promises and purposes revealed in Scripture gives the strength to endure trials and suffering. *Hupomonē* (**steadfastness**) and *makrothumia* (**patience**) are closely related. If there is a distinction, it is that *hupomonē* refers to being patient in circumstances, whereas *makrothumia* refers to patience with people (Richard C. Trench, *Synonyms of the New Testament* [Grand Rapids: Eerdmans, 1983], p. 198). Both refer to the patient enduring of trials.

Paul does not have in mind a stoic, teeth-gritting endurance. The strength provided by knowledge of God's Word allows the believer to endure trials **joyously,** literally "with joy" (*meta charis*). Commentators are divided on whether *meta charis* should be connected with **steadfastness** and **patience** in verse 11, or with **giving thanks** in verse 12. It seems best, however, to connect the phrase with verse 11. **Giving thanks** (v. 12) already includes the element of joy. Knowledge of God's truth gives us the ability to endure trials joyously, as did Paul himself (cf. Acts 16:25).

It was Paul's constant prayer for the Colossians that they be filled with the knowledge of God's will. He knew that only when believers are controlled by that knowledge can they walk worthy of the Lord and please Him. Paul knew further that such knowledge was required for a fruitful life, spiritual growth, strength, and joyful endurance of trials.

Paul Prays
for the Colossians
—part 2

3

giving thanks to the Father, who has qualified us to share in the inheritance of the saints in light. For He delivered us from the domain of darkness, and transferred us to the kingdom of His beloved Son, in whom we have redemption, the forgiveness of sins. (1:12-14)

Paul's prayer is a model or pattern for all believers to follow. Like his prayers here and elsewhere, our prayers should include praise as well as petitions. To the Philippians Paul wrote, "Be anxious for nothing, but in everything by prayer and supplication with thanksgiving let your requests be made known to God" (Phil. 4:6). In 1 Timothy 2:1 he urged that "entreaties and prayers, petitions and thanksgivings, be made on behalf of all men." Later he told the Colossians to "devote yourselves to prayer, keeping alert in it with an attitude of thanksgiving" (Col. 4:2). Paul constantly gave thanks in his prayers (cf. Acts 27:35; Rom. 1:8; 1 Tim. 1:12).

Giving thanks is too often demoted to a secondary place in the prayers of Christ's people. Our attitude in approaching God is often reminiscent of the leech's daughters: "Give, Give" (Prov. 30:15). We are quick to make our requests and slow to thank God for His answers. Because God so often answers our prayers, we come to expect it. We forget that it is only by His grace that we receive anything from Him.

The Bible repeatedly stresses the importance of giving thanks. "Offer to God a sacrifice of thanksgiving" (Ps. 50:14). "Let them give thanks to the Lord for His lovingkindness, and for His wonders to the sons of men! Let them also offer sacrifices of thanksgiving, and tell of His works with joyful singing" (Ps. 107:21-22). "It is good to give thanks to the Lord, and to sing praises to Thy name, O Most High" (Ps. 92:1). "Always giving thanks for all things in the name of our Lord Jesus Christ to God, even the Father" (Eph. 5:20). "Whatever you do in word or deed, do all in the name of the Lord Jesus, giving thanks through Him to God the Father" (Col. 3:17). "Through Him then, let us continually offer up a sacrifice of praise to God, that is, the fruit of lips that give thanks to His name" (Heb. 13:15). Thanksgiving should permeate our speech, our songs, and our prayers.

Our Lord knew the importance of giving thanks. In Matthew 11:25 He said, "I praise Thee, O Father, Lord of heaven and earth, that Thou didst hide these things from the wise and intelligent and didst reveal them to babes." Before feeding the five thousand, Jesus "took the loaves; and having given thanks, He distributed to those who were seated" (John 6:11). Just before raising Lazarus from the dead, "Jesus raised His eyes, and said, 'Father, I thank Thee that Thou heardest Me'" (John 11:41).

Revelation 7:11 tells us that the angels give thanks: "All the angels were standing around the throne and around the elders and the four living creatures; and they fell on their faces before the throne and worshiped God, saying, 'Amen, blessing and glory and wisdom and thanksgiving and honor and power and might, be to our God forever and ever. Amen.'"

David (2 Sam. 22:50; Ps. 28:7), the Levites (1 Chron. 16:4; Neh. 12:24), Asaph and his relatives (1 Chron. 16:7), Daniel (Dan. 6:10), and the priests, Levites, and descendants of Asaph (Ezra 3:10-11) also gave thanks to God.

In addition to those positive examples, the Bible teaches that failing to give thanks characterizes the wicked. One indictment of unbelievers is that "even though they knew God, they did not honor Him as God, or give thanks" (Rom. 1:21). Evil men are marked by ungratefulness (Luke 6:35; 2 Tim. 3:2).

Scripture instructs us to thank God for many things. We are to thank Him for who He is. Psalm 30:4 says, "Sing praise to the Lord, you His godly ones, and give thanks to His holy name" (cf. Ps. 97:12). We should also thank God for His nearness. "We give thanks to Thee, O God, we give thanks, for Thy name is near" (Ps. 75:1). Paul gave thanks to God for his salvation and his opportunity to serve Him: "I thank Christ

Jesus our Lord, who has strengthened me, because He considered me faithful, putting me into service; even though I was formerly a blasphemer and a persecutor and a violent aggressor. And yet I was shown mercy, because I acted ignorantly in unbelief" (1 Tim. 1:12-13).

The apostle also gave thanks for the spiritual growth of others: "We ought always to give thanks to God for you, brethren, as is only fitting, because your faith is greatly enlarged, and the love of each one of you toward one another grows ever greater" (2 Thess. 1:3).

Even mundane things like food call for giving thanks (1 Tim. 4:3-4). First Thessalonians 5:18 sums it up: "In everything give thanks; for this is God's will for you in Christ Jesus."

What makes Christians most thankful is the work of Christ. In 2 Corinthians 9:15, Paul exclaims, "Thanks be to God for His indescribable gift!" He gave thanks for the result of the work of Christ, which is our salvation (cf. 1 Cor. 1:4). That is also his theme in Colossians 1:12-14. Paul sums up the doctrine of salvation in three great truths: inheritance, deliverance, and transference. They are both a description of salvation and a cause for thanksgiving. He unfolds the specifics of his gratitude in those verses.

INHERITANCE

giving thanks to the Father, who has qualified us to share in the inheritance of the saints in light. (1:12)

Father emphasizes the personal, relational aspect of our union with God. Before our salvation, God was our Judge. We stood condemned before Him for violating His holy, just laws. But when, through the grace of God, we placed our faith in Christ, God ceased being our sentencing Judge and became our gracious Father.

Not only has God adopted us as His sons, but He has also **qualified us to share in the inheritance of the saints in light. Qualified** is from *hikanoō*, a word used only here and in 2 Corinthians 3:6 in the New Testament. It means "to make sufficient, to empower, to authorize, to make fit." We are not qualified through our own efforts. God has qualified us through the finished work of Christ.

Before God saved us by His grace we were truly unqualified for our inheritance. Several passages in Ephesians describe our helpless condition:

You were dead in your trespasses and sins, in which you formerly walked according to the course of this world, according to the prince of the power of the air, of the spirit that is now working in the sons of disobedience. Among them we too all formerly lived in the lusts of our flesh, indulging the desires of the flesh and of the mind, and were by nature children of wrath, even as the rest. (2:1-3)

Remember that you were at that time separate from Christ, excluded from the commonwealth of Israel, and strangers to the covenants of promise, having no hope and without God in the world. (2:12)

This I say therefore, and affirm together with the Lord, that you walk no longer just as the Gentiles also walk, in the futility of their mind, being darkened in their understanding, excluded from the life of God, because of the ignorance that is in them, because of the hardness of their heart; and they, having become callous, have given themselves over to sensuality, for the practice of every kind of impurity with greediness. (4:17-19)

Before our salvation, we were dominated by the evil world system; its wicked ruler, Satan; and our own fallen, sinful, human natures. We were Christless, stateless, covenantless, hopeless, godless. Our minds were given to futility; our understanding was darkened. We were cut off from the life of God, ignorant, hardhearted, callous, immoral, impure, and greedy. The only thing we were qualified to receive from God was His wrath. And that is what we would have received, if not for God's mercy toward us.

God has by grace **qualified** the unqualified to share in the inheritance. The Greek text literally reads, "for the portion of the lot" (*eis tēn merida tou klērou*). The partitive genitive (*tou klērou*) means that we each receive our own individual allotment or portion of the total inheritance. Paul here alludes to the partitioning of Israel's inheritance in Canaan (cf. Num. 26:52-56; 33:51-54; Josh. 14:1-2). Just as the Israelites received their inheritance in the Promised Land, so also do we receive our portion of the divine inheritance.

The Bible has much to say about our **inheritance.** It consists first of eternal life. Jesus said in Matthew 19:29, "Everyone who has left houses or brothers or sisters or father or mother or children or farms for My name's sake, shall receive many times as much, and shall inherit eternal life." Eternal life is far more than endless existence. It is a quality of life; Christ's life lived in the believer (Gal. 2:20; cf. 1 John 5:20). Second, our inheritance includes the earth. In the Sermon on the Mount, our Lord said that believers would inherit the earth (Matt. 5:5). That focuses on the future aspect of our inheritance, when we will rule with Christ in the millennial kingdom (Rev. 20:6). The knowledge that we will inherit the restored earth should free us from the present pursuit of material possessions. Someday we will receive far more than we could ever gain in this life. Third, we inherit all the promises of God. The writer of Hebrews exhorts us to be "imitators of those who through faith and patience inherit the promises" (Heb. 6:12).

When do we receive our inheritance? The present tense participle *hikanōsanti* (**qualified**) indicates we have it now (cf. Eph. 1:11). We have already been transferred from the domain of darkness into Christ's kingdom (Col. 1:13). We are already fellow heirs with Christ (Rom. 8:16-17). The full possession of that inheritance, however, is yet future. Peter refers to it as "an inheritance which is imperishable and undefiled and will not fade away, reserved in heaven for you" (1 Pet. 1:4). It will be ours forever. Hebrews 9:15 depicts it as an eternal inheritance.

Paul further defines our inheritance as that of **the saints in light.** *Hagiōn* (**saints**) refers to those who have been separated from the world and set apart to God. The inheritance belongs to that group alone. First Corinthians 6:9-10 asks the rhetorical question, "Do you not know that the unrighteous shall not inherit the kingdom of God? Do not be deceived; neither fornicators, nor idolaters, nor adulterers, nor effeminate, nor homosexuals, nor thieves, nor the covetous, nor drunkards, nor revilers, nor swindlers, shall inherit the kingdom of God."

Ephesians 5:5 echoes that thought: "For this you know with certainty, that no immoral or impure person or covetous man, who is an idolater, has an inheritance in the kingdom of Christ and God." And Galatians 5:21 adds that "those who practice such things [the deeds of the flesh in vv. 19-21] shall not inherit the kingdom of God."

The saints' inheritance is **in the light.** Light represents two things biblically. Intellectually, it represents truth (Ps. 119:130). Morally, it represents purity (Eph. 5:8-14). In contrast to Israel's earthly inheritance, the saints' inheritance is in the light—the spiritual realm of truth and purity where God Himself dwells (1 Tim. 6:16). In his defense before King Agrippa in Acts 26, Paul spoke of the Lord's commissioning him to preach to the Gentiles. The Lord told Paul that He was sending him "to open their eyes so that they may turn from darkness to light and from the dominion of Satan to God, in order that they may receive forgiveness of sins and an inheritance among those who have been sanctified by faith in Me" (v. 18). Paul no doubt had that event in mind when he wrote Colossians 1:12-14. The saints are those who have turned from sinful darkness to righteous light (cf. Eph. 5:8; 1 John 1:7).

God has graciously given us a guarantee for our inheritance. That guarantee is the indwelling Holy Spirit. In Ephesians 1:13-14, Paul writes, "You were sealed in Him with the Holy Spirit of promise, who is given as a pledge of our inheritance." "Pledge" translates *arrabōn*, which is similar to the modern Greek word for engagement ring. *Arra-*

bōn could also be translated "guarantee," or "down-payment." God has given us the Holy Spirit as the first installment on our future inheritance. That is an objective fact, not dependent on our feelings. Studying "the word of His grace, which is able to build you up and to give you the inheritance among all those who are sanctified" (Acts 20:32) results in a greater richness and understanding of our glorious inheritance.

So He has given us the Spirit and the Word to give us confidence and understanding of that inheritance. No wonder Paul prayed "that the eyes of your heart may be enlightened, so that you may know what is the hope of His calling, what are the riches of the glory of His inheritance in the saints" (Eph 1:18).

DELIVERANCE

For He delivered us from the domain of darkness, (1:13*a*)

A second cause for thanksgiving is our spiritual liberation. **Delivered** is from *ruomai*, which means "to draw to oneself," or "to rescue." God drew us out of Satan's kingdom to Himself. That event was the new birth. We are not gradually, progressively delivered from Satan's power. When we placed our faith in Christ, we were instantly delivered. "Therefore if any man is in Christ, he is a new creature; the old things passed away; behold, new things have come" (2 Cor. 5:17). Believers do not need deliverance from the dominion of sin and Satan; they need to act as those who have been delivered (cf. Rom. 6:2, 7, 11).

Those who receive the Lord Jesus Christ have been rescued from **the domain of darkness.** *Exousias* (**domain**) could be translated "power," "jurisdiction," or "authority." Our Lord used the phrase **domain of darkness** (*exousias tou skotous*) to refer to the supernatural forces of Satan marshalled against Him at His arrest (Luke 22:53). The triumph of the domain of darkness was short-lived, however. A few hours later, Jesus forever shattered Satan's power by His death on the cross. You need not fear that power, for "greater is He who is in you than he who is in the world" (1 John 4:4). Through His death, Jesus crushed Satan and delivered us from his dark kingdom.

TRANSFERENCE

and transferred us to the kingdom of His beloved Son, in whom we have redemption, the forgiveness of sins. (1:13*b*, 14)

Paul continues the litany of blessings that draw out his gratitude by describing our new domain. *Methistēmi* (**transferred**) means to remove or change. It is used in Acts 13:22 to speak of God's removing Saul from being king. It was used in the ancient world to speak of the displacement of a conquered people to another land. The verb speaks here of our total removal from the domain of satanic darkness to the glorious light of the kingdom of Christ.

Kingdom refers to more than the future millennial kingdom, when Jesus will reign on earth for a thousand years. Nor does it speak merely of the general rule of God over His creation. The kingdom is a spiritual reality right now. Paul gives us a definition of it in Romans 14:17: "The kingdom of God is not eating and drinking, but righteousness and peace and joy in the Holy Spirit." The kingdom is the special relationship men in this age have with God through Jesus Christ. A kingdom in its most basic sense is a group of people ruled by a king. Christians have acknowledged Christ as their King and are subjects in His kingdom. They have been **transferred . . . to the kingdom of His beloved Son.** The Greek text literally reads, "the Son of His love" (*tou huiou tēs agapēs autou*). The Father gives the kingdom to the Son He loves, then to everyone who loves the Son (Luke 12:32).

Although Christ does not yet rule on earth, He is no less a king. In response to Pilate's question, "Are You the King of the Jews?" Jesus replied, "It is as you say" (Matt. 27:11). He reigns in eternity, rules now over His church, and one day will return to rule the earth as King of kings.

There is a tremendous responsibility that accompanies being part of Christ's kingdom. As subjects of that kingdom, we must properly represent the King. Paul admonished the Thessalonians to "walk in a manner worthy of the God who calls you into His own kingdom and glory" (1 Thess. 2:12). Even their persecution was a plain indication of God's righteous judgment so they might be considered worthy of the kingdom of God, for which indeed they were suffering (2 Thess. 1:5). The writer of Hebrews reminds us, "Since we receive a kingdom which cannot be shaken, let us show gratitude, by which we may offer to God an acceptable service with reverence and awe" (Heb. 12:28).

Before we could be fit subjects for Christ's kingdom we needed **redemption, the forgiveness of sins.** *Apolutrōsis* (**redemption**) is one of the magnificent New Testament words expressing a blessed aspect of the work of Christ on our behalf. Alongside such terms as *sacrifice, offering, propitiation, ransom, justification, adoption,* and *reconciliation,* it attempts to describe the riches of our salvation. It means "to deliver by payment of a ransom," and was used to speak of freeing slaves from bondage. The meaning of *apolutrōsis* is expressed in our English word *emancipation.* The Septuagint uses a related word to speak of Israel's deliverance from bondage in Egypt. *Apolutrōsis* is used in several places in the New Testament to speak of Christ's freeing us from slavery to sin. In Ephesians 1:7, Paul writes, "In Him we have redemption through His blood, the forgiveness of our trespasses, according to the riches of His grace." To the Corinthians he wrote, "By His doing you are in Christ Jesus, who became to us wisdom from God, and righteousness and sanctification, and redemption" (1 Cor. 1:30). In the midst of perhaps the most thorough soteriological passage in the New Testament, Paul writes that we are "justified as a gift by His grace through the redemption which is in Christ Jesus" (Rom. 3:24).

Redemption results in **the forgiveness of sins.** *Aphesin* (**forgiveness**) refers to pardon, or remission of penalty. It is a composite of two Greek words, *apo*, "from," and *hiēmi*, "to send." Because Christ redeemed us, God has sent away our sins; they will never be found again. "As far as the east is from the west, so far has He removed our transgressions from us" (Ps. 103:12). "He will again have compassion on us; He will tread our iniquities under foot. Yes, Thou wilt cast all their sins into the depths of the sea" (Mic. 7:19).

So Christ's death on our behalf paid the price to redeem us. On that basis, God forgave our sins, granted us an inheritance, delivered us from the power of darkness, and made us subjects of Christ's kingdom. Those wonderful truths should cause us to give thanks to God continually, as did Paul in his prayer. And when we contemplate all He has done for us, how can we do any less than pray to be filled with the knowledge of His will?

The Pre-eminence of Jesus Christb

4

And He is the image of the invisible God, the first-born of all creation. For by Him all things were created, both in the heavens and on earth, visible and invisible, whether thrones or dominions or rulers or authorities—all things have been created by Him and for Him. And He is before all things, and in Him all things hold together. He is also head of the body, the church; and He is the beginning, the first-born from the dead; so that He Himself might come to have first place in everything. For it was the Father's good pleasure for all the fulness to dwell in Him, (1:15-19)

The Bible is supremely the book about the Lord Jesus Christ. The Old Testament records the preparation for His coming. The gospels present Him as God in human flesh, come into the world to save sinners. In Acts, the message of salvation in Christ begins to be spread throughout the world. The epistles detail the theology of Christ's work and personification of Christ in His Body, the church. Finally, Revelation presents Christ on the throne, reigning as King of kings and Lord of lords.

Every part of Scripture testifies about Jesus Christ. Luke 24:27 says, "Beginning with Moses and with all the prophets, [Jesus] explained to them the things concerning Himself in all the Scriptures." In John 5:39, Jesus said of the Scriptures, "It is these that bear witness of Me." Philip preached Christ to the Ethiopian eunuch by using the book of Isaiah (Acts 8:35).

But of all the Bible's teaching about Jesus Christ, none is more significant than Colossians 1:15-19. This dramatic and powerful passage removes any needless doubt or confusion over Jesus' true identity. It is vital to a proper understanding of the Christian faith.

As mentioned in the introduction, much of the heresy threatening the Colossian church centered on the Person of Christ. The heretics, denying His humanity, viewed Christ as one of many lesser descending spirit beings that emanated from God. They taught a form of philosophic dualism, postulating that spirit was good and matter was evil. Hence, a good emanation like Christ could never take on a body composed of evil matter. The idea that God Himself could become man was absurd to them. Thus, they also denied His deity.

Nor was Christ adequate for salvation, according to the errorists. Salvation required a superior, mystical, secret knowledge, beyond that of the gospel of Christ. It also involved worshiping the good emanations (angels) and keeping the Jewish ceremonial laws.

In the first three chapters of Colossians, Paul confronts the Colossian heresy head on. He rejects their denial of Christ's humanity, pointing out that it is in Him that "all the fulness of Deity dwells in bodily form" (2:9). Paul also rejects their worship of angels (2:18), and their ceremonialism (2:16-17). He emphatically denies that any secret knowledge is required for salvation, pointing out that in Christ "are hidden all the treasures of wisdom and knowledge" (2:3; cf. 1:27; 3:1-4).

By far the most serious aspect of the Colossian heresy was its rejection of Christ's deity. Before getting to the other issues, Paul makes an emphatic defense of that crucial doctrine. Christians would do well to follow his example in their confrontations with cultists. The primary focus of discussions with them should be the deity of Jesus Christ.

In Colossians 1:15-19, Paul reveals our Lord's true identity by viewing Him in relation to four things: God, the universe, the unseen world, and the church.

JESUS CHRIST IN RELATION TO GOD

And He is the image of the invisible God, the first-born of all creation. (1:15)

As already noted, the heretics viewed Jesus as one among a series of lesser spirits descending in sequential inferiority from God. Paul refutes that with two powerful descriptions of who Jesus really is. First, Paul describes Him as **the image of the invisible God.** *Eikōn* (**image**) means "image" or "likeness." From it we get our English word *icon*, referring to a statue. It is used in Matthew 22:20 of Caesar's portrait on a coin, and in Revelation 13:14 of the statue of Antichrist.

Although man is also the *eikōn* of God (1 Cor. 11:7; cf. Gen. 1:26-27), man is not a perfect image of God. Humans are made in God's image in that they have rational personality. Like God, they possess intellect, emotion, and will, by which they are able to think, feel, and choose. We humans are not, however, in God's image morally, because He is holy, and we are sinful. Nor are we created in His image essentially. We do not possess His incommunicable attributes, such as omniscience, omnipotence, immutability, or omnipresence. We are human, not divine.

The Fall marred the original image of God in man. Before the Fall, Adam and Eve were innocent, free of sin, and incapable of dying. They forfeited those qualities when they sinned. When someone puts faith in Christ, however, that person is promised that the image of God will be restored in him or her. "For whom He foreknew, He also predestined to become conformed to the image of His Son" (Rom. 8:29; cf. 2 Cor. 3:18; Col. 3:10). God will make believers sinless like Christ when they enter the final phase of their eternal life.

Unlike man, Jesus Christ is the perfect, absolutely accurate image of God. He did not become the image of God at the incarnation, but has been that from all eternity. Hebrews 1:3 describes Jesus as "the radiance of [God's] glory." Christ reflects God's attributes, as the sun's light reflects the sun. Further, He is said to be "the exact representation of [God's] nature." *Charaktēr* ("exact representation") refers to an engraving tool, or stamp. Jesus is the exact likeness of God. He is in the very form of God (Phil. 2:6). That is why He could say, "He who has seen Me has seen the Father" (John 14:9). In Christ, the invisible God became visible, "and we beheld His glory, glory as of the only begotten from the Father" (John 1:14).

By using the term *eikōn*, Paul emphasizes that Jesus is both the representation and manifestation of God. He is the full, final, and complete revelation of God. He is God in human flesh. That was His claim (John 8:58; 10:30-33), and the unanimous testimony of Scripture (cf. John 1:1; 20:28; Rom. 9:5; Phil. 2:6; Col. 2:9; Titus 2:13; Heb. 1:8; 2 Pet. 1:1). To think anything less of Him is blasphemy and gives evidence of a mind blinded by Satan (2 Cor. 4:4).

Paul further describes Jesus as **the first-born of all creation.** From the Arians of the early church to the Jehovah's Witnesses of our own day, those who would deny our Lord's deity have sought support from this phrase. They argue that it speaks of Christ as a created being, and hence He could not be the eternal God. Such an interpretation completely misunderstands the sense of *prōtotokos* (**first-born**) and ignores the context.

Although *prōtotokos* can mean firstborn chronologically (Luke 2:7), it refers primarily to position, or rank. In both Greek and Jewish culture, the firstborn was the son who had the right of inheritance. He was not necessarily the first one born. Although Esau was born first chronologically, it was Jacob who was the "firstborn" and received the inheritance. Jesus is the One with the right to the inheritance of all creation (cf. Heb. 1:2; Rev. 5:1-7, 13).

Israel was called God's firstborn in Exodus 4:22 and Jeremiah 31:9. Though not the first people born, they held first place in God's sight among all the nations. In Psalm 89:27, God says of the Messiah, "I also shall make him My first-born," then defines what He means—"the highest of the kings of the earth." In Revelation 1:5, Jesus is called "the first-born of the dead," even though He was not the first person to be resurrected chronologically. Of all ever raised, He is the preeminent One. Romans 8:29 refers to Him as the firstborn in relation to the church. In all the above cases, firstborn clearly means highest in rank, not first created.

There are many other reasons for rejecting the idea that the use of **first-born** makes Jesus a created being. Such an interpretation cannot be harmonized with the description of Jesus as *monogenēs* ("only begotten," or "unique") in John 1:18. We might well ask with the early church Father Theodoret how, if Christ was only-begotten, could He be first-begotten? And how, if He were first-begotten, could He be only-begotten? How could He be the first of many in His class, and at the same time the only member of His class? Yet such confusion is inevitable if we assign the meaning "first created" to "firstborn." Further, when the *prōtotokos* is one of the class referred to, the class is plural (cf. Col. 1:18; Rom. 8:29). Yet, creation is singular. Finally, if Paul meant to convey that Christ was the first created being, why did he not use the Greek word *prōtoktistos*, which means "first created?"

Such an interpretation of *prōtotokos* is also foreign to the context—both the general context of the epistle and the specific context of the passage. If Paul were here teaching that Christ is a created being, he would be agreeing with the central point of the Colossian errorists. They taught that Christ was a created being, the most prominent of the emanations from God. That would run counter to his purpose in writing Colossians, which was to refute the false teachers at Colossae.

Interpreting *prōtotokos* to mean that Christ is a created being is also out of harmony with the immediate context. Paul has just finished describing Christ as the perfect and complete image of God. In the next verse, he refers to Christ as the creator of everything that exists. How then could Christ Himself be a created being? Further, verse 17 states, "He is before all things." Christ existed before anything else was created (cf. Micah 5:2). And only God existed before the creation.

Far from being one of a series of emanations descending from God, Jesus is the perfect image of God. He is the preeminent inheritor over all creation (the genitive *ktiseōs* is better translated "over" than "of"). He both existed before the creation and is exalted in rank above it. Those truths define who Jesus is in relation to God. They also devastate the false teachers' position. But Paul is not finished—his next point undermines another false teaching of the Colossian errorists.

JESUS CHRIST IN RELATION TO THE UNIVERSE

For by Him all things were created, both in the heavens and on earth, visible and invisible, whether thrones or dominions or rulers or authorities—all things have been created by Him and for Him. And He is before all things, and in Him all things hold together. (1:16-17)

Paul gives three reasons for Jesus' primacy over creation. First, He is the Creator. The false teachers at Colossae viewed Jesus as the first and most important of the emanations from God, but they were convinced it had to be a lesser being much further down the chain who eventually created the material universe. But Paul rejects that blasphemy, insisting that by Him all things were created. That truth is affirmed by the apostle John (John 1:3) and the writer of Hebrews (Heb. 1:2). Because the Colossian errorists viewed matter as evil, they argued that neither the good God nor a good emanation could have created it. But Paul maintains that Jesus made all things, both in the heavens and on earth, visible and invisible. He refutes the false philosophic dualism of the Colossian heresy. Jesus is God, and He created the material universe.

By studying the creation, one can gain a glimpse of the power, knowledge, and wisdom of the Creator. The sheer size of the universe is staggering. The sun, for example, has a diameter of 864,000 miles (one hundred times that of earth's) and could hold 1.3 million planets the size of earth inside it. The star Betelgeuse, however, has a diameter of 100 million miles, which is larger than the earth's orbit around the sun. It takes sunlight, traveling at 186,000 miles per second, about 8.5 minutes to reach earth. Yet that same light would take more than four years to reach the nearest star, Alpha Centauri, some 24 trillion miles from earth. The galaxy to which our sun belongs, the Milky Way, contains hundreds of billions of stars. And astronomers estimate there are millions, or even billions of galaxies. What they can see leads them to estimate the number of stars in the universe at 10^{25}. That is roughly the number of all the grains of sand on all the world's beaches.

The universe also bears witness to the tremendous wisdom and knowledge of its Creator. Scientists now speak of the Anthropic Principle, "which states that the universe appears to be carefully designed for the well-being of mankind" (Donald B. DeYoung, "Design in Nature: The Anthropic Principle," *Impact*, no. 149 [November 1985]: p. ii). A change in the rate of Earth's rotation around the sun or on its axis would be catastrophic. The Earth would become either too hot or too cold to support life. If the moon were much nearer to the Earth, huge tides would inundate the continents. A change in the composition of the gases that make up our atmosphere would also be fatal to life. A slight change in the mass of the proton would result in the dissolution of hydrogen atoms. That would result in the destruction of the universe, because hydrogen is its dominant element.

The creation gives mute testimony to the intelligence of its Creator. Max Planck, winner of the Nobel Prize and one of the founders of modern physics, wrote, "According to everything taught by the exact sciences about the immense realm of nature, a certain order prevails —one independent of the human mind . . . this order can be formulated in terms of purposeful activity. There is evidence of an intelligent order of the universe to which both man and nature are subservient" (cited in DeYoung, "Design in Nature," p. iii). It is no wonder that the psalmist wrote, "The heavens are telling of the glory of God; and their expanse is declaring the work of His hands. Day to day pours forth speech, and night to night reveals knowledge. There is no speech, nor are there words; their voice is not heard. Their line has gone out through all the earth, and their utterances to the end of the world" (Ps. 19:1-4).

The testimony of nature to its Creator is so clear that it is only through willful unbelief that men can reject it. Paul writes in Romans 1:20, "Since the creation of the world His invisible attributes, His eternal power and divine nature, have been clearly seen, being understood through what has been made, so that they are without excuse." Like those who deny Christ's deity, those who reject Him as Creator give evidence of a mind darkened by sin and blinded by Satan.

Jesus also has primacy over the creation because He is before all things. When the universe began, He already existed (John 1:1-2; 1 John 1:1). He told the Jews in John 8:58, "Before Abraham was born, I am" (not "I was"). He is saying that He is Yahweh, the eternally existing God. The prophet Micah said of Him, "His goings forth are from long ago, from the days of eternity" (Mic. 5:2). Revelation 22:13 describes Him as "the Alpha and the Omega, the first and the last, the beginning and the end." As was previously mentioned, anyone existing before time began at the creation is eternal. And only God is eternal.

A third reason for Jesus' primacy over creation is that in Him all things hold together. Not only did Jesus create the universe, He also sustains it. He maintains the delicate balance necessary to life's existence. He quite literally holds all things together. He is the power behind every consistency in the universe. He is gravity and centrifugal and centripetal force. He is the One who keeps all the entities in space in their motion. He is the energy of the universe. In his book *The Atom Speaks*, D. Lee Chesnut describes the puzzle of why the nucleus of the atom holds together:

> Consider the dilemma of the nuclear physicist when he finally looks in utter amazement at the pattern he had now drawn of the oxygen nucleus. . . . For here are eight positively charged protons closely associated together within the confines of this tiny nucleus. With them are eight neutrons—a total of sixteen particles—eight positively charged, eight with no charge.
>
> Earlier physicists had discovered that like charges of electricity and like magnetic poles repel each other, and unlike charges or magnetic poles attract each other. And the entire history of electrical phenomena and electrical equipment had been built up on these principles known as Coulomb's law of electrostatic force and the law of magnetism. What was wrong? What holds the nucleus together? Why doesn't it fly apart? And therefore, why do not all atoms fly apart? ([San Diego: Creation-Science Research Center, 1973], pp. 31-33)

Chesnut goes on to describe the experiments performed in the 1920s and 1930s that proved Coulomb's law applied to atomic nuclei. Powerful "atom smashers" were used to fire protons into the nuclei of atoms. Those experiments also gave scientists an understanding of the incredibly powerful force that held protons together within the nucleus. Scientists have dubbed that force the "strong nuclear force," but have no explanation for why it exists. The physicist George Gamow, one of the founders of the Big Bang theory of the origin of the universe, wrote,

> The fact that we live in a world in which practically every object is a potential nuclear explosive, without being blown to bits, is due to the extreme difficulties that attend the starting of a nuclear reaction. (cited in Chesnut, *The Atom Speaks*, p. 38)

Karl K. Darrow, a physicist at the Bell (AT & T) Laboratories, agrees:

You grasp what this implies. It implies that all the massive nuclei have no right to be alive at all. Indeed, they should never have been created, and, if created, they should have blown up instantly. Yet here they all are. . . . Some inflexible inhibition is holding them relentlessly together. The nature of the inhibition is also a secret . . . one thus far reserved by Nature for herself. (cited in Chesnut, *The Atom Speaks*, p. 38)

One day in the future God will dissolve the strong nuclear force. Peter describes that day as the one when "the heavens will pass away with a roar and the elements will be destroyed with intense heat, and the earth and its works will be burned up" (2 Pet. 3:10). With the strong nuclear force no longer operative, Coulomb's law will take effect, and the nuclei of atoms will fly apart. The universe will literally explode. Until that time, we can be thankful that Christ "upholds all things by the word of His power" (Heb. 1:3). Jesus Christ must be God. He made the universe, existed outside and before it, and preserves it.

Jesus Christ in Relation to the Unseen World

whether thrones or dominions or rulers or authorities (1:16b)

Thrones, dominions, rulers, and **authorities** refer to the various ranks of angels. Far from being an angel, as the Colossian errorists taught, Christ created the angels. The writer of Hebrews also makes a clear distinction between Christ and the angels: "Of the angels He says, 'Who makes His angels winds, and His ministers a flame of fire.' But of the Son He says, 'Thy throne, O God, is forever and ever, and the righteous scepter is the scepter of His kingdom'" (Heb. 1:7-8). Jesus has been exalted "far above all rule and authority and power and dominion, and every name that is named, not only in this age, but also in the one to come" (Eph. 1:21). As a result, "At the name of Jesus every knee should bow, of those who are in heaven, and on earth, and under the earth" (Phil. 2:10). With that truth the apostle Peter agrees: "[Christ] is at the right hand of God, having gone into heaven, after angels and authorities and powers had been subjected to Him" (1 Pet. 3:22).

Scripture is clear that Jesus is not an angel, but the Creator of the angels. He is above the angels, who in fact worship Him and are under His authority. Jesus' relation to the unseen world, like His relation to the visible universe, proves He is God.

JESUS CHRIST IN RELATION TO THE CHURCH

He is also head of the body, the church; and He is the beginning, the first-born from the dead; so that He Himself might come to have first place in everything. (1:18)

Paul presents four great truths in this verse about Christ's relation to the church.

CHRIST IS THE HEAD OF THE CHURCH

There are many metaphors used in Scripture to describe the church. It is called a family, a kingdom, a vineyard, a flock, a building, and a bride. But the most profound metaphor, one having no Old Testament equivalent, is that of a Body. The church is a Body, and Christ is the head of the Body. This concept is not used in the sense of the head of a company, but rather looks at the church as a living organism, inseparably tied together by the living Christ. He controls every part of it and gives it life and direction. His life lived out through all the members provides the unity of the Body (cf. 1 Cor. 12:12-20). He energizes and coordinates the diversity within the Body, a diversity of spiritual gifts and ministries (1 Cor. 12:4-13). He also directs the Body's mutuality, as the individual members serve and support each other (1 Cor. 12:15-27).

Christ is not an angel who serves the church (cf. Heb. 1:14). He is the head of His church.

CHRIST IS THE SOURCE OF THE CHURCH

Archē (**beginning**) is used here in the twofold sense of source and primacy. The church has its origins in Jesus. God "chose us in Him before the foundation of the world" (Eph. 1:4). It is He who gives life to His church. His sacrificial death and resurrection on our behalf provided our new life. As head of the Body, Jesus holds the chief position, or highest rank in the church. As the beginning, He is its originator.

CHRIST IS THE FIRSTBORN FROM THE DEAD

First-born again translates *prōtotokos.* Of all those who have been raised from the dead, or ever will be, Christ is the highest in rank.

CHRIST IS THE PRE-EMINENT ONE

As a result of His death and resurrection, Jesus has come to have first place in everything. Paul summarizes for emphasis in verse 18. He wants to drive home the point as forcefully as he can that Jesus is not merely another emanation from God. Because

> He humbled Himself by becoming obedient to the point of death, even death on a cross . . . God highly exalted Him, and bestowed on Him the name which is above every name, that at the name of Jesus every knee should bow, of those who are in heaven, and on earth, and under the earth, and that every tongue should confess that Jesus Christ is Lord, to the glory of God the Father. (Phil. 2:8-11)

Jesus reigns supreme over the visible world, the unseen world, and the church. Paul sums up his argument in verse 19: **For it was the Father's good pleasure for all the fulness to dwell in Him.** *Plērōma* (**fulness**) was a term used by the later Gnostics to refer to the divine powers and attributes, which they believed were divided among the various emanations. That is likely the sense in which the Colossian errorists used the term. Paul counters that false teaching by stating that all the fulness of deity is not spread out in small doses to a group of spirits, but fully dwells in Christ alone (cf. 2:9). The commentator J. B. Lightfoot wrote about Paul's use of *plērōma*,

> On the one hand, in relation to Deity, He is the visible image of the invisible God. He is not only the chief manifestation of the Divine nature: He exhausts the Godhead manifested. In Him resides the totality of the Divine powers and attributes. For this totality Gnostic teachers had a technical term, the *pleroma* or *plenitude*. . . . In contrast to their doctrine, [Paul] asserts and repeats the assertion, that the *pleroma* abides absolutely and wholly in Christ as the Word of God. The entire light is concentrated in Him. (*St. Paul's Epistles to the Colossians and to Philemon* [1879; reprint, Grand Rapids: Zondervan, 1959], p. 102)

Paul tells the Colossians they do not need angels to help them get saved. Rather in Christ, and Him alone, they are complete (2:10). Christians share in His fulness: "For of His fulness we have all received, and grace upon grace" (John 1:16). All the fulness of Christ becomes available to believers.

What should the response be to the glorious truths about Christ in this passage? The Puritan John Owen astutely wrote,

The revelation made of Christ in the blessed gospel is far more excellent, more glorious, more filled with rays of divine wisdom and goodness than the whole creation, and the just comprehension of it, if attainable, can contain or afford. Without this knowledge, the mind of man, however priding itself in other inventions and discoveries, is wrapped up in darkness and confusion.

This therefore deserves the severest of our thoughts, the best of our meditations, and our utmost diligence in them. For if our future blessedness shall consist in living where He is, and beholding of His glory, what better preparation can there be for it than a constant previous contemplation of that glory as revealed in the gospel, that by a view of it we may be gradually transformed into the same glory? (John Owen, *The Glory of Christ* [reprint, Chicago: Moody, 1949], pp. 25-26)

Reconciled to God

5

and through Him to reconcile all things to Himself, having made peace through the blood of His cross; through Him, I say, whether things on earth or things in heaven. And although you were formerly alienated and hostile in mind, engaged in evil deeds, yet He has now reconciled you in His fleshly body through death, in order to present you before Him holy and blameless and beyond reproach—if indeed you continue in the faith firmly established and steadfast, and not moved away from the hope of the gospel that you have heard, which was proclaimed in all creation under heaven, and of which I, Paul, was made a minister. (1:20-23)

The word *reconcile* is one of the most significant and descriptive terms in all of Scripture. It is one of five key words used in the New Testament to describe the richness of salvation in Christ, along with *justification, redemption, forgiveness*, and *adoption.*

In justification, the sinner stands before God guilty and condemned, but is declared righteous (Rom. 8:33). In redemption, the sinner stands before God as a slave, but is granted his freedom (Rom. 6:18-22). In forgiveness, the sinner stands before God as a debtor, but the debt is paid and forgotten (Eph. 1:7). In reconciliation, the sinner stands before God as an enemy, but becomes His friend (2 Cor. 5:18-20). In adoption, the sinner stands before God as a stranger, but is made a son (Eph. 1:5). A complete understanding of the doctrine of salvation would involve a detailed study of each of those terms. In Colossians 1:20-23, Paul gives a concise look at reconciliation.

The verb *katallassō* (**to reconcile**) means "to change" or "exchange." Its New Testament usage speaks of a change in a relationship. In 1 Corinthians 7:11 it refers to a woman being reconciled to her husband. In its other two New Testament usages, Romans 5:10, and 2 Corinthians 5:18-20, it speaks of God and man being reconciled. When people change from being at enmity with each other to being at peace, they are said to be reconciled. When the Bible speaks of reconciliation, then, it refers to the restoration of a right relationship between God and man.

There is another term for reconcile that is used in Colossians 1:20, 22—*apokatallassō*. It is a compound word, made up of the basic word for reconcile, *katallassō*, with a preposition added to intensify the meaning. It means thoroughly, completely, or totally reconciled. Paul no doubt used this stronger term in Colossians as a counterattack against the false teachers. Because they held that Christ was merely another spirit being emanating from God, they also denied the possibility of man's being reconciled to God by Christ alone. In refuting that denial, Paul emphasizes that there is total, complete, and full reconciliation through the Lord Jesus. Inasmuch as He possesses all the fullness of deity (1:19; 2:9), Jesus is able to fully reconcile sinful men and women to God (1:20).

Paul defends Christ's sufficiency to reconcile men to God by discussing four aspects of reconciliation: the plan of reconciliation, the means of reconciliation, the aim of reconciliation, and the evidence of reconciliation.

THE PLAN OF RECONCILIATION

and through Him to reconcile all things to Himself, having made peace through the blood of His cross; through Him, I say, whether things on earth or things in heaven. And although you were formerly alienated and hostile in mind, engaged in evil deeds, (1:20-21)

God's ultimate plan for the universe is **to reconcile all things to Himself** through Jesus Christ. When His work of creation was finished, "God saw all that He had made, and behold, it was very good"

(Gen. 1:31). God's good creation, however, was soon marred by man's sin. The Fall resulted not only in fatal and damning tragedy for the human race, but also affected the entire creation. Sin destroyed the perfect harmony between creatures, and between all creation and the Creator. The creation was "subjected to futility" (Rom. 8:20) and "groans and suffers the pains of childbirth together until now" (Rom. 8:22). One evidence of that is the Second Law of Thermodynamics, which indicates that the universe is losing its usable energy. If God did not intervene, the universe would eventually suffer a heat death—all available energy would be used up, and the universe would become uniformly cold and dark.

We live on a cursed earth in a cursed universe. Both are under the baleful influence of Satan, who is both "the god of this world" (2 Cor. 4:4), and "the prince of the power of the air" (Eph. 2:2). The devastating effects of the curse and satanic influence will reach a terrifying climax in the events of the Tribulation. Some of the various bowl, trumpet, and seal judgments are demonic, others represent natural phenomena gone wild as God lets loose His wrath. At the culmination of that time of destruction and chaos, Christ returns and sets up His kingdom. During His millennial reign, the effects of the curse will begin to be reversed. The Bible gives us a glimpse of what the restored creation will be like.

There will be dramatic changes in the animal world. In Isaiah we learn that

> The wolf will dwell with the lamb, and the leopard will lie down with the kid, and the calf and the young lion and the fatling together; and a little boy will lead them. Also the cow and the bear will graze; their young will lie down together; and the lion will eat straw like the ox. And the nursing child will play by the hole of the cobra, and the weaned child will put his hand on the viper's den. They will not hurt or destroy in all My holy mountain. (Isa. 11:6-9)

> "The wolf and the lamb shall graze together, and the lion shall eat straw like the ox; and dust shall be the serpent's food. They shall do no evil or harm in all My holy mountain," says the Lord. (Isa. 65:25)

The changes in the animal world will be paralleled by changes in the earth and the solar system:

> Then the moon will be abashed and the sun ashamed, for the Lord of hosts will reign on Mount Zion and in Jerusalem, and His glory will be before His elders. (Isa. 24:23)

The light of the moon will be as the light of the sun, and the light of the sun will be seven times brighter, like the light of seven days, on the day the Lord binds up the fracture of His people and heals the bruise He has inflicted. (Isa. 30:26)

No longer will you have the sun for light by day, nor for brightness will the moon give you light; but you will have the Lord for an everlasting light, and your God for your glory. Your sun will set no more, neither will your moon wane; for you will have the Lord for an everlasting light. (Isa. 60:19-20)

Tremendous, dramatic changes will mark the reconciliation of the world to God. Paul writes, "The creation itself also will be set free from its slavery to corruption" (Rom. 8:21). God and the creation will be reconciled; the curse of Genesis 3 will be removed. We might say that God will make friends with the universe again. The universe will be restored to a proper relationship with its Creator. Finally, after the millennial kingdom, there will indeed be a new heaven and a new earth, as both Peter and John indicate:

According to His promise we are looking for new heavens and a new earth, in which righteousness dwells. (2 Pet. 3:13)

I saw a new heaven and a new earth; for the first heaven and the first earth passed away. (Rev. 21:1)

The Lord will make everything new.

Paul again takes direct aim at the false philosophical dualism of the Colossian heretics. They taught that all matter was evil and spirit was good. In their scheme, God did not create the physical universe, and He certainly would not wish to be reconciled to it. Paul declares that God will indeed reconcile the material world to Himself, and further, that He will do it through His Son, Jesus Christ. Far from being a spirit emanation unconcerned with evil matter, Jesus is the agent through which God will accomplish the reconciliation of the universe. The German theologian Erich Sauer comments,

The offering on Golgotha extends its influence into universal history. The salvation of mankind is only *one part* of the world-embracing counsels of God. . . . The "heavenly things" also will be cleansed through Christ's sacrifice of Himself (Heb. 9:23). A "cleansing" of the heavenly places is required if on no other ground than that they have been the dwelling of fallen spirits (Eph. 6:12; 2:2), and because Satan, their chief, has for ages had access to the highest regions of the heavenly world . . . the other side becomes this side; eternity transfigures time and this earth, the chief scene of the redemption, becomes the Residence of the universal kingdom of God (*The Triumph of the Crucified* [Grand Rapids: Eerdmans, 1960], pp. 179, 180 [italics in original]).

Some have imagined **all things** to include fallen men and fallen angels, and on that basis have argued for universalism, the ultimate salvation of everyone. By so doing they overlook a fundamental rule of interpretation, the *analogia Scriptura*. That principle teaches that no passage of Scripture, properly interpreted, will contradict any other passage. When we let Scripture interpret Scripture, it is clear that by all things Paul means all things for whom reconciliation is possible. That fallen angels and unregenerate men will spend eternity in hell is the emphatic teaching of Scripture. Our Lord will one day say to unbelievers, "Depart from Me, accursed ones, into the eternal fire which has been prepared for the devil and his angels," and they "will go away into eternal punishment" (Matt. 25:41, 46). In Revelation 20:10-15, the apostle John writes,

The devil who deceived them was thrown into the lake of fire and brimstone, where the beast and the false prophet are also; and they will be tormented day and night forever and ever. And I saw a great white throne and Him who sat upon it, from whose presence earth and heaven fled away, and no place was found for them. And I saw the dead, the great and the small, standing before the throne, and books were opened; and another book was opened, which is the book of life; and the dead were judged from the things which were written in the books, according to their deeds. And the sea gave up the dead which were in it, and death and Hades gave up the dead which were in them; and they were judged, every one of them according to their deeds. And death and Hades were thrown into the lake of fire. This is the second death, the lake of fire. And if anyone's name was not found written in the book of life, he was thrown into the lake of fire.

On the other hand, there is a sense in which even fallen angels and unredeemed men will be reconciled to God for judgment—but only in the sense of submitting to Him for final sentencing. Their relationship to Him will change from that of enemies to that of the judged. They will be sentenced to hell, unable any longer to pollute God's creation. They will be stripped of their power and forced to bow in submission to God. Paul writes in Colossians 2:15 that after Christ "disarmed the rulers and authorities [fallen angels], He made a public display of them, having triumphed over them." Because of Christ's victory, "the God of peace will soon crush Satan under your feet" (Rom. 16:20). And "at the name of Jesus every knee should bow, of those who are in heaven, and on earth, and under the earth" (Phil. 2:10). God has elevated Christ to a position above all things, whether things on earth or things in heaven. Paul wrote to the Ephesians that God "raised Him from the dead, and seated Him at His right hand in the heavenly places, far above all rule and authority and power and dominion, and every name that is named, not only in this age, but also in the one to come. And He put all things in subjection under His feet" (Eph. 1:21-22).

Though in the sacrifice of Christ, God made provision for the world (cf. John 3:16; 1 John 2:2), all persons will not be reconciled to God in the saving sense of being redeemed. The benefits of Christ's atonement are applied only to the elect, who alone come to saving faith in Him.

From God's general plan to reconcile all things to Himself, Paul turns to the specific reconciliation of believers like the Colossians. That they had been reconciled was evidence enough that Christ was sufficient to reconcile men and women to God. Their reconciliation foreshadowed the ultimate reconciliation of the universe.

To impress on them Christ's power to reconcile men to God, Paul reminds the Colossians of what they were like before their reconciliation. They **were formerly alienated and hostile in mind, engaged in evil deeds.** *Apallotrioō* (**alienated**) means "estranged," "cut off," or "separated." Before their reconciliation, the Colossians were completely estranged from God. In a similar passage, Paul writes, "You were at that time separate from Christ, excluded from the commonwealth of Israel, and strangers to the covenants of promise, having no hope and without God in the world. But now in Christ Jesus you who formerly were far off have been brought near by the blood of Christ" (Eph. 2:12-13). Non-Christians are detached from God because of sin; there is no such thing as an "innocent heathen." All unbelievers suffer separation from God unless they receive the reconciliation provided in Jesus Christ.

The Colossians had also been **hostile in mind.** *Echthros* (**hostile**) could also be translated "hateful." Unbelievers are not only alienated from God by condition, but also hateful of God by attitude. They hate Him and resent His holy standards and commands because they are **engaged in evil deeds.** Scripture teaches that unbelievers "loved the darkness rather than the light; for their deeds were evil. For everyone who does evil hates the light, and does not come to the light, lest his deeds should be exposed" (John 3:19-20). Their problem is not ignorance, but willful love of sin.

Even though they knew God, they did not honor Him as God, or give thanks; but they became futile in their speculations, and their foolish heart was darkened. Professing to be wise, they became fools, and exchanged the glory of the incorruptible God for an image in the form of corruptible man and of birds and four-footed animals and crawling creatures. Therefore God gave them over in the lusts of their hearts to impurity, that their bodies might be dishonored among them. (Rom. 1:21-24)

Although "that which is known about God is evident within them; for God made it evident to them" (Rom. 1:19), they "suppress the truth in unrighteousness" (Rom. 1:18). As Isaiah wrote to wayward Israel, "Your iniquities have made a separation between you and your God, and your sins have hidden His face from you, so that He does not hear" (Isa. 59:2). Sin is the root cause of man's alienation from God. Because God cannot fellowship with sin (cf. Hab. 1:13; 1 John 1:6), it is sin that needs to be dealt with before God and man can be reconciled.

The question arises as to whether man is reconciled to God, or God to man. There is a sense in which both occur. Since "the mind set on the flesh is hostile toward God" (Rom. 8:7), and "those who are in the flesh cannot please God" (Rom. 8:8), reconciliation cannot take place until man is transformed. "Therefore if any man is in Christ, he is a new creature; the old things passed away; behold, new things have come. Now all these things are from God, who reconciled us to Himself through Christ" (2 Cor. 5:17-18).

There is also God's side to reconciliation. From His holy perspective, His just wrath against sin must be appeased. Far from being the harmless, tolerant grandfather that many today imagine Him to be, God "takes vengeance on His adversaries, and He reserves wrath for His enemies" (Nah. 1:2). "At His wrath the earth quakes, and the nations cannot endure His indignation" (Jer. 10:10). The one who refuses to obey the Son will find that "the wrath of God abides on him" (John 3:36). Because of their sin, "the wrath of God comes upon the sons of disobedience" (Eph. 5:6). Man and God could never be reconciled unless God's wrath was appeased. The provision for that took place through Christ's sacrifice. "Much more then, having now been justified by His blood, we shall be saved from the wrath of God through Him" (Rom. 5:9). It is "Jesus who delivers us from the wrath to come" (1 Thess. 1:10). He bore the full fury of God's wrath against our sins (cf. 2 Cor. 5:21; 1 Pet. 2:24). After all, "God has not destined us for wrath, but for obtaining salvation through our Lord Jesus Christ" (1 Thess. 5:9).

Christ's death on the cross reconciled us to God (Eph. 2:16), something we could never have done on our own. In Romans 5:6-10, Paul gives four reasons for that. First, lack of strength: "we were still helpless" (v. 6). Second, lack of merit: we were "the ungodly" (v. 6). Third, lack of righteousness: "we were yet sinners" (v. 8). Finally, lack of peace with God: "we were enemies" (v. 10). It is only through the atoning work of the Lord Jesus Christ that anyone can receive reconciliation (v. 11).

The Means of Reconciliation

having made peace through the blood of His cross . . . He has now reconciled you in His fleshly body through death (1:20*b*, 22*a*)

Those two phrases sum up the specific means whereby Christ effected our reconciliation with God. Paul says first that Christ made peace between God and man through the blood of His cross. Blood speaks metaphorically of His atonement. It connects Christ's death with the Old Testament sacrificial system (cf. 1 Pet. 1:18-19). It is also a term that graphically notes violent death, such as that suffered by the sacrificial animals. The countless thousands of animals sacrificed under the Old Covenant pointed ahead to the violent, blood-shedding death the final sacrificial Lamb would suffer. The writer of Hebrews informs us that "the bodies of those animals whose blood is brought into the holy place by the high priest as an offering for sin, are burned outside the camp. Therefore Jesus also, that He might sanctify the people through His own blood, suffered outside the gate" (Heb. 13:11-12).

The reference to Christ's blood again stresses the link between His violent death and the violent deaths of the animals sacrificed under the Old Covenant. Unlike many of them, however, Jesus did not bleed to death (cf. John 19:34). No man took His life. He was not a helpless victim, but willingly offered up His life to God.

> For this reason the Father loves Me, because I lay down My life that I may take it again. No one has taken it away from Me, but I lay it down on My own initiative. I have authority to lay it down, and I have authority to take it up again. This commandment I received from My Father. (John 10:17-18)

Jesus chose the moment of His death: "When Jesus therefore had received the sour wine, He said, 'It is finished!' And He bowed His head, and gave up His spirit" (John 19:30).

There is nothing mystical, however, about the blood of Christ. It saves us only in the sense that His death was the sacrificial death of the final Lamb. It was that death that reconciled us to God (Rom. 5:10).

Proper biblical teaching on the blood of Christ simply is that His physical blood has no magical or mystical saving power. It is not some supernaturally preserved form of the actual blood of Christ that literally washes believers of their sin. The blood of Christ is applied to the believer in a symbolic sense, by faith, in the same way that we "see" Christ by faith, and we are seated with Him in the heavenlies—not in a physical sense.

How could the red and white corpuscles be literally applied to believers in salvation? To our physical bodies? Could it be otherwise with literal blood? Where is that literal, tangible blood kept? How much of it is applied, and why is it not used up? To one degree or another, we must acknowledge that there is symbolism in what Scripture says about the blood. Otherwise we will wind up with an obviously unbiblical doctrine like transubstantiation to explain how literal blood can be applied to all believers for salvation. (I have recently heard that some believe the blood of Jesus is kept in a bottle in heaven to be literally used in some way to apply to the soul!)

A strictly physical interpretation of what Scripture says about the blood of Christ cannot adequately deal with such passages as John 6:53-54: "Truly, truly, I say to you, unless you eat the flesh of the Son of Man and drink His blood, you have no life in yourselves. He who eats My flesh and drinks My blood has eternal life, and I will raise him up on the last day."

It would be equally hard to explain how physical blood is meant in Matthew 23:30-35 ("We would not have been partakers with them in the blood of the prophets"); 27:24-25 ("His blood be on us, and on our children"); Acts 5:28 ("[you] intend to bring this man's blood upon us"); 18:6 ("Your blood be upon your own heads"); 20:26, 28 ("I am pure from the blood of all men"); and 1 Corinthians 10:16 ("The cup of blessing . . . is it not the communion of the blood of Christ?").

The literal blood of Christ ran into the dirt and dust, and nothing in Scripture hints that it now exists in any tangible or visible form. Communion wine does not change into blood. There is no way the actual blood of Christ could be applied to all of us. We must acknowledge at some point that the sprinkling with blood under the New Covenant is symbolic.

"Without shedding of blood there is no forgiveness" (Heb. 9:22). I affirm that truth and have never denied it. But the "shedding of blood" in Scripture is an expression that means much more than just bleeding. It refers to violent sacrificial death. If just bleeding could buy salvation, why did not Jesus simply bleed without dying? Of course, He had to die to be the perfect sacrifice, and without His death our redemption could not have been purchased by His blood.

The meaning of Scripture in this matter is not all that difficult to understand. Romans 5:9-10 clarifies the point; those two verses side by side show that to be "justified by His blood" (v. 9) is the same as being "reconciled to God by the death of His Son" (v. 10). The critical element in salvation is the sacrificial death of Christ on our behalf. The shedding of His blood was the visible manifestation of His life being poured out in sacrifice, and Scripture consistently uses the term "shedding of blood" as a metonym for atoning death. (A metonym is a figure of speech in which the part is used to represent or designate the whole.)

Bloodshed was God's design for all Old Testament sacrifices. They were bled to death rather than clubbed or burnt. God designed that sacrificial death was to occur with blood loss as a vivid manifestation of life being poured out ("the life of the flesh is in the blood"). Nevertheless, those who were too poor to bring animals for sacrifices were allowed to bring one-tenth of an ephah (about two quarts) of fine flour instead (Lev. 5:11). Their sins were covered just as surely as the sins of those who could afford to offer a lamb, goat, turtledove, or pigeon (Lev. 5:6-7). Christ's blood was precious—but as precious as it was, only when it was poured out in death could the penalty of sin be paid.

Thus, if Christ had bled without dying, salvation would not have been purchased. In that sense, it is not His blood but His death that saves us. And when Scripture talks about the shedding of blood, the point is not mere bleeding, but dying by violence as a sacrifice. That is not heresy, and nothing in Protestant church history would support the notion that it is. The only major group to insist that the application of the blood is literal is the Roman Catholic Church.

Christ died not only as a sacrifice, but also as our substitute. He has now reconciled you in His fleshly body through death. In Romans 8:3, Paul tells us that God sent "His own Son in the likeness of sinful flesh and as an offering for sin, He condemned sin in the flesh." He took the place of sinners, dying a substitutionary death that paid the full penalty for the sin of all who believe. This death satisfied God's wrath. Once again Paul hammers away at the false teaching of the Colossian heretics that Christ was a mere spirit being. On the contrary, Paul insists, He died as a man for men. Were that not true, there could be no reconciliation for any person.

The Aim of Reconciliation

in order to present you before Him holy and blameless and beyond reproach (1:22*b*)

God's ultimate goal in reconciliation is to present His elect holy and pure before Him. Paul expressed a similar desire for the Corinthians: "I am jealous for you with a godly jealousy; for I betrothed you to one husband, that to Christ I might present you as a pure virgin" (2 Cor. 11:2). Jude tells us that we will one day "stand in the presence of His glory blameless with great joy" (Jude 24). Such purification is necessary if sinners are to stand in the presence of a holy God.

Holy (*hagios*) means to be separated from sin and set apart to God. It has to do with the believer's relationship with Him. As a result of a faith union with Jesus Christ, God sees Christians as holy as His Son. God "chose us in Him before the foundation of the world, that we should be holy and blameless before Him" (Eph. 1:4). "He made Him who knew no sin to be sin on our behalf, that we might become the righteousness of God in Him" (2 Cor. 5:21).

Blameless (*amōmos*) means without blemish. It was used in the Septuagint to speak of sacrificial animals (Num. 6:14). It is used in the New Testament to refer to Christ as the spotless Lamb of God (Heb. 9:14; 1 Pet. 1:19). In reference to ourselves, reconciliation gives us a blameless character.

Beyond reproach (*anegklētos*) goes beyond blameless. It means not only that we are without blemish, but also that no one can bring a charge against us (cf. Rom. 8:33). Satan, the accuser of the brethren (Rev. 12:10), cannot make a charge stick against those whom Christ has reconciled.

Christ's reconciliation makes believers holy, blameless, and beyond reproach **before Him.** God sees us now as we will be in heaven when we are glorified. He views us clothed with the very righteousness of Jesus Christ. The process of spiritual growth involves becoming in practice what we are in reality before God. We "have put on the new self" and that new self "is being renewed to a true knowledge according to the image of the One who created him" (Col. 3:10). The Christian life involves "beholding as in a mirror the glory of the Lord [which covers us before God, and] being transformed into the same image from glory to glory, just as from the Lord, the Spirit" (2 Cor. 3:18).

The Evidence of Reconciliation

if indeed you continue in the faith firmly established and steadfast, and not moved away from the hope of the gospel that you have heard, which was proclaimed in all creation under heaven, and of which I, Paul, was made a minister. (1:23)

One of the most sobering truths in the Bible is that not all who profess to be Christians are in fact saved. Our Lord warned, "'Many will say to Me on that day, "Lord, Lord, did we not prophesy in Your name, and in Your name cast out demons, and in Your name perform many miracles?" And then I will declare to them, "I never knew you; depart from Me, you who practice lawlessness"'" (Matt. 7:22-23).

Of all the marks of a genuine Christian presented in Scripture, none is more significant than the one Paul mentions here. People give evidence of being truly reconciled when they **continue in the faith firmly established and steadfast.** The Bible repeatedly testifies that those who are truly reconciled will continue in the faith. In the parable of the soils, Jesus described those represented by the rocky soil as "'those who, when they hear, receive the word with joy; and these have no firm root; they believe for a while, and in time of temptation fall away'" (Luke 8:13). By falling away they gave evidence that they were never truly saved. In John 8:31, "Jesus therefore was saying to those Jews who had believed Him, 'If you abide in My word, then you are truly disciples of Mine.'" Speaking of apostates, the apostle John writes in 1 John 2:19, "They went out from us, but they were not really of us; for if they had been of us, they would have remained with us; but they went out, in order that it might be shown that they all are not of us."

After hearing some difficult and challenging teaching from Him, many of Jesus' so-called disciples "withdrew, and were not walking with Him anymore" (John 6:66). By so doing, they gave evidence that they had never truly been His disciples. Perseverance is the hallmark of the true saint. (I discuss the issue further in my books *The Gospel According to Jesus* [Grand Rapids: Zondervan, 1988] and *Saved Without a Doubt* [Wheaton, Ill.: Victor, 1992].)

Lest there be any confusion about what they were to continue in, Paul specifies the content of their faith as **the gospel that you have heard, which was proclaimed in all creation under heaven, and of which I, Paul, was made a minister.** The Colossians are to hold fast to the apostolic gospel they had heard; the gospel that had been proclaimed throughout the world; the gospel of which Paul was a minister, commissioned to preach. Those who, like the Colossian errorists, preach any other gospel stand cursed before God (Gal. 1:8).

Perhaps no passage stresses the vital importance of reconciliation more than 2 Corinthians 5:17-21:

> If any man is in Christ, he is a new creature; the old things passed away; behold, new things have come. Now all these things are from God, who reconciled us to Himself through Christ, and gave us the ministry of reconciliation, namely, that God was in Christ reconciling

the world to Himself, not counting their trespasses against them, and He has committed to us the word of reconciliation. Therefore, we are ambassadors for Christ, as though God were entreating through us; we beg you on behalf of Christ, be reconciled to God. He made Him who knew no sin to be sin on our behalf, that we might become the righteousness of God in Him.

In that powerful text we can discern five truths about reconciliation. First, reconciliation transforms men: "If any man is in Christ, he is a new creature; the old things passed away; behold, new things have come" (v. 17). Second, it appeases God's wrath: "He made Him who knew no sin to be sin on our behalf, that we might become the righteousness of God in Him" (v. 21). Third, it comes through Christ: "All these things are from God, who reconciled us to Himself through Christ" (v. 18). Fourth, it is available to all who believe: "God was in Christ reconciling the world to Himself" (v. 19). Finally, every believer has been given the ministry of proclaiming the message of reconciliation: God "gave us the ministry of reconciliation" (v. 18), and "He has committed to us the word of reconciliation" (v. 19).

God sends His people forth as ambassadors into a fallen, lost world, bearing unbelievably good news. People everywhere are hopelessly lost and doomed, cut off from God by sin. But God has provided the means of reconciliation through the death of His Son. Our mission is to plead with people to receive that reconciliation, before it is too late. Paul's attitude, expressed in verse 20, should mark every Christian: "Therefore, we are ambassadors for Christ, as though God were entreating through us; we beg you on behalf of Christ, be reconciled to God."

Paul's View of the Ministry

6

Now I rejoice in my sufferings for your sake, and in my flesh I do my share on behalf of His body (which is the church) in filling up that which is lacking in Christ's afflictions. Of this church I was made a minister according to the stewardship from God bestowed on me for your benefit, that I might fully carry out the preaching of the word of God, that is, the mystery which has been hidden from the past ages and generations; but has now been manifested to His saints, to whom God willed to make known what is the riches of the glory of this mystery among the Gentiles, which is Christ in you, the hope of glory. And we proclaim Him, admonishing every man and teaching every man with all wisdom, that we may present every man complete in Christ. And for this purpose also I labor, striving according to His power, which mightily works within me. (1:24-29)

The ministry is a topic that was dear to the heart of the apostle Paul, and it is a frequent theme in his letters. He never lost the sense of wonder that God would call him to the ministry, and he never tired of talking about it. Toward the end of his life, he wrote to his protegé and fellow minister Timothy, "I thank Christ Jesus our Lord, who has strengthened me, because He considered me faithful, putting me into service; even though I was formerly a blasphemer and a persecutor and a violent aggressor" (1 Tim. 1:12-13).

Like Jeremiah, who spoke of the Word of God as a burning fire in his bones (Jer. 20:9), Paul felt compelled to carry out his ministry. To the Corinthians he wrote, "For if I preach the gospel, I have nothing to boast of, for I am under compulsion; for woe is me if I do not preach the gospel" (1 Cor. 9:16).

Paul often spoke of his ministry when he needed to establish his authority and credibility. That was his aim in this passage. Colossians was written in part as a polemic against false teachers, and it was essential for Paul to defend his authority to speak for God. Otherwise, the false teachers would have dismissed what he wrote as merely his own opinion. Having begun the epistle with a statement of his apostolic authority (1:1), Paul now gives a detailed look at the divine character of his ministry. He recites eight aspects of that ministry: the source of the ministry, the spirit of the ministry, the suffering of the ministry, the scope of the ministry, the subject of the ministry, the style of the ministry, the sum of the ministry, and the strength of the ministry.

THE SOURCE OF THE MINISTRY

the gospel . . . of which I, Paul, was made a minister . . . Of this church I was made a minister according to the stewardship from God bestowed on me for your benefit (1:23c, 25a)

Paul closed out the last section by describing the content of the Colossians' faith, namely the gospel, the saving truth of which he **was made a minister** (1:23). In 1:25 he repeats the thought, saying again that he **was made a minister** of Christ's church. The source of his ministry was God.

Becoming a minister of Jesus Christ was not what Saul of Tarsus planned to do with his life. On the contrary, he appeared headed for the upper echelons of Judaism. His credentials were impressive. He was "circumcised the eighth day, of the nation of Israel, of the tribe of Benjamin, a Hebrew of Hebrews; as to the Law, a Pharisee; as to zeal, a persecutor of the church; as to the righteousness which is in the Law, found blameless" (Phil. 3:5-6). Although born in Tarsus, he was brought up in Jerusalem, "educated under Gamaliel, strictly according to the law of our fathers, being zealous for God" (Acts 22:3). He said, "[I was] advancing in Judaism beyond many of my contemporaries among my countrymen, being more extremely zealous for my ancestral traditions" (Gal. 1:14). It was that zeal that led him to become a persecutor of Christians.

New Testament readers first meet Paul under his Jewish name, Saul, at Stephen's martyrdom. "When they had driven him out of the city, they began stoning him, and the witnesses laid aside their robes at the feet of a young man named Saul" (Acts 7:58). Not content with a supporting role, he quickly became the leading persecutor of the church: "Now Saul, still breathing threats and murder against the disciples of the Lord, went to the high priest, and asked for letters from him to the synagogues at Damascus, so that if he found any belonging to the Way, both men and women, he might bring them bound to Jerusalem" (Acts 9:1-2). He "persecuted this Way to the death, binding and putting both men and women into prisons" (Acts 22:4). As he described it in his testimony before King Agrippa,

> So then, I thought to myself that I had to do many things hostile to the name of Jesus of Nazareth. And this is just what I did in Jerusalem; not only did I lock up many of the saints in prisons, having received authority from the chief priests, but also when they were being put to death I cast my vote against them. And as I punished them often in all the synagogues, I tried to force them to blaspheme; and being furiously enraged at them, I kept pursuing them even to foreign cities. (Acts 26:9-11)

It was while engaged in his one-man crusade to wipe out the church that he had the experience which turned his world upside down:

> As I was journeying to Damascus with the authority and commission of the chief priests, at midday, O King, I saw on the way a light from heaven, brighter than the sun, shining all around me and those who were journeying with me. And when we had all fallen to the ground, I heard a voice saying to me in the Hebrew dialect, "Saul, Saul, why are you persecuting Me? It is hard for you to kick against the goads." And I said, "Who art Thou, Lord?" And the Lord said, "I am Jesus whom you are persecuting. But arise, and stand on your feet; for this purpose I have appeared to you, to appoint you a minister and a witness not only to the things which you have seen, but also to the things in which I will appear to you; delivering you from the Jewish people and from the Gentiles, to whom I am sending you, to open their eyes so that they may turn from darkness to light and from the dominion of Satan to God, in order that they may receive forgiveness of sins and an inheritance among those who have been sanctified by faith in Me." (Acts 26:12-18)

Paul did not volunteer to become a minister of Jesus Christ; he was appointed one by the Lord Himself. Blinded and terrified by the majesty of

Christ's glorious appearance, all he could say was "What shall I do, Lord?" (Acts 22:10).

Paul often stressed the marvelous fact that God had chosen him for the ministry. To the Romans he wrote that he was a minister to the Gentiles because of God's gracious choice of him: "I have written very boldly to you on some points, so as to remind you again, because of the grace that was given me from God, to be a minister of Christ Jesus to the Gentiles, ministering as a priest the gospel of God, that my offering of the Gentiles might become acceptable, sanctified by the Holy Spirit" (Rom. 15:15-16). He was eager to affirm that it was God who gave him the ministry of reconciliation (2 Cor. 5:18) and put him into the service of Jesus Christ (1 Tim. 1:12). He said to Timothy, "There is one God, and one mediator also between God and men, the man Christ Jesus, who gave Himself as a ransom for all, the testimony borne at the proper time. And for this I was appointed a preacher and an apostle (I am telling the truth, I am not lying) as a teacher of the Gentiles in faith and truth" (1 Tim. 2:5-7; cf. 2 Tim. 1:11).

All Christians have been called to serve God in one capacity or another. As God is sovereign in calling men to salvation, so is He in calling them to service. The Holy Spirit gives spiritual gifts, which are enablements for the service to which one is called, according to His sovereign will (1 Cor. 12:11). Like Paul, the believer's responsibility is to be obedient to that calling (Acts 26:19).

Because he was made a minister by sovereign call, Paul viewed his ministry as a **stewardship from God. Stewardship** translates *oikonomia*, a compound word made up of *oikos* ("house") and *nemō* ("manage"). It means to manage a household as a steward of someone else's possessions. The steward had oversight of the other servants and handled the business and financial affairs of the household. That freed the owner to travel and pursue other interests. Being a steward was thus a position of great trust and responsibility in the ancient world.

Unlike many who have held high offices throughout the church's history, Paul sought no glory for himself. He wanted to be regarded "in this manner, as [a servant] of Christ, and [a steward] of the mysteries of God. In this case, moreover, it is required of stewards that one be found trustworthy" (1 Cor. 4:1-2). He had a God-given task that he was obligated to fulfill (cf. 1 Cor. 9:16-17; Gal. 2:7; Eph. 3:2, 7-8). There is no stronger passage to show Paul's firm sense of the divine call in his life than 1 Corinthians 9:16-17. He writes, "If I preach the gospel, I have nothing to boast of, for I am under compulsion; for woe is me if I do not preach the gospel. For if I do this voluntarily, I have a reward; but if against my will, I have a stewardship entrusted to me." "I am under compulsion" is strong language. "Woe is me" is even stronger. He operated under the knowledge of a divine mandate that was not even voluntary initially. All who are called to preach should feel the compulsion, the fear of judgment, and the sense of stewardship Paul felt. The church is the household of God (1 Tim. 3:15), and all believers have the responsibility to manage the ministries the Lord has given them. Contrary to much popular teaching today, our spiritual gifts are not intended for our own edification. They are given to help us minister to others. Paul told the Colossians that his stewardship was **bestowed on me for your benefit.** Peter echoed the same truth when he wrote, "As each one has received a special gift, employ it in serving one another, as good stewards of the manifold grace of God" (1 Pet. 4:10). Leaders have a special stewardship: "The overseer must be above reproach as God's steward" (Titus 1:7). Every Christian will one day give account to Christ of his stewardship. May none of us be found poor stewards, like the lazy slave in the parable of the talents (Matt. 25:24-25).

THE SPIRIT OF THE MINISTRY

Now I rejoice (1:24a)

As challenging and demanding as it is, ministry was never intended to be an arduous and unbearable burden. Paul's attitude of joy should be the spirit of ministry for every Christian. The sad reality is, however, that many Christians (even some pastors) have lost the joy of serving the Lord. They grudgingly carry out their responsibilities, with solemn faces and somber spirits. Like Jonah, they are hesitant, angry, bitter, and resentful. They are reminiscent of Elijah, who "requested for himself that he might die, and said, 'It is enough; now, O Lord, take my life, for I am not better than my fathers'" (1 Kings 19:4).

The writer of Hebrews rebukes those pseudo-martyrs in no uncertain terms. He reminds them of "Jesus, the author and perfecter of faith, who for the joy set before Him endured the cross, despising the shame, and has sat down at the right hand of the throne of God. For consider Him who has endured such hostility by sinners against Himself, so that you may not grow weary and lose heart" (Heb. 12:2-3). Jesus never lost the joy of His ministry, even when faced with the terrible reality of the cross. And, unlike Him, most believers "have not yet resisted to the point of shedding blood" (v. 4). A Christian who has lost the joy of the ministry does not have bad circumstances, but bad connections. You do not lose the joy of serving Christ unless your communion with Him breaks down.

Christian joy is internal. Paul was sometimes discouraged by his circumstances, but he maintained his joy. He described himself as "afflicted in every way, but not crushed; perplexed, but not despairing; persecuted, but not forsaken; struck down, but not destroyed" (2 Cor. 4:8-9). He knew "great sorrow and unceasing grief" (Rom. 9:2) over the plight of unbelieving Israel. Whatever Paul's circumstances, he never lost his deep-seated confidence that God is in control.

Joy is generated by humility. People lose their joy when they become self-centered, thinking they deserve better circumstances or treatment than they are getting. That was never a problem for Paul. Like all of God's great servants, he was conscious of his unworthiness. Imprisoned in Rome, while other preachers got the glory, he wrote, "Christ is proclaimed; and in this I rejoice, yes, and I will rejoice" (Phil. 1:18). Facing the possibility of martyrdom, he wrote, "Even if I am being poured out as a drink offering upon the sacrifice and service of your faith, I rejoice and share my joy with you all" (Phil. 2:17). Beaten and imprisoned in Philippi, he sang hymns of praise to God (Acts 16:25). Because he believed he deserved nothing, no circumstance could shake his joyous confidence that God was in control of his life (cf. Col. 2:5; 1 Thess. 2:19-20; Philem. 7).

The joy of the early church was a dramatic testimony to the world. The second-century apologist Aristides wrote to the Roman emperor Antonius Pius a description of Christians that said if any righteous person from among them passed from this world the Christians would rejoice and give thanks to God. When a child was born to Christian parents, they would praise God. If it died in infancy, according to Aristides, the parents thanked God even more because the child would be one who had passed through the world without encountering sin. (See *The Apology of Aristides*, trans. Rendel Harris [London: Cambridge, 1893].)

Circumstances, people, and worry are the thieves that are eager to steal the joy of the ministry. Humility, devotion to Christ, and trust in God protect the joy that is Christ's legacy to every Christian (cf. John 15:11; 17:13).

THE SUFFERING OF THE MINISTRY

in my sufferings for your sake, and in my flesh I do my share on behalf of His body (which is the church) in filling up that which is lacking in Christ's afflictions. (1:24*b*)

To emphasize that joy is independent of circumstances, Paul tells the Colossians that he rejoices **in my sufferings for your sake. Sufferings** refers to his present imprisonment (Acts 28:16, 30), from which he wrote Colossians. Paul could rejoice despite his imprisonment because he always viewed himself as a prisoner of Jesus Christ, not the Roman Empire (cf. Philem. 1, 9, 23).

The early church considered it a privilege to suffer for the name of Christ. In Acts 5:41, the apostles "went on their way from the presence of the Council, rejoicing that they had been considered worthy to suffer shame for His name." To the Philippians Paul wrote, "To you it has been granted for Christ's sake, not only to believe in Him, but also to suffer for His sake" (Phil. 1:29). Why was suffering a cause for joy? The New Testament suggests at least five reasons.

First, suffering brings believers closer to Christ. Paul wrote, "That I may know Him, and the power of His resurrection and the fellowship of His sufferings" (Phil. 3:10). Suffering in the cause of Christ yields the fruit of better understanding of what Jesus went through in His suffering.

Second, suffering assures the believer that he belongs to Christ. Jesus said, "If the world hates you, you know that it has hated Me before it hated you" (John 15:18). Because "a disciple is not above his teacher, nor a slave above his master" (Matt. 10:24), we will suffer. Paul warned Timothy, "Indeed, all who desire to live godly in Christ Jesus will be persecuted" (2 Tim. 3:12). Peter tells suffering Christians, "If you are reviled for the name of Christ, you are blessed, because the Spirit of glory and of God rests upon you" (1 Pet. 4:14). Suffering causes believers to sense the presence of the Holy Spirit in their lives, which gives assurance of salvation.

Third, suffering brings a future reward. "If indeed we suffer with [Christ] in order that we may also be glorified with Him. For I consider that the sufferings of this present time are not worthy to be compared with the glory that is to be revealed to us" (Rom. 8:17-18). "For momentary, light affliction is producing for us an eternal weight of glory far beyond all comparison" (2 Cor. 4:17).

Fourth, suffering can result in the salvation of others. Church history is filled with accounts of those who came to Christ after watching other Christians endure suffering.

Fifth, suffering frustrates Satan. He wants suffering to harm us, but God brings good out of it.

The statement **in my flesh I do my share on behalf of His body (which is the church) in filling up that which is lacking in Christ's afflictions** has been the subject of much controversy. Roman Catholics have imagined here a reference to the suffering of Christians in purgatory. Christ's suffering, they maintain, was not enough to purge us completely from our sins. Christians must make up what was lacking in Christ's suffering on their behalf by their own suffering after death. That can hardly be Paul's point, however. He has just finished demonstrating that Christ alone is sufficient to reconcile us to God (1:20-23). To do an about face now and teach that believers must help pay for their sins would undermine his whole argument. The New Testament is clear that Christ's sufferings need nothing added to them. In Jesus' death on the cross, the work of salvation was completed. Further, the Colossian heretics taught that human works were necessary for salvation. To teach that believers' suffering was necessary to help expiate their sins would be to play right into the errorists' hands. The idea that Paul refers to suffering in purgatory is ruled out by both the general content of the epistle and the immediate context, as well as the obvious absence of any mention of a place like purgatory in Scripture. Finally, *thlipsis* (**afflictions**) is used nowhere in the New Testament to speak of Christ's sufferings.

In my flesh refers to Paul's physical pain. When he says **I do my share on behalf of His body (which is the church)** he is indicating that the physical pain he endures at the hands of Christ-hating persecutors is the result of what he does to benefit and build the church. It was not his personality that offended and brought hostile injury to him, but his ministry for the Body of Christ.

In what sense were Paul's sufferings **filling up that which is lacking in Christ's afflictions**? In that Paul was receiving the persecution that was intended for Christ. Jesus, having ascended to heaven, was out of their reach. But because His enemies had not filled up all the injuries they wanted to inflict on Him, they turned their hatred on those who preached the gospel. It was in that sense that Paul filled up what was lacking in Christ's afflictions. In 2 Corinthians 1:5 he wrote that "the sufferings of Christ are ours in abundance." He bore in his body the marks of the blows intended for Christ (Gal. 6:17; cf. 2 Cor. 11:23-28). He not only suffered for Christ, but also for the sake of the church (2 Tim. 2:10). Those who wish to represent Christ and serve His church must be willing to suffer for His Name.

THE SCOPE OF THE MINISTRY

that I might fully carry out the preaching of the word of God, (1:25*b*)

Paul was driven to fulfill his ministry. He told the Ephesian elders, "I do not consider my life of any account as dear to myself, in order that I may finish my course, and the ministry which I received from the Lord Jesus, to testify solemnly of the gospel of the grace of God" (Acts 20:24). That ministry consisted primarily of **the preaching of the word of God,** of "declaring . . . the whole purpose of God" (Acts 20:27). And Paul fulfilled that ministry. Near the end of his life he exclaimed triumphantly, "I have fought the good fight, I have finished the course, I have kept the faith" (2 Tim. 4:7). His economy of effort, his single-minded devotion, and clear, direct focus on the task God had given him enabled him to carry out his ministry fully. He set himself to do God's will, nothing more or less, and stayed within that narrow prescription. He desired to preach the whole counsel of God to those to whom God called him, never shirking his duty or mitigating the divine message.

Some in the Lord's service think they have to win the entire world. As a result, they spread themselves so thin that they accomplish little. Paul was led by the Holy Spirit to make only three missionary journeys, all to the same general area. Yet few people in history have affected the world the way he did. Jesus never left Palestine, yet no one has come remotely close to having the impact on the world that He has. Jesus' ministry was effective because He limited it to doing what God wanted.

First, Jesus limited His ministry to God's will. He said in John 5:30, "I do not seek My own will, but the will of Him who sent Me." Too many men in the ministry are busy building their own empires, rather than seeking to fulfill God's will.

Second, Jesus limited His ministry to God's timing. The gospel of John repeatedly speaks of Jesus' hour as having not yet come (cf. 2:4; 7:30; 8:20; 12:27; 13:1; 17:1). Jesus carried out His ministry conscious of God's timing. He refused to do things until the right time.

Third, Jesus limited His ministry to God's objective. He knew that God had not sent Him to reach the entire world by Himself. In Matthew 15:24 He said, "I was sent only to the lost sheep of the house of Israel."

Fourth, Jesus limited His ministry to God's kingdom. He refused to be drawn into the political controversies of His day. When His opponents tried to embroil Him in one such controversy, He replied, "Render to Caesar the things that are Caesar's; and to God the things that are God's" (Matt. 22:21). He kept the political realm and the spiritual realm separate. That is a lesson many in the contemporary church seem to have missed.

Fifth, Jesus limited Himself to God's people. He realized He could pour His life into only a few men. Out of the larger group of His followers, He chose the twelve and spent most of His time with them. And even among the twelve, He spent more time with Peter, James, and John than with the rest.

Those who desire truly effective ministries must learn the importance of limits. If they concentrate on the depth of their ministries, God will take care of the breadth.

THE SUBJECT OF THE MINISTRY

that is, the mystery which has been hidden from the past ages and generations; but has now been manifested to His saints, to whom God willed to make known what is the riches of the glory of this mystery among the Gentiles, which is Christ in you, the hope of glory. (1:26-27)

The message Paul proclaimed in his ministry was **the mystery which has been hidden from the past ages and generations; but has now been manifested to His saints.** There are some things God reveals to no one. Deuteronomy 29:29 says, "The secret things belong to the Lord our God." God reveals other things only to certain people. "The secret of the Lord is for those who fear Him" (Ps. 25:14). Proverbs 3:32 says, "He is intimate with the upright." Still other things were hidden in the Old Testament but have now been revealed in the New. The New Testament calls them mysteries (*mustērion*). Paul's use of this word is not to indicate a secret teaching, rite, or ceremony revealed only to some elite initiates (as in the mystery religions), but truth revealed to all believers in the New Testament. This truth, that has now **been manifested to His saints,** is that **which has been hidden from the past ages and generations,** namely the Old Testament era and people. **Now** refers to the time of the writing of the New Testament. Such newly revealed truth includes the mystery of the incarnate God (Col. 2:2-3, 9); of Israel's unbelief (Rom. 11:25); of lawlessness(2 Thess. 2:7; cf. Rev. 17:5, 7); of the unity of Jew and Gentile in the church (Eph. 3:3-6); and of the rapture (1 Cor. 15:51). This mystery truth is available only for those who are saints—true believers (cf. 1 Cor. 2:7-16). The phrase **to whom God willed to make known** clearly indicates that the mysteries are not discovered by the genius of man, but are revealed by the will and act of God. It is God's purpose that His people know this truth.

Of all the mysteries God has revealed in the New Testament, the most profound is **Christ in you, the hope of glory.** The Old Testament predicted the coming of the Messiah. But the idea that He would actually live in His redeemed church, made up mostly of Gentiles, was not revealed. The New Testament is clear that Christ, by the Holy Spirit, takes up permanent residence in all believers (cf. Rom. 8:9; 1 Cor. 6:19, 20; Eph. 2:22). The revelation of the riches of the glory of this mystery among the Gentiles awaited the New Testament (Eph. 3:3-6). Believers, both Jew and Gentile, now possess the surpassing riches of the indwelling Christ (John 14:23; Rom. 8:9-10; Gal. 2:20; Eph. 1:7, 17-18; 3:8-10, 16-19; Phil. 4:19). The church is described as "the temple of the living

God; just as God said, 'I will dwell in them and walk among them; and I will be their God, and they shall be My people'" (2 Cor. 6:16). That Christ indwells all believers is the source for their **hope of glory** and is the subject or theme of the gospel ministry. What makes the gospel attractive is not just that it promises present joy and help, but that it promises eternal honor, blessing, and glory. When Christ comes to live in a believer, His presence is the anchor of the promise of heaven—the guarantee of future bliss eternally (cf. 2 Cor. 5:1-5; Eph. 1:13-14). In the reality that Christ is living in the Christian is the experience of new life and hope of eternal glory.

THE STYLE OF THE MINISTRY

And we proclaim Him, admonishing every man and teaching every man with all wisdom, (1:28a)

Paul's passion was to **proclaim Him** who had done so much for him. *Katangellō* (**proclaim**) means to publicly declare a completed truth or happening. It is a general term and is not restricted to formal preaching. Paul's proclamation included two aspects, one negative, one positive.

Admonishing is from *noutheteō*. It speaks of encouraging counsel in view of sin and coming punishment. It is the responsibility of church leaders. In Acts 20:31, Paul described his ministry at Ephesus: "Night and day for a period of three years I did not cease to admonish each one with tears." But it is also the responsibility of every believer. Paul wrote to the Thessalonians, "If anyone does not obey our instruction in this letter, take special note of that man and do not associate with him, so that he may be put to shame. And yet do not regard him as an enemy, but admonish him as a brother" (2 Thess. 3:14-15).

Colossians 3:16 commands, "Let the word of Christ richly dwell within you, with all wisdom teaching and admonishing one another." Paul expressed his confidence that the Romans were "full of goodness, filled with all knowledge, and able also to admonish one another" (Rom. 15:14). If there is sin in the life of a believer, other believers have the responsibility to lovingly, gently admonish them to forsake that sin.

Teaching refers to imparting positive truth. It, too, is the responsibility of every believer (Col. 3:16), and is part of the Great Commission (Matt. 28:20). It is especially the responsibility of church leaders. "An overseer, then, must be . . . able to teach" (1 Tim. 3:2).

Admonishing and teaching must be done **with all wisdom.** This is the larger context. As discussed in chapter 2, **wisdom** refers to practical discernment—understanding the biblical principles for holy conduct. The consistent pattern of Paul's ministry was to link teaching and admonishment and bring them together in the context of the general doctrinal truths of the Word. Doctrinal teaching was invariably followed by practical admonitions. That must also be the pattern for all ministries.

THE SUM OF THE MINISTRY

that we may present every man complete in Christ. (1:28*b*)

The goal of the ministry is the maturity of the saints. Paul expressed that clearly in Ephesians 4:11-13: "[Christ] gave some as apostles, and some as prophets, and some as evangelists, and some as pastors and teachers, for the equipping of the saints for the work of service, to the building up of the body of Christ; until we all attain to the unity of the faith, and of the knowledge of the Son of God, to a mature man, to the measure of the stature which belongs to the fulness of Christ." That goal was shared by Epaphras, the founder of the Colossian church: "Epaphras, who is one of your number, a bondslave of Jesus Christ, sends you his greetings, always laboring earnestly for you in his prayers, that you may stand perfect and fully assured in all the will of God" (Col. 4:12). Our aim is not merely to win people to Christ, but to bring them to spiritual maturity. They will then be able to reproduce their faith in others. In 2 Timothy 2:2 Paul charged Timothy, "The things which you have heard from me in the presence of many witnesses, these entrust to faithful men, who will be able to teach others also."

To be **complete,** or mature, is to be like Christ. Although all Christians strive for that lofty end, no one on earth has arrived there yet (cf. Phil. 3:12). Every believer, however, will one day attain it. "Beloved, now we are children of God, and it has not appeared as yet what we shall be. We know that, when He appears, we shall be like Him, because we shall see Him just as He is" (1 John 3:2). Christians move toward maturity by feeding on God's Word: "All Scripture is inspired by God and profitable for teaching, for reproof, for correction, for training in righteousness; that the man of God may be adequate, equipped for every good work" (2 Tim. 3:16-17).

The Colossian heretics believed perfection was only for the elite, a view shared by many others throughout history. The American journalist Walter Lippmann wrote,

As yet, no teacher has ever appeared who was wise enough to know how to teach his wisdom to all mankind. In fact, the great teachers have attempted nothing so utopian. They were quite well aware how difficult for most men is wisdom, and they have confessedly stated that the perfect life was for the select few.

In contrast, Christ offers spiritual maturity to every man and woman.

The Strength of the Ministry

And for this purpose also I labor, striving according to His power, which mightily works within me. (1:29)

Kopiaō (**labor**) means to work to the point of exhaustion. People sometimes tell me that I work too hard. But compared to Paul, I am not working hard enough. It saddens me to hear of pastors or seminary students who are looking for an easy pastorate. When I was a young pastor, a lady (who did not know I was a pastor) advised me to go into the ministry. When I asked her why, she replied that ministers did not have to do anything and could make lots of money.

No one would get that idea by observing Paul. Concerning those who denigrated his ministry, he wrote:

> Are they servants of Christ? (I speak as if insane) I more so; in far more labors, in far more imprisonments, beaten times without number, often in danger of death. Five times I received from the Jews thirty-nine lashes. Three times I was beaten with rods, once I was stoned, three times I was shipwrecked, a night and a day I have spent in the deep. I have been on frequent journeys, in dangers from rivers, dangers from robbers, dangers from my countrymen, dangers from the Gentiles, dangers in the city, dangers in the wilderness, dangers on the sea, dangers among false brethren; I have been in labor and hardship, through many sleepless nights, in hunger and thirst, often without food, in cold and exposure. Apart from such external things, there is the daily pressure upon me of concern for all the churches. (2 Cor. 11:23-28)

No one can successfully serve Jesus Christ without working hard. Lazy pastors, Christian leaders, or laymen will never fulfill the ministry the Lord has called them to. **Striving** is from *agōnizomai*, which refers to competing in an athletic event. Our English word *agonize* is derived from it. Success in serving the Lord, like success in sports, demands maximum effort.

Lest anyone misunderstand him, Paul says that he strives **according to His power, which mightily works within me.** All his toil and hard labor would have been useless apart from God's power in his life. To the Corinthians he wrote, "By the grace of God I am what I am, and His grace toward me did not prove vain; but I labored even more than all of them, yet not I, but the grace of God with me" (1 Cor. 15:10). God gave Paul the strength to work hard at his ministry. Galatians 2:20 really sums up the two components in this human-divine action: "I have been crucified with Christ; and it is no longer I who live, but Christ lives in me; and the life which I now live in the flesh I live by faith in the Son of God, who loved me, and delivered Himself up for me."

These eight aspects of Paul's ministry should characterize every believer. All Christians serve Christ in some capacity. Paul's message to all in this passage is, "The things you have learned and received and heard and seen in me, practice these things" (Phil. 4:9).

Paul's Love for the Church

7

For I want you to know how great a struggle I have on your behalf, and for those who are at Laodicea, and for all those who have not personally seen my face, that their hearts may be encouraged, having been knit together in love, and attaining to all the wealth that comes from the full assurance of understanding, resulting in a true knowledge of God's mystery, that is, Christ Himself, in whom are hidden all the treasures of wisdom and knowledge. I say this in order that no one may delude you with persuasive argument. For even though I am absent in body, nevertheless I am with you in spirit, rejoicing to see your good discipline and the stability of your faith in Christ. As you therefore have received Christ Jesus the Lord, so walk in Him, having been firmly rooted and now being built up in Him and established in your faith, just as you were instructed, and overflowing with gratitude. (2:1-7)

If someone were to ask you to suggest the most important qualities a minister can possess, you might argue for intelligence, education, leadership ability, boldness, holiness, or speaking ability. Although all those are essential components, perhaps the most necessary ingredient in the life of any minister of Jesus Christ is love for the church. No one can truly serve God in the church without that motivation.

Jesus loved the church so much that He gave His life for it. Paul charged the Ephesian elders to "shepherd the church of God which He purchased with His own blood" (Acts 20:28). In Ephesians 5:25 he said that husbands should love their wives "just as Christ also loved the church and gave Himself up for her."

Paul, too, had a deep love for the church and gave his life in service to it. He frequently expressed his love in his epistles. To the Corinthians he wrote, "You are our letter, written in our hearts, known and read by all men" (2 Cor. 3:2); "Our mouth has spoken freely to you, O Corinthians, our heart is opened wide" (2 Cor. 6:11); "I will most gladly spend and be expended for your souls" (2 Cor. 12:15). He told the Philippians, "I have you in my heart" (Phil. 1:7).

Paul loved the church because he loved Christ. He knew well the truth expressed in 1 John 4:21, "This commandment we have from Him, that the one who loves God should love his brother also." It was his love for Christ and His church that enabled Paul to endure the physical suffering he went through (cf. 2 Cor. 11:23-27). It also allowed him to bear "the daily pressure . . . of concern for all the churches" (2 Cor. 11:28). Because of that love he could endure defections, false teachers, and personal abuse. Indeed, he could "endure all things for the sake of those who are chosen, that they also may obtain the salvation which is in Christ Jesus and with it eternal glory" (2 Tim. 2:10).

Paul's love for the church caused him to write this letter to the churches of the Lycus Valley (cf. 4:15-16). He wanted them to know of the great struggle he had on their behalf and their sister church in Laodicea, even though they had not all personally seen his face. Paul's love was not selective; he loved the whole church, not just those personally known by or close to him. That kind of unselfish love should characterize every spiritual leader. **Struggle** translates *agōn*, from which we get our English word *agony*. It is a different form of the same word he used in 1:29 to speak of his striving in the ministry. Paul's deep love even for those he had never met reflects his love for Christ, the Head of the church.

Just as loving parents have goals for their children, so Paul had goals for the church. He lists five of them for which he had struggled. He desired the Colossians to be strong in heart, united in love, settled in understanding, walking in Christ, and overflowing with gratitude.

STRONG IN HEART

that their hearts may be encouraged, (2:2*a*)

The basic meaning of *parakaleō* (**encouraged**) is "to call alongside." Because a person can be called alongside for many purposes, the word has a wide range of meanings. They include to entreat, appeal to, summon, comfort, exhort, or encourage. In the present context, however, it could be translated "strengthen" because the Colossians were beset by false teachers and needed strengthening rather than comfort.

Commentator William Barclay cites an example of *parakaleō* from classical Greek that parallels its usage here.

> There was a Greek regiment which had lost heart and was utterly dejected. The general sent a leader to talk to it to such purpose that courage was reborn and a body of dispirited men became fit again for heroic action. That is what [*parakaleō*] means here. It is Paul's prayer that the Church may be filled with that courage which can cope with any situation. (*The Letters to the Philippians, Colossians, and Thessalonians* [Louisville, Ky.: Westminster, 1975], p. 129)

When Paul expressed his desire that their hearts be strengthened, he was not referring just to their emotions. The biblical writers associated the emotions with what the King James Version picturesquely calls the "bowels" (cf. Ps. 22:14; Song of Sol. 5:4; Lam. 2:11; 1 John 3:17). They did so because strong emotions produce physical reactions in the lower part of the abdomen. Even today someone who is anxious feels what are called butterflies in the stomach. The abstract concept of emotions was viewed in terms of the concrete physical effects they produced.

When used figuratively in the Bible, the word *heart* is usually more general and refers broadly to the inner person, the center of life. It often equates specifically to the mind. In Revelation 2:23 the Lord describes Himself as "He who searches the minds and hearts; and . . .will give to each one of you according to your deeds." The heart here is a synonym for the mind. Using the term *heart* as the general term for the thinking faculty, Jeremiah 17:9 says, "The heart is more deceitful than all else and is desperately sick; who can understand it?" Revelation 18:7 says of Babylon, "For she says in her heart, 'I sit as a queen and I am not a widow, and will never see mourning.'" "The fool," Psalm 53:1 says, "has said in his heart, 'There is no God.'" As those verses indicate, the heart refers to the mind, where thinking takes place (cf. Isa. 47:8; Zeph. 2:15; Matt. 24:48).

The emotions respond to what goes on in the heart, to what the mind perceives. The way to control the emotions, then, is through the mind. When the mind is filled with biblical truth, the emotions respond properly. For that reason the Bible counsels to "watch over your heart with all diligence, for from it flow the springs of life" (Prov. 4:23). Scripture also says to "direct your heart in the way" (Prov. 23:19). Believers are to guide their hearts, that they may follow the path of pleasing God. For that we need His help. "Examine me, O Lord, and try me; test my mind and my heart" (Ps. 26:2). "Search me, O God, and know my heart; try me and know my anxious thoughts; and see if there be any hurtful way in me, and lead me in the everlasting way" (Ps. 139:23-24). What fills the heart will inevitably issue in behavior. "For the mouth speaks out of that which fills the heart. The good man out of his good treasure brings forth what is good; and the evil man out of his evil treasure brings forth what is evil" (Matt. 12:34-35).

What is the means of a strong mind? Ephesians 3:16 says, "That He would grant you, according to the riches of His glory, to be strengthened with power through His Spirit in the inner man." The Spirit strengthens the hearts of those who yield their lives to His control. One of His names is *Helper* (cf. John 14:16, 26; 15:26; 16:7). *Helper* in the Greek is the noun form of *parakaleō* and could be translated "Strengthener" in those passages. True inner strength comes only from being filled with the Spirit.

After his conversion, Paul enjoyed the experience of being strengthened: "Saul kept increasing in strength and confounding the Jews who lived at Damascus by proving that this Jesus is the Christ" (Acts 9:22). As he lived his life in the power of the Spirit, he experienced strength. Eventually, he could say, "We are afflicted in every way, but not crushed; perplexed, but not despairing; persecuted, but not forsaken; struck down, but not destroyed" (2 Cor. 4:8-9). He could endure all that because he was strong in heart.

Although the Spirit is the divine strengthener, He also uses human instruments. Jesus told Peter "Once you have turned again, strengthen your brothers" (Luke 22:32). "Judas and Silas, also being prophets themselves, encouraged and strengthened the brethren with a lengthy message" (Acts 15:32). Paul sent Timothy to the Thessalonians to strengthen their faith (1 Thess. 3:2). An important part of Paul's ministry was strengthening the believers. Acts 15:41 records his "traveling through Syria and Cilicia, strengthening the churches" (cf. Acts 14:21-22; 18:23). God uses gifted men to teach and strengthen the church (cf. Eph. 4:11-14).

Strong hearts result in a powerful Christian life. When believers are strengthened by the Spirit, Christ will dwell in their hearts, they will be rooted and grounded in love, they will know the love of Christ and be filled with all the fullness of God (Eph. 3:16-19). Then Christ, through them, will do "exceeding abundantly beyond all [they can] ask or think" (Eph. 3:20).

UNITED IN LOVE

having been knit together in love, (2:2*b*)

Fervent love is the necessary balance to a strong mind. Christianity is not mindless enthusiasm, but neither is it lifeless intellectual orthodoxy. Paul eloquently states the centrality of love in 1 Corinthians 13:1-3:

> If I speak with the tongues of men and of angels, but do not have love, I have become a noisy gong or a clanging cymbal. And if I have the gift of prophecy, and know all mysteries and all knowledge; and if I have all faith, so as to remove mountains, but do not have love, I am nothing. And if I give all my possessions to feed the poor, and if I deliver my body to be burned, but do not have love, it profits me nothing.

Sumbibazō (**knit together**) means to unite, or bring together. This aorist participle explains the main verb (**may be encouraged**) by further defining the strengthened heart as one filled with love. It refers in Ephesians 4:16 and Colossians 2:19 to the various parts that unite to form the human body. Believers share a common life with love as its basis. All believers possess the same eternal life, all come to Christ in the same way, and all were placed into the Body of Christ by the same Spirit (cf. 1 Cor. 12:11-13). The church's unity is not organizational, but organic. Believers are "all one in Christ Jesus" (Gal. 3:28; cf. Rom. 10:12).

Certainly this prayer of Jesus was answered in the unity of the Body:

> I do not ask in behalf of [My disciples] alone, but for those also who believe in Me through their word; that they may all be one; even as Thou, Father, art in Me, and I in Thee, that they also may be in Us; that the world may believe that Thou didst send Me. And the glory which Thou hast given Me I have given to them; that they may be one, just as We are one; I in them, and Thou in Me, that they may be perfected in unity, that the world may know that Thou didst send Me, and didst love them, even as Thou didst love Me. (John 17:20-23)

The late Francis Schaeffer called the unity of the church "the final apologetic" to the watching world (*The Mark of the Christian* [Downers Grove, Ill.: InterVarsity, 1970], p. 15). He went on to write,

> In John 13 the point was that, if an individual Christian does not show love toward other true Christians, the world has a right to judge that he is not a Christian. Here [in John 17:21] Jesus is stating something else which is much more cutting, much more profound: We cannot expect the world to believe that the Father sent the Son, that Jesus' claims are true, and that Christianity is true, unless the world sees some reality of the oneness of true Christians.
>
> Now that is frightening. Should we not feel some emotion at this point? (*The Mark of the Christian*, p. 15)

That Christians display their unity in practice was Paul's constant concern. He wrote to the quarrelsome Corinthians, "Now I exhort you, brethren, by the name of our Lord Jesus Christ, that you all agree, and there be no divisions among you, but you be made complete in the same mind and in the same judgment" (1 Cor. 1:10). Again, at the end of his second letter to them, he commanded them to "be like-minded, live in peace" (2 Cor. 13:11). He admonished the Philippians to "conduct yourselves in a manner worthy of the gospel of Christ; so that whether I come and see you or remain absent, I may hear of you that you are standing firm in one spirit, with one mind striving together for the faith of the gospel" (Phil. 1:27) and to "make my joy complete by being of the same mind, maintaining the same love, united in spirit, intent on one purpose" (Phil. 2:2).

The key to practical unity is found in Ephesians 4:3: "Being diligent to preserve the unity of the Spirit in the bond of peace." Preserving the unity the Spirit has created is accomplished by being peacemakers. Peacemakers love each other. Such love is evident when believers "put on a heart of compassion, kindness, humility, gentleness and patience; bearing with one another, and forgiving each other, whoever has a complaint against anyone; just as the Lord forgave you, so also should you" (Col. 3:12-13).

That kind of humble, practical love "is the perfect bond of unity" (Col. 3:14). Love is always linked with humility, because only humble people can love. After urging the Philippians to pursue unity in Philippians 2:2, Paul went on to show them how in verses 3-8:

> Do nothing from selfishness or empty conceit, but with humility of mind let each of you regard one another as more important than him-

self; do not merely look out for your own personal interests, but also for the interests of others. Have this attitude in yourselves which was also in Christ Jesus, who, although He existed in the form of God, did not regard equality with God a thing to be grasped, but emptied Himself, taking the form of a bond-servant, and being made in the likeness of men. And being found in appearance as a man, He humbled Himself by becoming obedient to the point of death, even death on a cross.

Humility is the key that opens the door of love and unity. The perfect illustration of it was Christ's self-emptying and obedience, even to the point of death. When believers practice such self-effacing humility, they will be "of the same mind, maintaining the same love, united in spirit, intent on one purpose" (Phil. 2:2).

The apostle John also saw Christ's offering of Himself as the supreme example of love: "We know love by this, that He laid down His life for us; and we ought to lay down our lives for the brethren" (1 John 3:16). But since most Christians will not have the opportunity to die for others, John gives a more practical test of love: "Whoever has the world's goods, and beholds his brother in need and closes his heart against him, how does the love of God abide in him? Little children, let us not love with word or with tongue, but in deed and truth" (1 John 3:17-18).

Loving someone is not defined by having warm feelings toward them, but by meeting their needs. The last time you made a sacrifice for someone was the last time you loved him or her. Love is first action, then the emotions follow. So the strengthened heart is a heart that has learned to love.

Settled in Understanding

and attaining to all the wealth that comes from the full assurance of understanding, resulting in a true knowledge of God's mystery, that is, Christ Himself, in whom are hidden all the treasures of wisdom and knowledge. I say this in order that no one may delude you with persuasive argument. For even though I am absent in body, nevertheless I am with you in spirit, rejoicing to see your good discipline and the stability of your faith in Christ. (2:2c-5)

Paul desires that the Colossians also experience all the **wealth** that comes from **full assurance.** Without that assurance, believers cannot enjoy all the blessings that are theirs in Christ. For example, no one can look forward with hope to the blessings of heaven who doubts whether he is going there. For that reason Peter says, "Be all the more diligent to make certain about His calling and choosing you" (2 Pet. 1:10). How?

> Applying all diligence, in your faith supply moral excellence, and in your moral excellence, knowledge; and in your knowledge, self-control, and in your self-control, perseverance, and in your perseverance, godliness; and in your godliness, brotherly kindness, and in your brotherly kindness, love. For if these qualities are yours and are increasing, they render you neither useless nor unfruitful in the true knowledge of our Lord Jesus Christ. (2 Pet. 1:5-8)

Sunesis (**understanding**) refers to applying biblical principles to everyday life. It is the exclusive property of Christians because "a natural man does not accept the things of the Spirit of God; for they are foolishness to him, and he cannot understand them, because they are spiritually appraised" (1 Cor. 2:14). Because "those who are according to the flesh set their minds on the things of the flesh" (Rom. 8:5), they are "darkened in their understanding" (Eph. 4:18).

When the believer experiences spiritual truth by living it, it becomes truly understood and leads to assurance of his or her salvation. The New Testament, then, concludes that knowing the truth and acting on it leads to **full assurance of understanding.** People often express to me doubts about their salvation, even though they have read books on assurance. Their primary problem is not a lack of knowledge, but a failure to apply the truths they know. Truth that finds solid footing in a strong heart and works itself out in love of fellow believers results in deep conviction. That is the basis for assurance.

In light of the heresy plaguing them, Paul stresses the need for the Colossians' understanding to include **a true knowledge of God's mystery, that is, Christ Himself, in whom are hidden all the treasures of wisdom and knowledge.** At the heart of this understanding, they need to have a settled conviction about Christ's deity and sufficiency. In **Christ Himself** the hidden God was manifested to mankind. In that sense, He is **God's mystery.** First Timothy 3:16 records what may be a first-century hymn:

> And by common confession great
> is the mystery of godliness:
> He who was revealed in the flesh,
> Was vindicated in the Spirit,

Beheld by angels,
Proclaimed among the nations,
Believed on in the world,
Taken up in glory.

All those phrases refer to Christ. In the early church, as in our own day, it was vitally important to have a grasp on Christ's deity. No person can be a Christian at all without this true knowledge of Jesus Christ as the incarnate God. Yet so many Christians who affirm the deity of Christ live as if He were not the One in whom all spiritual sufficiency resides.

But Jesus is the One in whom are hidden all the treasures of wisdom and knowledge. He alone is sufficient. Hidden is from *apokruphos*, from which we get our English word apocrypha. It was used by the heretics to refer to the writings containing their secret knowledge. But there is no hidden spiritual knowledge necessary to salvation and sanctification outside of Christ. The treasures of wisdom and knowledge in Christ, however, are hidden from all but Christians.

Because Christ is sufficient, there is no need for the writings of any cult, philosophy, or psychology to supplement the Bible. He is the source of all true spiritual knowledge. That knowledge is also crucial to assurance because doubts about Christ's sufficiency bring doubts about His ability to do what He promised.

Paul expresses the reason for his concern about knowing Christ in verse 4: **I say this in order that no one may delude you with persuasive argument.** Lightfoot paraphrases Paul's thought as follows: "I wish to warn you against any one who would lead you astray by specious argument and persuasive rhetoric" (*St. Paul's Epistles to the Colossians and to Philemon* [1879; reprint, Grand Rapids: Zondervan, 1959], p. 175). The basic attack of all false systems throughout history has been to deny either Christ's deity, His sufficiency to save and sanctify, or both. Any group or person doing so is guilty of teaching "doctrines of demons" (1 Tim. 4:1). As purveyors of another gospel, they are accursed (Gal. 1:8). Believers need to have a settled conviction about Christ's deity and sufficiency to be able to withstand the onslaughts of such false teaching.

Having warned the Colossians to continue to stand firm, Paul rejoices that they are doing so. Although **absent in body** due to his imprisonment, Paul was present with them **in spirit.** Their **good discipline** and the **stability** of their **faith in Christ** caused him to rejoice. *Taxis* (**good discipline**) and *stereōma* (**stability**) are both military terms, perhaps suggested by Paul's close contact with Roman soldiers during his imprisonment (cf. Acts 28:16; Phil. 1:13). *Taxis* refers to a line of soldiers drawn up for battle, whereas *stereōma* refers to the solidity of a formation of soldiers. Taken together, they express Paul's joy that individually and collectively the Colossians were standing firm against the attacks of false teaching. His goal for them is that they remain settled in their present true understanding, and not yield to doubt from those attacks.

WALKING IN CHRIST

As you therefore have received Christ Jesus the Lord, so walk in Him, having been firmly rooted and now being built up in Him and established in your faith, just as you were instructed, (2:6-7a)

Therefore builds the concluding exhortation on what Paul has said in verses 2-5. The Colossians have received Christ Jesus the Lord, they have settled convictions about His deity and sufficiency, and are standing firm against the attacks of false teachers, so they must continue to **walk in Him.** The familiar term **walk** refers to daily conduct. In this context it means primarily to continue believing the truth about Christ, not allowing their Christology to waver.

In broader terms, however, walking in Christ means living in union with Him. It means to maintain a lifestyle patterned after His. "The one who says he abides in Him," the apostle John writes, "ought himself to walk in the same manner as He walked" (1 John 2:6). When faced with the dilemmas that confront Christians in their daily lives, the guideline should be, "What would Jesus do in this situation?" The hymn "O to Be Like Thee" expresses what should be the desire of every Christian:

> O to be like Thee!
> Blessed Redeemer, this is my constant longing and prayer;
> Gladly I'll forfeit all of earth's treasures,
> Jesus Thy perfect likeness to wear.
>
> O to be like Thee!
> O to be like Thee, Blessed Redeemer, pure as Thou art!
> Come in Thy sweetness, come in Thy fullness;
> Stamp Thine own image deep on my heart.

Like a tree with deep roots in rich soil, believers have been **firmly rooted** in Christ. That eternal planting took place at salvation, as the perfect tense of the participle *errizōmenoi* (**having been firmly**

rooted) suggests. Christ then became the source of our spiritual nourishment, growth, and fruit. As we walk in Christ, we are **now being built up in Him.** That connotes the process of being more and more like Jesus Christ. *Epoikodomoumenoi* (**being built up**) is a present-tense participle indicating continuous action. By studying the "word of His grace, which is able to build you up" (Acts 20:32), believers will "grow in the grace and knowledge of our Lord and Savior Jesus Christ" (2 Pet. 3:18). And they will come "to the measure of the stature which belongs to the fulness of Christ" (Eph. 4:13).

Being firmly rooted in Christ and growing in Him results in believers being **established** in their **faith.** The passive voice of the participle *bebaioumenoi* (**established**) indicates that it is God who will establish believers. Having such a firm foundation for faith based on walking in Christ is imperative for a healthy Christian life (cf. Rom. 16:25; 2 Thess. 2:16-17; 1 Pet. 5:10; Jude 24).

OVERFLOWING WITH GRATITUDE

overflowing with gratitude. (2:7*b*)

The last of the four participles in verse 7, *perisseuontes* (**overflowing**), is the only one in the active voice. It is a response to the other three. Believers who are firmly rooted in Christ, being built up in Him, and established in their faith, will overflow with gratitude to God. "Through Him then, let us continually offer up a sacrifice of praise to God, that is, the fruit of lips that give thanks to His name" (Heb. 13:15). A grateful heart for all God has given us in Christ will further strengthen our grip on the truth.

Praise completes the circle in which the blessings that flow to us from God return to Him in the form of our praise and adoration. By taking in the truth of the Word, believers get a strong mind. By living out those truths, they receive full assurance that Christ is who He claimed to be. Assured of that, they can appropriate the riches that are His legacy to believers, and walk in Him. As they walk in Him, they will grow in Him and become established in their faith. As a result, they will give praise to God.

Philosophy or Christ?

See to it that no one takes you captive through philosophy and empty deception, according to the tradition of men, according to the elementary principles of the world, rather than according to Christ. For in Him all the fulness of Deity dwells in bodily form, and in Him you have been made complete, and He is the head over all rule and authority; (2:8-10)

From the dawn of recorded history, man has pondered the questions of ultimate reality. He has sought an explanation for the universe around him and the meaning of his own existence. The questions "Who am I?", "Why am I here?", and "Where am I going?" are universal in the human race. Worldly philosophies ineptly try to answer those queries.

The word *philosophy* comes from two Greek words, *phileō*, "to love," and *sophia*, "wisdom." Philosophy is the love and pursuit of wisdom. Because everyone has a worldview, in one sense everyone is a philosopher. Throughout history there have also been those who specialized in the academic discipline of philosophy. The Greek thinker Thales, a contemporary of the prophet Jeremiah, is generally regarded as the first philosopher in the latter sense. From his time to our own day, there have been thousands of philosophers, each with his own explanation of the universe.

I remember taking a college course in European philosophy. Most of the philosophers we studied either denied the existence of God or held an unbiblical view of Him, such as deism or pantheism. It was a frustrating experience, studying the musings of unregenerate men desperately trying to determine ultimate truth apart from God. But as Francis Schaeffer in our own generation emphasized, man cannot begin with himself and arrive at ultimate reality (cf. *The God Who Is There, Escape from Reason*, and *He Is There and He Is Not Silent*). The apostle Paul agreed with that assessment. He wrote in 1 Corinthians 2:9 that ultimate truth is discoverable neither by empiricism nor by rationalism: "Things which eye has not seen and ear has not heard [empiricism], and which have not entered the heart of man [rationalism], all that God has prepared for those who love Him."

Os Guinness comments on the futility of modern man's search for truth apart from God:

> Contemporary man, with his self-drawn picture of society as the "closed room" with No Exit, is caught metaphysically and sociologically. In the darkness of the room evidently without windows, perhaps without doors, he gropes round and round the edges. Can one hope that someone will dare to wonder whether there is any light other than the feeble sparks of his own making? Or will he stubbornly persist in treading the barren circle of poor premises? (*The Dust of Death* [Downers Grove, Ill.: InterVarsity, 1973], p. 148)

Not surprisingly, many philosophers have expressed that futility. The seventeenth-century British philosopher David Hume said, "I am first affrighted and confounded with that forlorn solitude, in which I am plac'd in my philosophy" (cited in Guinness, *The Dust of Death*, p. 22).

The nineteenth-century German philosopher Friedrich Nietzsche scorned Christianity as the religion of weaklings. He was among the first to proclaim that God is dead. Yet he could not live with the implications of his philosophy. Guinness writes, "For Nietzsche to be consistent, he needed to become his own superman, but his views were overwhelming even for himself. As he poised over the abyss, he shivered with the horror of being 'responsible for everything alive.' In the impossibility of this situation, madness perhaps becomes his only possible freedom from the overbearing responsibility. 'Alas, grant me madness'" (*The Dust of Death*, p. 24). Tragically, Nietzsche's wish was granted. He spent the last eleven years of his life insane.

One of the leading twentieth-century philosophers was the

French existentialist Jean-Paul Sartre, also an atheist. In his novel *Nausea* he has the main character, Roquentin, say, "Every existing thing is born without reason, goes on living out of weakness, and dies by accident" (cited in Robert Denoon Cumming, ed., *The Philosophy of Jean-Paul Sartre* [New York: Random House, 1965], pp. 66-67). Roquentin expresses Sartre's belief that, apart from God, man is utterly meaningless:

> We were a heap of existences, uncomfortable, embarrassed at ourselves, we hadn't the slightest reason to be there, none of us, each one confused, vaguely alarmed, felt superfluous in relation to the others.
>
> And I myself . . . *I too was superfluous.* . . . I dreamed vaguely of killing myself to wipe out at least one of these superfluous existences. But even my death would have been *superfluous.* (in *The Philosophy of Jean-Paul Sartre*, pp. 61-62, italics in the original)

Commenting on Sartre's view of the absurdity of man apart from God, William Barrett writes, "Sartre's atheism states candidly . . . that man is an alien in the universe, unjustified and unjustifiable, absurd in the simple sense that there is no . . . reason sufficient to explain why he or his universe exists (*Irrational Man* [Garden City, N.Y.: Doubleday, 1962], p. 262).

Man's rebellion against God has, in Schaeffer's words, driven him beneath the line of despair. In the words of the apostle Paul, "They became futile in their speculations, and their foolish heart was darkened. Professing to be wise, they became fools" (Rom. 1:21-22). By eliminating God and His revelation from the picture, modern philosophy has plunged man into the abyss of ignorant darkness and hopeless despair.

The city of Colossae also had its philosophers. The church there faced the danger of being infiltrated by false teaching, as we do in our own day. The church has throughout its history fought to maintain its doctrinal purity. That the Colossians do so was Paul's great concern, and 2:8-23 thus becomes the heart of the epistle. In this, the polemical section of Colossians, he attacks the false teachers head on.

The specific heresy threatening the Colossians is unknown, in that Paul does not name it. We can, however, reconstruct some of its tenets from 2:8-23. It contained elements of philosophy (2:8-15), legalism (2:16-17), mysticism (2:18-19), and asceticism (2:20-23). Because those beliefs were shared by the first-century Jewish sect known as the Essenes, we noted in the introduction it is possible they (or a group holding similar beliefs) were the ones threatening the Colossian believers.

This heresy also had components that were early forms of Gnosticism, the belief that there was a transcendent kind of knowledge beyond Christian doctrine known only to elite initiates who had ascended to that level. Most damning, though, was its teaching that Jesus was neither God nor the source of all truth. That was the frontal attack on His deity and sufficiency.

In 2:1-7, Paul exhorts the Colossians to maintain their allegiance to both the deity and complete sufficiency of Jesus Christ. He reminds them that, in contrast to the claims of the false teachers, in Christ "are hidden all the treasures of wisdom and knowledge" (2:3). That statement is a profound summation of the sufficiency of the Lord Jesus. That positive teaching is counterbalanced with a negative treatment in 2:8-23, where Paul tells them what to avoid. In so doing, he fully refutes the claims of the Colossian errorists. Against their claim to a secret, superior knowledge, he has already pointed out that there is no hidden knowledge apart from Christ (2:3). Against their teaching that a series of lesser beings emanated from God, Paul emphasizes that "all the fullness of Deity dwells" in Christ (2:9). They worshiped those emanations, which Paul describes in 2:15 as demonic beings, whom Christ has already conquered. He speaks against the falsity of ceremonial, ritualistic legalism and mysticism in 2:16-19. Finally, in 2:20-23 Paul rejects their asceticism, since it is "of no value against fleshly indulgence" (2:23).

Paul gives here a model for dealing with heresy. He does not bitterly denounce the heresy by name. In fact, he does not even give it a name. Nor does he present in exhaustive detail what the heretics believed. He deals with the heresy by emphasizing those truths that refute its claims and similar claims by all other heresies no matter what their names. Commentator Charles R. Erdman wrote, "When he now reaches the very heart of his letter the apostle dwells so eloquently upon the deity of Christ and the dignity and completeness of believers that the reader is left in some uncertainty as to the exact system of error against which the Colossians were to be upon their guard" (*The Epistles of Paul to the Colossians and to Philemon* [Philadelphia: Westminster, 1956], p. 73). Any false system will collapse in the face of the truth.

In 2:8-10, Paul begins to attack the first element of the Colossian heresy: false philosophy. By way of a warning, he contrasts the deficiency of philosophy with the sufficiency of Christ.

THE DEFICIENCY OF PHILOSOPHY

See to it that no one takes you captive through philosophy and empty deception, according to the tradition of men, according to

the elementary principles of the world, rather than according to Christ. (2:8*a*)

Paul is concerned that those who have been transferred from Satan's domain to Christ's kingdom not become enslaved again. He voiced a similar concern in Galatians 5:1: "It was for freedom that Christ set us free; therefore keep standing firm and do not be subject again to a yoke of slavery." He calls the Colossians to constant watchfulness because danger is near, as the present tense imperative form of *blepō* (**see to it**) indicates. The church constantly faces the danger of false teachers. Jesus says in Matthew 7:15, "Beware of the false prophets, who come to you in sheep's clothing, but inwardly are ravenous wolves." In Matthew 16:6 he warns, "Watch out and beware of the leaven of the Pharisees and Sadducees."

The apostles also warned the church against false teachers. Paul cautioned the Ephesian elders that "after my departure savage wolves will come in among you, not sparing the flock; and from among your own selves men will arise, speaking perverse things, to draw away the disciples after them. Therefore be on the alert" (Acts 20:29-31). To the Philippians he wrote, "Beware of the dogs, beware of the evil workers, beware of the false circumcision" (Phil. 3:2). Peter also warns of the danger of false teachers. He writes in 2 Peter 3:1, "You therefore, beloved, knowing this beforehand, be on your guard lest, being carried away by the error of unprincipled men, you fall from your own steadfastness."

Paul specifically warns them to be careful **that no one takes you captive. Takes you captive** is from *sulagōgeō*, a rare word used only here in the New Testament and not at all found in extrabiblical Greek until long after Paul's time. *Sulagōgeō* is a compound word, made up of *sulē*, "booty," and *agō*, "to carry off." It literally means "to kidnap," or "to carry off as booty, or spoil of war." The same concept is found in 2 Timothy 3:6, where Paul warns of "those who enter into households and captivate weak women weighed down with sins, led on by various impulses." To Paul, it was unthinkable that those who had been ransomed and redeemed should be vulnerable by ignorance and thus in the spiritual war become prisoners of some spiritual predator with false doctrine.

Surely it grieves the heart of any pastor to learn of spiritual children who by immaturity are susceptible to the danger of false teaching and fall prey to a cult. Yet many have been duped into thinking they have found some truth, which in reality is a lie that has made them a captive to false teaching. One of the primary duties of church leaders is to guard the flock against wolves and perverse men (Acts 20:28-32) who assault flock members in an effort to kidnap them.

Paul describes the means the false teachers would use to kidnap the Colossians as **philosophy and empty deception.** *Philosophia* (**philosophy**) appears only here in the New Testament. As already noted, it means "to love wisdom." It is used here in a much broader sense than the academic discipline, since "philosophy is not reducible to the Judeo-Gnostic speculations about which Paul warned the Colossian Christians" (Mark M. Hanna, *Crucial Questions in Apologetics* [Grand Rapids: Baker, 1981], p. 11). Historian Adolf Schlatter noted that "everything that had to do with theories about God and the world and the meaning of human life was called 'philosophy' at that time, not only in pagan schools, but also in the Jewish schools of the Greek cities" (*The Church in the New Testament Period* [reprint, London: SPCK, 1955], pp. 150-54).

The first-century Jewish historian Josephus wrote, "There are three philosophical sects among the Jews. The followers of the first of whom are the Pharisees, of the second the Sadducees, and the third sect who pretends to be a severer discipline are called Essenes" (*Jewish Wars* 2.8.2). Thus, the term *philosophy* was broad enough to encompass religious sects. The use of the definite article with *philosophia* shows that Paul was referring here to the specific beliefs of the Colossian errorists. Most likely they used it to refer to the transcendent, higher knowledge they supposedly had attained through mystical experience.

Paul goes on to describe this philosophy as **empty deception.** Lightfoot wrote, "The absence of both preposition and article in the second clause shows that *kenēs apatēs* [empty deception] describes and qualifies philosophia" (*St. Paul's Epistles to the Colossians and to Philemon* [1879; reprint, Grand Rapids: Zondervan, 1959], p. 178). He translated the phrase, "Through his philosophy which is an empty deceit" (p. 178). Although the false teachers at Colossae considered their view the epitome of wisdom, Paul dismisses it as **empty deception.**

Apatēs (**deception**) means "a deceit, fraud, or trick." The philosophy of the Colossian false teachers was not what it appeared to be. It sounded good and seduced the minds of those deceived by it, but it was a vapid illusion. There is no value in such speculative human philosophy, no matter how deeply and profoundly religious it sounds.

Commentator Herbert Carson sounds an appropriate warning:

> With Paul it would no doubt be true to say that philosophy, in the simple sense of a love of knowledge and a desire for the truth, would be quite compatible with his position. But to philosophy in the developed sense with its emphasis on the primacy of human reason he would obviously be utterly opposed. . . . Hence, while the Christian may see a certain negative value in speculative philosophy, he will constantly be on his guard lest he come to study revelation, not as a believer, but as

a humanist. This does not mean that he should come with a blind un-reasoning faith. But it does mean that, instead of bringing philosophical presuppositions which will colour his study of Scripture and so prejudice his interpretation, he comes as one conscious of the finiteness of his intellect, and aware that his mind also is affected by his sinful nature. Thus he is willing to be taught by the Holy Spirit, and acknowledges that it is the Word of God rather than his own reason which is the final arbiter of truth. (*The Epistles of Paul to the Colossians and Philemon* [Grand Rapids: Eerdmans, 1976], p. 62)

Paul then gives two sources for such vain speculation. **The tradition of men** is the first. **Tradition** is *paradosis,* that which is given from one to another. Just because people have believed something and handed it down through the years does not make it true. Tradition usually serves merely to perpetuate error.

A study of the history of philosophy serves to illustrate that point. Most philosophers have built on the work of previous philosophers, either to refine their system, or to refute it. Francis Schaeffer remarked, "One man would draw a circle and say, 'You can live within this circle.' The next man would cross it out and would draw a different circle. The next man would come along and, crossing out the previous circle, draw his own—ad infinitum" (*The God Who Is There* [Downers Grove, Ill.: InterVarsity, 1973], p. 17).

First-century Judaism is another example of the effects of tradition. The Jewish leaders and teachers had encrusted the Word of God with so many customs, rituals, and teachings that they were no longer able to distinguish it from the traditions of men. Mark 7 records an exchange between the scribes and Pharisees and Jesus on this subject. In verse 5, they asked Jesus, "Why do Your disciples not walk according to the tradition of the elders?" Jesus replied in verses 8-9, "Neglecting the commandment of God, you hold to the tradition of men. . . . You nicely set aside the commandment of God in order to keep your tradition."

The Gentiles also had traditions. Peter used the same Greek word in a different form when he wrote to Gentiles in 1 Peter 1:18: "Knowing that you were not redeemed with perishable things like silver or gold from your futile way of life inherited [received by tradition] from your forefathers." In our own day, a common argument for evolution is the false assertion that it is "what scientists have always believed." In all the above examples, tradition was nothing more than ignorance and falsehood handed down from generation to generation. It was the tradition of men, not the tradition of God (2 Thess. 3:6), which is the only source of truth.

A second source for this false philosophy is **the elementary principles of the world.** It is difficult to reconstruct the exact meaning of that phrase. *Stoicheia* (**elementary principles**) refers primarily to the letters of the alphabet. It literally means "things in a row." Hence, Paul might be describing the false belief system of the Colossian errorists as rudimentary, too simplistic for mature spiritual adults. To accept their teaching would be to descend, to regress from the mature teaching of Scripture to the infantile teachings of an immature religion, based not on advanced thinking and wisdom but on silly and childish thoughts. To abandon biblical truth for empty philosophy is like returning to kindergarten after earning a doctorate. Paul writes:

> The word of the cross is to those who are perishing foolishness, but to us who are being saved it is the power of God. For it is written, "I will destroy the wisdom of the wise, and the cleverness of the clever I will set aside." Where is the wise man? Where is the scribe? Where is the debater of this age? Has not God made foolish the wisdom of the world? For since in the wisdom of God the world through its wisdom did not come to know God, God was well-pleased through the foolishness of the message preached to save those who believe. (1 Cor. 1:18-21)

This same phrase is also found in Galatians 4:3: "So also we, while we were children, were held in bondage under the elemental things of the world." There again, the element of immaturity is evident. Whether first-century Judaism, as in Galatians, or the false teaching threatening the Colossians, human religion is not advanced, erudite, higher, transcendent and lofty in its profundity. Rather, it is banal, elemental, and rudimentary. It does not convey any new and profound truths. And, fatally, at its core is an effort to achieve salvation by works.

There is a second possible, though less likely, meaning for *stoicheia*. It could refer to elemental spirits—either supposed emanations from God, or the spirit beings that the people of the ancient world associated with the stars and planets. Astrology is not new. Many of the great men of the ancient world, such as Alexander the Great and Julius Caesar, believed in it implicitly. People who believed in astrology were caught in the grip of a rigid determinism. The influence of the stars and planets controlled their destiny, unless they had the secret knowledge necessary to escape that control. It was precisely such knowledge that the false teachers may have claimed. Paul would then be warning the Colossians, some of whom had no doubt believed in astrology before their salvation, to avoid such false teaching. In either case, what these heretics offered was not an advance in spiritual knowledge, but a retreat to spiritual infancy and demonic doctrine (cf. 1 Tim. 4:1).

THE SUFFICIENCY OF CHRIST

rather than according to Christ. For in Him all the fulness of Deity dwells in bodily form, and in Him you have been made complete, and He is the head over all rule and authority; (2:8*b*-10)

This is one of the most blessed passages in all of Scripture. It presents the glorious majesty of Christ's Person and His complete sufficiency. Verse 9 is perhaps the most definitive statement of Christ's deity in the epistles. It is the rock upon which all attempts to disprove Christ's deity are shattered. Obviously, these heretics were saying Jesus was not God, and that was the most damning and disturbing element of their "satanology"—as it still is in any false system.

The false teaching just described was part of the satanically devised and humanly propagated religious system, and it was not according to Christ and what Scripture reveals about Him. It, like all false systems of religion, cannot save. That is the peak of its deadliness. In Christ alone **all the fulness of Deity dwells in bodily form.** He alone has the power to save. *Plērōma* (**fulness**) is the same term used in 1:19. As noted in the discussion of that passage, it was a term used by the Colossian errorists. They believed the divine *plērōma* was divided in its expression among the various emanations. Each got a decreasing share as they descended the ladder from good to bad. Paul, however, insists that all the fullness **of Deity,** not a part of it, dwells in Christ. *Katoikeō* (**dwells**) means "to settle down and be at home." The present tense indicates that the essence of Deity continually abides at home in Christ. Deity is a word emphasizing divine nature. That nature of God that continually abode in Jesus Christ was not some divine light that merely lit Him up for a while, but was not His own. He is fully God forever. And as the One possessing all the fullness of Deity, Christ **is the head over all rule and authority.** He was not one of a series of lesser beings emanating from God, as the false teachers maintained. Rather, He is God Himself and thus the head over all the angelic realm.

As we have noted, the Colossian false teachers also apparently taught a form of philosophic dualism, believing that spirit was good and matter was evil. Hence, it was unthinkable to them that God would take on a human body. Paul counters that false doctrine by emphasizing that all the fullness of Deity dwells in Christ **in bodily form.** The One who took upon Himself human nature at Bethlehem will keep that humanity for all eternity. He will forever be the God-Man.

Because Christ is who He is, we **have been made complete** in Him. His fullness is imparted to us. *Peplērōmenoi* (**been made com-**

plete) is a form of the verb *plēroō*, from which the noun *plērōma* is derived. Christ is the *plērōma* of God, and we are filled with His *plērōma*. John wrote, "For of His fulness we have all received" (John 1:16). The perfect tense of the participle *peplērōmenoi* indicates that the results of our having been filled are eternal.

As a result of the Fall, man is in a sad state of incompleteness. He is spiritually incomplete because He is totally out of fellowship with God. He is morally incomplete because he lives outside of God's will. He is mentally incomplete because he does not know ultimate truth.

At salvation, believers become "partakers of the divine nature" (2 Pet. 1:4) and are made complete. Believers are spiritually complete because they have fellowship with God. They are morally complete in that they recognize the authority of God's will. They are mentally complete because they know the truth about ultimate reality.

To maintain, as the Colossian errorists did, that those who were made complete in Christ still lacked anything is absurd. Those who are "partakers of the divine nature" have, through "His divine power," been "granted . . . everything pertaining to life and godliness" (2 Pet. 1:3). All true believers are complete in Christ and do not need the teachings of any cult or false teacher.

Everyone has a choice, whether to follow human wisdom or to come to Christ. To follow human wisdom is to be kidnapped by the emissaries of Satan and his false system, which leaves a person spiritually incomplete. To come to Christ is to come to the One who alone offers completeness. May those of us who have found Christ never doubt His sufficiency by turning aside to follow any human wisdom. (For a more thorough treatment of the matter of our sufficiency in Christ, see my book, *Our Sufficiency in Christ* [Dallas: Word, 1991].)

Complete in Christ

9

and in Him you were also circumcised with a circumcision made without hands, in the removal of the body of the flesh by the circumcision of Christ; having been buried with Him in baptism, in which you were also raised up with Him through faith in the working of God, who raised Him from the dead. And when you were dead in your transgressions and the uncircumcision of your flesh, He made you alive together with Him, having forgiven us all our transgressions, having canceled out the certificate of debt consisting of decrees against us and which was hostile to us; and He has taken it out of the way, having nailed it to the cross. When He had disarmed the rulers and authorities, He made a public display of them, having triumphed over them through Him. (2:11-15)

Healings were an essential element of our Lord's earthly ministry. They established His messianic credentials, showed the tender compassion of God, and foreshadowed the millennial kingdom, when He will banish disease. Our Lord's healings also illustrate an important principle about salvation. When Jesus healed someone, He made them completely healthy. In Matthew 9:22 we read, "But Jesus turning and seeing her said, 'Daughter, take courage; your faith has made you well.' And at once the woman was made well." Matthew 15:28 records the healing of a Canaanite woman's daughter: "Then Jesus answered and said to her, 'O woman, your faith is great; be it done for you as you wish.' And her daughter was healed at once." When the centurion's servants returned to the house, "they found the slave in good health" (Luke 7:10). Jesus said to the multitude in the Temple, "If a man receives circumcision on the Sabbath that the Law of Moses may not be broken, are you angry with Me because I made an entire man well on the Sabbath?" (John 7:23). Our Lord's healing ministry can be summarized in the words of Matthew 15:31: "The multitude marveled as they saw the dumb speaking, the crippled restored, and the lame walking, and the blind seeing; and they glorified the God of Israel."

Just as Jesus made people completely well when He healed physically, so also does He provide complete salvation when He heals spiritually. That salvation does not need to be supplemented by false human philosophy or psychology, ritualism, mysticism, self-denial, or any other human work. In Christ we "have been made complete" (Col. 2:10; cf. 2 Pet. 1:3). When a person comes to saving faith in Jesus Christ, "he is a new creature; the old things passed away; behold, new things have come" (2 Cor. 5:17; cf. Gal. 6:15).

Having stated the truth that Christians are complete in Christ in 2:10, Paul gives three aspects of that completeness in 2:11-15. In Christ we have complete salvation, complete forgiveness, and complete victory.

COMPLETE SALVATION

and in Him you were also circumcised with a circumcision made without hands, in the removal of the body of the flesh by the circumcision of Christ; having been buried with Him in baptism, in which you were also raised up with Him through faith in the working of God, who raised Him from the dead. (2:11-12)

As already noted, the Colossian heresy was a mixture of pagan philosophy with Jewish legalism. Not surprisingly, the Colossian false teachers, like the Judaizers Paul confronted in Galatia, were teaching that circumcision was necessary for salvation.

Every Jewish boy was circumcised on the eighth day after his birth (Lev. 12:2-3). It was the sign that he belonged to the covenant nation (Gen. 17:10-14). Throughout Israel's history there had been two schools of thought about circumcision. Some held that circumcision alone was enough to save, since it granted membership in the covenant nation. That view was wrong, since "they are not all Israel who are descended from Israel" (Rom. 9:6). Membership in the covenant community did not guarantee individual salvation. Paul writes in Romans 2:25, 28, "For indeed circumcision is of value, if you practice the Law; but if you are a transgressor of the Law, your circumcision has become uncircumcision. . . . For he is not a Jew who is one outwardly; neither is circumcision that which is outward in the flesh."

The second view recognized that circumcision was only the outward demonstration that man was born sinful and needed cleansing. The cutting away of the male foreskin on the reproductive organ was a graphic way to demonstrate that man needed cleansing at the deepest level of his being. No other part of the human anatomy so demonstrates that depth of sin, inasmuch as that is the part of man that produces life—and all that he produces is sinful. That is the biblical view. From the beginning, circumcision was used symbolically to illustrate the desperate need man had for cleansing of the heart. In Deuteronomy 10:16 Moses commanded the people of Israel, saying "Circumcise then your heart, and stiffen your neck no more." Deuteronomy 30:6 adds, "Moreover the Lord your God will circumcise your heart and the heart of your descendants, to love the Lord your God with all your heart and with all your soul, in order that you may live." The Lord commanded the Israelites of Jeremiah's time to circumcise themselves to the Lord and remove the foreskins of their hearts (Jer. 4:4; cf. 9:26). God was always concerned with the heart, not with the physical rite.

The experience of Abraham illustrates the truth that circumcision does not save. Paul writes in Romans 4:11 that Abraham "received the sign of circumcision, a seal of the righteousness of the faith which he had while uncircumcised." Abraham was not circumcised until many years after "he believed in the Lord; and [God] reckoned it to him as righteousness" (Gen. 15:6). His circumcision was the outward sign of a heart already made righteous by faith.

The New Testament also emphasizes circumcising the heart. Stephen accused the Sanhedrin of being "men who are stiff-necked and uncircumcised in heart" (Acts 7:51). Paul defined true circumcision in Romans 2:29: "He is a Jew who is one inwardly; and circumcision is that which is of the heart."

For Christians, the physical rite of circumcision is unnecessary because we have already been **circumcised with a circumcision made without hands.** The object of **the circumcision of Christ** is **the removal of the body of the flesh.** The **body of the flesh** refers to the sinful, fallen human nature totally dominating believers before salvation. Christians have been cleansed of that sinful dominance and been given a new nature created in righteousness, having been **circumcised with a circumcision made without hands,** that is, not physical but spiritual. At salvation, "our old self was crucified with Him, that our body of sin might be done away with, that we should no longer be slaves to sin" (Rom. 6:6). As a result, "if any man is in Christ, he is a new creature; the old things passed away; behold, new things have come" (2 Cor. 5:17). Nowhere is it expressed any better than in the words of Paul when he wrote, "We are the true circumcision, who worship in the Spirit of God and glory in Christ Jesus and put no confidence in the flesh" (Phil. 3:3). Believers have been freed from sin's dominance and judgment, though not yet from its presence.

The question arises as to why Christians still sin if their sinful self has died. Paul gives the answer in a personal way in Romans 7:15-23:

> That which I am doing, I do not understand; for I am not practicing what I would like to do, but I am doing the very thing I hate. But if I do the very thing I do not wish to do, I agree with the Law, confessing that it is good. So now, no longer am I the one doing it, but sin which indwells me. For I know that nothing good dwells in me, that is, in my flesh; for the wishing is present in me, but the doing of the good is not. For the good that I wish, I do not do; but I practice the very evil that I do not wish. But if I am doing the very thing I do not wish, I am no longer the one doing it, but sin which dwells in me. I find then the principle that evil is present in me, the one who wishes to do good. For I joyfully concur with the law of God in the inner man, but I see a different law in the members of my body, waging war against the law of my mind, and making me a prisoner of the law of sin which is in my members.

The new disposition, which desires to do good and obey God, resides in the unredeemed flesh—humanness. That flesh is still subject to temptation from "all that is in the world, the lust of the flesh and the lust of the eyes and the boastful pride of life" (1 John 2:16). Paul's new self wished to obey God, but, he said, "I see a different law in the members of my body, waging war against the law of my mind, and making me a prisoner of the law of sin which is in my members." (Rom. 7:23). The new creation is pure and holy. As believers we await only the redemption of our bodies (Rom. 8:23) to make them fully fit for heaven. (A fuller treatment of this marvelous truth is given in one of my other commentaries in this series, *Romans 1-8*, in the section on chapters 6-8.)

When viewed as a rite necessary for salvation, **baptism** is as superfluous as circumcision. Some see support in 2:12 for baptismal regeneration, but Paul would hardly replace one rite with another (cf. 1 Cor. 1:13-17). Arguing that the change from spiritual death to spiritual life is effected by water baptism would make Paul as much of a ritualist as those he was condemning. Water baptism is no more in view in 2:12

than physical circumcision was in 2:11. Both verses speak of spiritual realities.

Baptism pictures believers' union with Christ. They have been buried with Him in baptism, the spiritual union of the believer with Christ that takes place at salvation (cf. 1 Cor. 12:13). Water baptism is only a picture of that reality. It symbolizes the believer's identification with Christ's death, burial, and resurrection (cf. Rom. 6:3-4).

Such a spiritual transformation can only be achieved **through faith in the working of God. Working** translates *energeia*, from which we get our English word *energy*. It refers to God's active power—the same power that **raised** Jesus **from the dead.** Those who believe that God raised Jesus from the dead will also be raised with Him. "If you confess with your mouth Jesus as Lord, and believe in your heart that God raised Him from the dead, you shall be saved" (Rom. 10:9).

COMPLETE FORGIVENESS

And when you were dead in your transgressions and the uncircumcision of your flesh, He made you alive together with Him, having forgiven us all our transgressions, having canceled out the certificate of debt consisting of decrees against us and which was hostile to us; and He has taken it out of the way, having nailed it to the cross. (2:13-14)

Paul here approaches the same truth he discussed in 2:11-12 from a different perspective. In 2:11-12 he emphasized that salvation is complete apart from any religious ritual. In these verses he emphasizes that forgiveness is complete apart from any human work. Forgiveness is perhaps the most exciting and comforting doctrine in all of Scripture, because it is what guilty sinners need to be made right with God.

Like all of sinful mankind, the Colossians **were dead in** their **transgressions** before their salvation (cf. Eph. 2:1). The Greek construction is a locative of sphere. Unbelievers exist in the sphere or realm of spiritual death. To be spiritually dead means to be devoid of any sense, unable to respond to spiritual stimuli, just as to be physically dead means to be unable to respond to physical stimuli. It is to be so locked in sin's grasp that one is unable to respond to God. The Bible and spiritual truth make no sense to one in such a state. Those who are spiritually dead are dominated by the world, the flesh, and Satan and possess no spiritual, eternal life.

Paul describes the Colossians in their prior unsaved state as being dead not only in their sins, but also in **the uncircumcision of** their

flesh. That phrase designates Gentiles, whose condition of uncircumcision demonstrated that they were outside the covenant. Paul wrote about them in Ephesians 2:11-12: "Remember, that formerly you, the Gentiles in the flesh, who are called 'Uncircumcision' by the so-called 'Circumcision,' which is performed in the flesh by human hands—remember that you were at that time separate from Christ, excluded from the commonwealth of Israel, and strangers to the covenants of promise, having no hope and without God in the world." The Gentiles were therefore in a much worse state than the unbelieving Jews, who at least were a part of the covenant community that possessed the law of God. It is no wonder, then, that Paul describes them as "having no hope and without God in the world" (Eph. 2:12).

Fortunately, the story did not end there. Because God is "rich in mercy" (Eph. 2:4), **He made** us **alive together with Him.** Paul again stresses the believer's union with Christ (cf. 2:10, "in Him"; 2:11, "in Him"; 2:12, "with Him"). Those who were hopelessly dead in sin received new life through that union. God initiates the salvation process, because spiritually dead people cannot make themselves alive.

As a result of being made alive with Christ, believers have been **forgiven** of **all** their **transgressions.** The knowledge that all our sins have been forgiven brings great joy. "How blessed is he whose transgression is forgiven, whose sin is covered!" (Ps. 32:1).

That God forgives the sins of those who trust in Him and includes them in His eternal kingdom and glory is the most important truth of Scripture. The psalmist wrote, "If Thou, Lord, shouldst mark iniquities, O Lord, who could stand? But there is forgiveness with Thee, that Thou mayest be feared" (Ps. 130:3-4). In Isaiah 1:18 we read, "Come now, and let us reason together," says the Lord, "Though your sins are as scarlet, they will be as white as snow; though they are red like crimson, they will be like wool." Isaiah says in Isaiah 55:7, "Let the wicked forsake his way, and the unrighteous man his thoughts; and let him return to the Lord, and He will have compassion on him; and to our God, for He will abundantly pardon." "Who is a God like Thee," exclaimed the prophet Micah, "who pardons iniquity and passes over the rebellious act of the remnant of His possession?" (Mic. 7:18).

God's forgiveness is also a prominent theme in the New Testament. Our Lord told His disciples at the Last Supper, "This is My blood of the covenant, which is poured out for many for forgiveness of sins" (Matt. 26:28). Peter told those assembled in Cornelius's house that "through [Jesus'] name everyone who believes in Him receives forgiveness of sins" (Acts 10:43). In Acts 13:38-39 Paul said, "Let it be known to you, brethren, that through Him forgiveness of sins is proclaimed to you, and through Him everyone who believes is freed from all things, from which you could not be freed through the Law of Moses." To the

Ephesians Paul wrote, "In Him we have redemption through His blood, the forgiveness of our trespasses, according to the riches of His grace" (Eph. 1:7). In Hebrews 8:12 the Lord says, "I will be merciful to their iniquities, and I will remember their sins no more."

What are the characteristics of God's forgiveness? First, it is gracious. It is not earned, but is a free gift. Romans 3:24 says people are "justified as a gift by His grace through the redemption which is in Christ Jesus." Paul echoes that thought in Titus 3:4-7: "When the kindness of God our Savior and His love for mankind appeared, He saved us, not on the basis of deeds which we have done in righteousness, but according to His mercy, by the washing of regeneration and renewing by the Holy Spirit, whom He poured out upon us richly through Jesus Christ our Savior, that being justified by His grace we might be made heirs according to the hope of eternal life."

Second, God's forgiveness is complete. Forgiveness, Ephesians 1:7 tells us, is "according to the riches of His grace." God's grace will always be greater than sin, because "where sin increased, grace abounded all the more" (Rom. 5:20). The apostle John flatly states, "I am writing to you, little children, because your sins are forgiven you for His name's sake" (1 John 2:12).

Third, God's forgiveness is eager. "'Do I have any pleasure in the death of the wicked,' declares the Lord God, 'rather than that he should turn from his ways and live?'" (Ezek. 18:23; cf. 33:11). "Thou, Lord, art good, and ready to forgive, and abundant in lovingkindness to all who call upon Thee" (Ps. 86:5). Far from begrudging His forgiveness, God is anxious to give it.

Fourth, God's forgiveness is certain. In Acts 26:18 Paul says that God sent him to the Gentiles "to open their eyes so that they may turn from darkness to light and from the dominion of Satan to God, in order that they may receive forgiveness of sins and an inheritance among those who have been sanctified by faith in [Jesus]." Forgiveness is certain because it is based on God's promise.

Fifth, God's forgiveness is unequalled. The prophet Micah said, "Who is a God like Thee, who pardons iniquity and passes over the rebellious act of the remnant of His possession?" (Mic. 7:18). The answer to his question is that there is none. None of the gods of false religion offers such forgiveness.

Sixth, God's forgiveness is motivating. Ephesians 4:32 commands us to "be kind to one another, tender-hearted, forgiving each other, just as God in Christ also has forgiven you." God has forgiven us the huge, unpayable debt we owed Him. How can we do any less than forgive others the trivial debts they owe us (cf. Matt. 18:23-35)? That verse is further confirmation of God's complete forgiveness. How could He command us to forgive others if He has not forgiven us?

Paul then illustrates God's forgiveness. When God forgave us, He **canceled out the certificate of debt consisting of decrees against us and which was hostile to us; and He has taken it out of the way, having nailed it to the cross.** **Certificate of debt** translates *cheirographos*, which literally means "something written with the hand," or "an autograph." It was used to refer to a certificate of indebtedness handwritten by the debtor in acknowledgment of his debt. Paul describes that certificate as **consisting of decrees against us.** *Dogmasin* (**decrees**) refers to the Mosaic law (cf. Eph. 2:15). All peoples (including Gentiles, cf. Rom. 2:14-15) owe God a debt because they have violated His law. The certificate was **hostile to us,** that is, it was enough to condemn us to judgment and hell, because "cursed is everyone who does not abide by all things written in the book of the law, to perform them" (Gal. 3:10). *Exaleiphō* (**canceled out**) means "to wipe off," like erasing a blackboard. Ancient documents were commonly written either on papyrus, a paper-like material made from the bulrush plant, or vellum, which was made from an animal's hide. The ink used then had no acid in it and did not soak into the writing material. Since the ink remained on the surface, it could be wiped off if the scribe wanted to reuse the material. Paul says here that God has wiped off our certificate of debt, **having nailed it to the cross.** Not a trace of it remains to be held against us. Our forgiveness is complete.

COMPLETE VICTORY

When He had disarmed the rulers and authorities, He made a public display of them, having triumphed over them through Him. (2:15)

Having **disarmed** Satan (literally "stripping him") and **the rulers and authorities** (fallen angels), **He made a public display of them, having triumphed over them through Him.** The imagery here is like that of a triumphant Roman general, parading his defeated captives through the streets of Rome. Christ's victory on the cross halted the demons in their attempts to stop His redemptive work and stripped Satan of his powers. Hebrews 2:14 says, "Since then the children share in flesh and blood, He Himself likewise also partook of the same, that through death He might render powerless him who had the power of death, that is, the devil; and might deliver those who through fear of death were subject to slavery all their lives."

To worship such defeated and humiliated beings would be the height of folly. The cross is the answer to the Colossian errorists' insistence on worshiping angelic beings. Through the Lord Jesus and His work on the cross (cf. Eph. 1:20-23; 3:10), God canceled the believer's debt, defeating Satan and his fallen angels. That is why Paul can affirm in Romans 8:37-39, "In all these things we overwhelmingly conquer through Him who loved us. For I am convinced that neither death, nor life, nor angels, nor principalities, nor things present, nor things to come, nor powers, nor height, nor depth, nor any other created thing, shall be able to separate us from the love of God, which is in Christ Jesus our Lord." Though we still wrestle against the forces of evil (Eph. 6:12), they cannot be victorious. Christ, the crucified, risen Lord of all, reigns supreme in the universe. To be united with Him is to be free from Satan's dominion.

The death of Christ brings transformation, pardon, and victory. That adds up to complete salvation with complete forgiveness and triumph. No wonder Paul said, "May it never be that I should boast, except in the cross of our Lord Jesus Christ, through which the world has been crucified to me, and I to the world" (Gal. 6:14).

Spiritual Intimidation

10

Therefore let no one act as your judge in regard to food or drink or in respect to a festival or a new moon or a Sabbath day—things which are a mere shadow of what is to come; but the substance belongs to Christ. Let no one keep defrauding you of your prize by delighting in self-abasement and the worship of the angels, taking his stand on visions he has seen, inflated without cause by his fleshly mind, and not holding fast to the head, from whom the entire body, being supplied and held together by the joints and ligaments, grows with a growth which is from God. If you have died with Christ to the elementary principles of the world, why, as if you were living in the world, do you submit yourself to decrees, such as, "Do not handle, do not taste, do not touch!" (which all refer to things destined to perish with the using)— in accordance with the commandments and teachings of men? These are matters which have, to be sure, the appearance of wisdom in self-made religion and self-abasement and severe treatment of the body, but are of no value against fleshly indulgence. (2:16-23)

Today, with advanced media capability, there is an onslaught of false teaching of unprecedented proportions. On every side, the sufficiency of Jesus Christ is either openly or implicitly denied. False philosophy has infiltrated the church in the guise of psychology, which is all too often viewed as a necessary supplement to God's Word. Many lean toward mysticism, claiming to receive visions and extrabiblical revelations. Others are legalists, equating holiness with observing a list of cultural taboos. Still others urge the practice of asceticism, arguing that poverty or physical deprivation is the path to godliness. Pastors, elders, and other church leaders, who are responsible to warn the church against false teaching, are often the very ones proclaiming those errors.

The churches in the Lycus Valley also faced the danger of spiritual intimidation. False teachers were telling them that Jesus Christ was not sufficient, that they needed something more. These people believed they were privy to a higher level of spiritual knowledge and the secrets of spiritual illumination. This higher, hidden truth was beyond Jesus Christ and the Word. These heretics formed an elite, exclusive group that disdained "unenlightened" and "simplistic" Christians. They effectively beguiled some Christians and drew them away from confidence in Christ alone. The "something more" that the false teachers offered was a syncretism of pagan philosophy, Jewish legalism, mysticism, and asceticism. As noted earlier, Paul wrote the Colossians to refute that false teaching and to present the absolute sufficiency of Jesus Christ for salvation and sanctification. Because the Colossians had Christ, and He is sufficient, they did not need to be intimidated by the false teachers.

In 2:8-23, Paul mounts a frontal attack on the Colossian heresy. He has already dealt with philosophy (2:8-10) and presented Christ's sufficiency (2:11-15). He continues his refutation of the Colossian heresy by dealing with legalism (2:16-17), mysticism (2:18-19), and asceticism (2:20-23).

LEGALISM

Therefore let no one act as your judge in regard to food or drink or in respect to a festival or a new moon or a Sabbath day—things which are a mere shadow of what is to come; but the substance belongs to Christ. (2:16-17)

Legalism is the religion of human achievement. It argues that spirituality is based on Christ plus human works. It makes conformity to man-made rules the measure of spirituality. Believers, however, are complete in Christ, who has provided complete salvation, forgiveness, and victory. **Therefore,** Paul tells the Colossians, **let no one act as your judge.** Do not sacrifice your freedom in Christ for a set of man-made rules. Inasmuch as "Christ is the end of the law for righteousness to everyone who believes" (Rom. 10:4), to become entangled again in a legalistic system is pointless and harmful. Paul reminded the Galatians, who were also beguiled by legalism, "It was for freedom that Christ set us free; therefore keep standing firm and do not be subject again to a yoke of slavery" (Gal. 5:1).

Legalism is useless because it cannot restrain the flesh. It is also dangerously deceptive, because inwardly rebellious and disobedient Christians, or even non-Christians, can conform to a set of external performance standards or rituals. The nineteenth-century American pastor Gardiner Spring warned,

> A merely moral man may be very scrupulous of duties he owes to his fellowmen, while the infinitely important duties he owes to God are kept entirely out of sight. Of loving and serving God, he knows nothing. Whatever he does or whatever he leaves undone, he does nothing for God. He is honest in his dealings with all except God, he robs none but God, he is thankless and faithless to none but God, he feels contemptuously, and speaks reproachfully of none but God. A just perception of the relations he sustains to God constitutes no part of his principles, and the duties which result from those relations constitute no part of his piety. He may not only disbelieve the Scriptures, but may never read them; may not only disregard the divine authority, but every form of divine worship, and live and die as though he had no concern with God and God had not concern with him. The character of the young man in the Gospel presents a painful and affecting view of the deficiencies of external morality (see Mt. 19:16-22). He was not dishonest, nor untrue; he was not impure nor malignant; and not a few of the divine commands he had externally observed. Nay, he says, "All these have I kept." Nor was his a mere sporadic goodness, but steady and uniform. He had performed these services "from his youth up." Nor was this all. He professed a willingness to become acquainted with his whole duty. "What lack I yet?" And yet when brought to the test, this poor youth saw that, with all his boasted morality, he could not deny himself, take up his cross, and follow Christ. (*The Distinguishing Traits of Christian Character* [Phillipsburg, N.J.: Presby. & Ref., n.d.], pp. 7-8)

That Christians not be intimidated by such legalism was Paul's constant concern. He commanded Titus not to pay attention to "Jewish myths and commandments of men who turn away from the truth," because "to the pure, all things are pure; but to those who are defiled and unbelieving, nothing is pure, but both their mind and their conscience are defiled" (Titus 1:14-15). Romans 14-15 and 1 Corinthians 8-10 also discuss Christian liberty and the only legitimate reason for restraining it: to protect a weaker Christian brother or sister.

The false teachers were telling the Colossians that it was not enough to have Christ; they also needed to keep the Jewish ceremonial law. The false teachers' prohibitions about **food** and **drink** were probably based on the Old Testament dietary laws (cf. Lev. 11). Those laws were given to mark Israel as God's distinct people and to discourage them from intermingling with the surrounding nations.

Because the Colossians were under the New Covenant, the dietary laws of the Old Covenant were no longer in force. Jesus made that clear in Mark 7:

> After He called the multitude to Him again, He began saying to them, "Listen to Me, all of you, and understand: there is nothing outside the man which going into him can defile him; but the things which proceed out of the man are what defile the man. If any man has ears to hear, let him hear." And when leaving the multitude, He had entered the house, His disciples questioned Him about the parable. And He said to them, "Are you so lacking in understanding also? Do you not understand that whatever goes into the man from outside cannot defile him; because it does not go into his heart, but into his stomach, and is eliminated?" (Thus He declared all foods clean.) (vv. 14-19)

Paul reminded the Romans that "the kingdom of God is not eating and drinking, but righteousness and peace and joy in the Holy Spirit" (Rom. 14:17). That the dietary laws are no longer in force was illustrated by Peter's vision (Acts 10:9-16) and formally ratified by the Jerusalem Council (Acts 15:28-29).

A **festival** was one of the annual Jewish celebrations, such as Passover, Pentecost, the Feast of Tabernacles, or the Feast of Lights (cf. Lev. 23). Sacrifices were also offered on the **new moon,** or first day of the month (Num. 28:11-14).

Contrary to the claims of some today, Christians are not required to worship on the **Sabbath day.** It, like the other Old Covenant holy days Paul mentions, is not binding under the New Covenant. There is convincing evidence for that in Scripture. First, the Sabbath was the sign to Israel of the Old Covenant (Ex. 31:16-17; Neh. 9:14; Ezek. 20:12). Because we are now under the New Covenant (Heb. 8), we are no longer required to keep the sign of the Old Covenant.

Second, the New Testament nowhere commands Christians to observe the Sabbath.

Third, in our only glimpse of an early church worship service in the New Testament, we find the church meeting on Sunday, the first day of the week (Acts 20:7).

Fourth, we find no hint in the Old Testament that God expected the Gentile nations to observe the Sabbath, nor are they ever condemned for failing to do so. That is certainly strange if He expected all peoples to observe the Sabbath.

Fifth, there is no evidence of anyone's keeping the Sabbath before the time of Moses, nor are there any commands to keep the Sabbath before the giving of the law at Mount Sinai.

Sixth, the Jerusalem Council did not impose Sabbath keeping on the Gentile believers (Acts 15).

Seventh, Paul warned the Gentiles about many different sins in his epistles, but never about breaking the Sabbath.

Eighth, Paul rebuked the Galatians for thinking God expected them to observe special days (including the Sabbath) (Gal. 4:10-11).

Ninth, Paul taught that keeping the Sabbath was a matter of Christian liberty (Rom. 14:5).

Tenth, the early church Fathers, from Ignatius to Augustine, taught that the Old Testament Sabbath had been abolished and that the first day of the week (Sunday) was the day when Christians should meet for worship. That disproves the claim of some that Sunday worship was not instituted until the fourth century.

The dietary laws, festivals, sacrifices, and Sabbath-day worship were all **things which are a mere shadow of what is to come; but the substance belongs to Christ.** A shadow has no reality; the reality is what makes the shadow. Jesus Christ is the reality to which the shadows pointed. For example, regarding food regulations, He is "the bread that came down out of heaven" (John 6:41). There is no need for Christians to observe the Passover either, because "Christ our Passover also has been sacrificed" (1 Cor. 5:7). What justification could there be for demanding that Gentiles observe the Sabbath when God has granted them eternal rest (Heb. 4:1-11)? Any continuing preoccupation with the shadows once the reality has come is pointless.

Paul's point is simple: true spirituality does not consist merely of keeping external rules, but of having an inner relationship with Jesus Christ.

MYSTICISM

Let no one keep defrauding you of your prize by delighting in self-abasement and the worship of the angels, taking his stand on visions he has seen, inflated without cause by his fleshly mind, and not holding fast to the head, from whom the entire body, being supplied and held together by the joints and ligaments, grows with a growth which is from God. (2:18-19)

Mysticism may be defined as the pursuit of a deeper or higher subjective religious experience. It is the belief that spiritual reality is perceived apart from the human intellect and natural senses. It looks for truth internally, weighing feelings, intuition, and other internal sensations more heavily than objective, observable, external data. Mysticism ultimately derives its authority from a self-actualized, self-authenticated light rising from within. This irrational and anti-intellectual approach is the antithesis of Christian theology. The false teachers claimed a mystical union with God. Paul exhorts the Colossians not to allow those false teachers to **keep defrauding** them of their **prize.** It was as if the heretics assumed the role of spiritual referees and disqualified the Colossians for not abiding by their rules.

Self-abasement translates *tapeinophrosunē*, which is usually rendered "humility." The NASB translation emphasizes the negative use of the term in the present context. The humility of the Colossian errorists was a false humility. They were **delighting** in it, meaning their supposed humility was nothing but ugly pride. It was like that of Uriah Heep, one of the most contemptible characters of English literature, who said, "I am well aware that I am the 'umblest person going" (chapter 16 of Charles Dickens's *David Copperfield*).

The false teachers had a far more serious problem than false humility, however. They also engaged in **the worship of the angels,** thus denying the truth that there is "one mediator also between God and men, the man Christ Jesus" (1 Tim. 2:5).

The worship of angels was a heresy that was to plague the Phrygian region (where Colossae was located) for centuries. Commentator William Hendriksen notes that in A.D. 363 a church synod was held in Colossae's sister city of Laodicea. It declared, "It is not right for Christians to abandon the church of God and go away to invoke angels" (Canon 25) (cited in *Philippians, Colossians, and Philemon*. New Testament Commentary [Grand Rapids: Baker, 1981], p. 126). The early Church Father Theodoret, commenting on Colossians 2:18, wrote, "The disease which St. Paul denounces, continued for a long time in Phrygia and Pisidia" (cited in Hendriksen, p. 126). The archangel Michael was worshiped in Asia Minor as late as A.D. 739. He was also given credit for miraculous cures.

The Bible strictly forbids the worship of angels. "It is written," Jesus told Satan, "'You shall worship the Lord your God, and serve Him only'" (Matt. 4:10).

The angels themselves worship God, as Isaiah noted in his vision:

In the year of King Uzziah's death, I saw the Lord sitting on a throne, lofty and exalted, with the train of His robe filling the temple. Seraphim stood above Him, each having six wings; with two he covered his face, and with two he covered his feet, and with two he flew. And one called out to another and said, "Holy, Holy, Holy, is the Lord of hosts, the whole earth is full of His glory." And the foundations of the thresholds trembled at the voice of him who called out, while the temple was filling with smoke. (Isa. 6:1-4)

In Revelation 5:11-12, John writes, "I looked, and I heard the voice of many angels around the throne and the living creatures and the elders; and the number of them was myriads of myriads, and thousands of thousands, saying with a loud voice, 'Worthy is the Lamb that was slain to receive power and riches and wisdom and might and honor and glory and blessing.'"

When John tried to worship an angel, he was rebuked for doing so: "I fell at his feet to worship him. And he said to me, 'Do not do that; I am a fellow servant of yours and your brethren who hold the testimony of Jesus; worship God'" (Rev. 19:10; cf. Rev. 22:9).

In addition to practicing false humility and worshiping angels, the false teachers were taking their stand on visions they had seen. Like many heretics and cultists down through the ages, they claimed support for their aberrant teachings in visions they had supposedly seen. Some of the worst excesses in the modern-day charismatic movement are derived from such visions. There is no need for extrabiblical revelation through visions, because "God, after He spoke long ago to the fathers in the prophets in many portions and in many ways, in these last days has spoken to us *in His Son*" (Heb. 1:1-2, italics added).

Paul warns the Colossians not to be intimidated by the false teachers' claims. Far from being the spiritual elite they thought themselves to be, they were inflated without cause by their **fleshly minds.** Being guilty of gross spiritual pride, they were devoid of the Holy Spirit. Having gone beyond the teaching of Christ (cf. 2 John 9), they were not **holding fast to the head,** that is, Christ (cf. Col. 1:18). He is the One **from whom the entire body, being supplied and held together by the joints and ligaments, grows with a growth which is from God.** Spiritual growth comes from union with Christ. Jesus says in John 15:4-5, "Abide in Me, and I in you. As the branch cannot bear fruit of itself, unless it abides in the vine, so neither can you, unless you abide in Me. I am the vine, you are the branches; he who abides in Me, and I in him, he bears much fruit; for apart from Me you can do nothing."

There is a tendency in human nature to move from objectivity to subjectivity—to shift the focus from Christ to experience. This has always intimidated weak believers and threatened the church.

Today this brand of mysticism is most commonly seen in the charismatic movement—where Scripture is a distant second in importance to visions and revelations.

When such intimidation came from the sixteenth-century mystical charismatics of Martin Luther's day, the great Reformer was very firm with them, clinging to biblical revelation and the centrality and sufficiency of Christ. In particular, the followers of Thomas Münzer and the radical Anabaptists gave great prominence to the work and gifts of the Spirit—and to mystical knowledge. Their cry, expressing their suprabiblical experience, was "The Spirit, the Spirit!" Luther replied, "I will not follow where their spirit leads." When they were granted the privilege of an interview with Luther, they gave their cry "The Spirit, the Spirit!" The great Reformer was not impressed and thundered, "I slap your spirit on the snout."

We, like the Colossians, must not be intimidated by those who would make something other than knowing Christ through His Word a requirement for spiritual maturity. Christ is all sufficient, "seeing that His divine power has granted to us everything pertaining to life and godliness, through the true knowledge of Him who called us by His own glory and excellence" (2 Pet. 1:3).

ASCETICISM

If you have died with Christ to the elementary principles of the world, why, as if you were living in the world, do you submit yourself to decrees, such as, "Do not handle, do not taste, do not touch!" (which all refer to things destined to perish with the using)—in accordance with the commandments and teachings of men? These are matters which have, to be sure, the appearance of wisdom in self-made religion and self-abasement and severe treatment of the body, but are of no value against fleshly indulgence. (2:20-23)

An ascetic is one who lives a life of rigorous self-denial. In addition to practicing legalism and mysticism, the Colossian errorists were attempting to gain righteousness through self-denial.

The church has been intimidated for centuries by those who advocated poverty as a means to spirituality. It has not always remembered that money itself is not the root of evil, but the love of it (cf. 1 Tim. 6:10). Many of God's choicest servants in the Old Testament, such as Abraham, Job, and Solomon, were extremely wealthy.

If you have died with Christ to the elementary principles of the world, why, Paul asks, **as if you were living in the world, do you submit yourself to decrees, such as, "Do not handle, do not taste, do not touch!"** Through their union with Christ, the redeemed are set free from man-made rules designed to promote spirituality. To practice asceticism, Paul writes, is to adopt a worldly system of religion, based on **elementary principles.**

As already noted, the false teachers taught a form of philosophical dualism. They practiced asceticism in an attempt to free the spirit from the prison of the body.

The view that the body was evil eventually found its way into the church. According to the church Father Athanasius, Anthony, the founder of Christian monasticism, never changed his vest or washed his feet (*Life of Anthony*, para. 47). He was outdone, however, by Simeon Stylites (c. 390-459), who spent the last thirty-six years of his life atop a fifty-foot pillar. Simeon mistakenly thought the path to spirituality lay in exposing his body to the elements and withdrawing from the world. Their feats have been emulated by monks throughout church history. Even Martin Luther, before discovering the truth of justification by faith, nearly wrecked his health through asceticism.

God may call some to a life of self-denial. Many missionaries, for example, have by necessity led ascetic lives. They did not do so, however, as an attempt to gain spirituality.

Asceticism is useless in that it focuses attention on **things destined to perish with the using.** "Food is for the stomach, and the stomach is for food;" writes Paul to the Corinthians, "but God will do away with both of them" (1 Cor. 6:13). There is no spiritual value in keeping **the commandments and teachings of men.**

The reason for asceticism's impotency is seen in 2:23. Although it has **the appearance of wisdom in self-made religion and self-abasement and severe treatment of the body,** it is **of no value against fleshly indulgence.** Asceticism might make a person appear spiritual, because of its emphasis on humility and poverty, but it serves only to gratify the flesh. It is a vain attempt to appear more holy than others. Jesus warned His disciples against it: "Whenever you fast, do not put on a gloomy face as the hypocrites do, for they neglect their appearance in order to be seen fasting by men. Truly I say to you, they have their reward in full. But you, when you fast, anoint your head, and wash your face so that you may not be seen fasting by men, but by your Father who is in secret; and your Father who sees in secret will repay you" (Matt. 6:16-18).

Commenting on the futility of asceticism, the great nineteenth-century Scottish preacher Alexander McClaren wrote, "Any asceticism is a great deal more to men's taste than abandoning self. They will rather stick hooks in their backs and do the 'swinging poojah' than give up their sins and yield up their wills. There is only one thing that will put the collar on the neck of the animal within us and that is the power of the indwelling Christ. Ascetic religion is godless, for its practitioners essentially worship themselves. As such, we are not to be intimidated by it.

Paul's message to the Colossians is also a warning to us. We are not to be intimidated by false human philosophy, legalism, mysticism, or asceticism. Those are but "broken cisterns that can hold no water" (Jer. 2:13). We must hold fast to Christ, in whom we "have been made complete" (Col. 2:10).

Living the Risen Life **11**

If then you have been raised up with Christ, keep seeking the things above, where Christ is, seated at the right hand of God. Set your mind on the things above, not on the things that are on earth. For you have died and your life is hidden with Christ in God. When Christ, who is our life, is revealed, then you also will be revealed with Him in glory. (3:1-4)

Jesus said in John 17:18, "As Thou didst send Me into the world, I also have sent them into the world." He commanded His disciples, saying, "Go therefore and make disciples of all the nations, baptizing them in the name of the Father and the Son and the Holy Spirit, teaching them to observe all that I commanded you; and lo, I am with you always, even to the end of the age" (Matt. 28:19-20). It is the privilege and sober responsibility of the church to proclaim the good news of the gospel "even to the remotest part of the earth" (Acts 1:8).

Paradoxically, before Christians can reach the world, they must first leave it. In Galatians 1:4 Paul affirmed that Christ "gave Himself for our sins, that He might deliver us out of this present evil age." Christians are of Christ's kingdom, which is not of this world (John 18:36). We have overcome the world through faith in Christ (1 John 5:4-5). Although we exist in this world physically, spiritually we are already citizens of heaven (Eph. 2:6).

Our spiritual growth, joy, and fruitfulness require that we maintain a proper perspective on this world. We are "strangers and exiles on the earth" (Heb. 11:13), because "here we do not have a lasting city, but we are seeking the city which is to come" (Heb. 13:14). "Our citizenship is in heaven, from which also we eagerly wait for a Savior, the Lord Jesus Christ" (Phil. 3:20). We are "aliens and strangers" on this earth (1 Pet. 2:11). We are in the world, but not of the world. Until we realize that basic truth and live it, we will be ineffective in reaching the world with the truth of the gospel.

Of Robert Murray McCheyne, the devout nineteenth-century Scottish pastor and evangelist, a friend once said, "The man of whom I speak seemed to have got up to the full height . . . and to have entered into the secret places of the holiness of God." When McCheyne preached the gospel, "you could see strong men, hard and stern, melt as wax before the fire. Their breasts would swell and heave as if they would burst and the whole place became a place of weepers." He learned to live in the heavenlies to reach souls on earth. He was fulfilling the command of Romans 12:2: "Do not be conformed to this world, but be transformed by the renewing of your mind."

It is only when we rise above the world that we can both appreciate the appalling spiritual poverty in which most people live and learn to fix our minds on heavenly realities. Our blessings are in heaven (Eph. 1:3); the angels are there (Eph. 3:10); Christ is there (Eph. 1:20); and we, through our union with Him in His resurrection, exist in the heavenly realm (Eph. 2:6). Because the things most important to us are in heaven, we must not be entangled in this present world. All those Scriptures provide the backdrop for Paul's message in 3:1-4 as he moves to the practical side of the epistle. He begins by calling the readers to that preoccupation with heavenly reality that is the hallmark of true spirituality, and the starting point of practical holiness. Five features will help unfold the power of heavenly living on earth: the reminder, the responsibility, the resource, the reason, and the revelation.

THE REMINDER

If then you have been raised up with Christ (3:1a)

If denotes reality, as in 2:20, and is better translated "since." Believers having been **raised up with Christ** is not in doubt. The verb actually means "to be co-resurrected." It is an accomplished fact.

Believers spiritually are entered into Christ's death and resurrection at the moment of their salvation. Galatians 2:20 says, "I have been crucified with Christ; and it is no longer I who live, but Christ lives in me; and the life which I now live in the flesh I live by faith in the Son of God, who loved me, and delivered Himself up for me." In that verse, the apostle shows the union of the believer with the Lord, so that they have a shared life. Romans 6:3-4 teaches the same truth: "Do you not know that all of us who have been baptized into Christ Jesus have been baptized into His death? Therefore we have been buried with Him through baptism into death, in order that as Christ was raised from the dead through the glory of the Father, so we too might walk in newness of life."

The "baptism" here is not into water, but an immersing into the Savior's death and resurrection. Through their union with Christ, believers have died, have been buried, and have risen with Him. By saving faith they have entered into a new dimension. They possess divine and eternal life, which is not merely endless existence, but a heavenly quality of life brought to them by the indwelling Lord. They are thus alive in Christ to the realities of the divine realm.

Consequently, Christians have an obligation to live consistently with those realities. Paul delineates the specifics of that obligation in Romans 6:11-19:

> Even so consider yourselves to be dead to sin, but alive to God in Christ Jesus. Therefore do not let sin reign in your mortal body that you should obey its lusts, and do not go on presenting the members of your body to sin as instruments of unrighteousness; but present yourselves to God as those alive from the dead, and your members as instruments of righteousness to God. For sin shall not be master over you, for you are not under law, but under grace. What then? Shall we sin because we are not under law but under grace? May it never be! Do you not know that when you present yourselves to someone as slaves for obedience, you are slaves of the one whom you obey, either of sin resulting in death, or of obedience resulting in righteousness? But thanks be to God that though you were slaves of sin, you became obedient from the heart to that form of teaching to which you were committed, and having been freed from sin, you became slaves of righteousness. I am speaking in human terms because of the weakness of your flesh. For just as you presented your members as slaves to impurity and to lawlessness, resulting in further lawlessness, so now present your members as slaves to righteousness, resulting in sanctification.

This new life is real and powerful, but so is remaining sin. Though it no longer is our master, it can still overpower us if we are not presenting ourselves to God as servants of righteousness. (For a fuller treatment of this rich teaching, see my comments on Romans 6-8 in *Romans 1-8*, MacArthur New Testament Commentary [Chicago: Moody, 1991].)

Spirituality, as Paul says in Philippians 2:12, is working that inner life out, the process of living the reality of our union with Christ. In Him we have all the resources necessary for living the Christian life (cf. 2 Pet. 1:3). Paul emphasizes the centrality of Christ throughout Colossians 3:1-4. By using such phrases as **with Christ** (3:1); **where Christ** (3:1); **with Christ** (3:3); **when Christ** (3:4); and **with Him** (3:4), he stresses again Christ's total sufficiency (cf. 2:10). Unfortunately, many Christians fail to understand and pursue the fullness of Christ. Consequently, because of not knowing what Scripture says, or not applying it properly, they are intimidated into thinking they need something more than Him alone to live the Christian life. They fall prey to false philosophy, legalism, mysticism, or asceticism.

Paul reminds the Colossians that they have risen with Christ. This is the path to holiness, not self-denial, angelic experience, or ceremony. They are no longer living the old life they lived before their salvation, but possess the eternal life of Christ and have been raised to live on another plane. They must not be ignorant or forgetful of who they are and how they are to live. All sinful passion is controlled and conquered by the power of the indwelling Christ and our union with Him.

The Responsibility

keep seeking the things above, where Christ is, seated at the right hand of God. Set your mind on the things above, not on the things that are on earth. (3:1*b*, 2)

The present tense of *zēteō* (**keep seeking**) indicates continuous action. Preoccupation with the eternal realities that are ours in Christ is to be the pattern of the believer's life. Jesus put it this way: "Seek first His kingdom and His righteousness; and all these things shall be added to you" (Matt. 6:33). Paul is not advocating a form of mysticism. Rather, he desires that the Colossians' preoccupation with heaven govern their earthly responses. To be preoccupied with heaven is to be preoccupied with the One who reigns there and His purposes, plans, provisions, and power. It is also to view the things, people, and events of this world through His eyes and with an eternal perspective.

The things above refers to the heavenly realm and hones in on the spiritual values that characterize Christ, such as tenderness, kindness, meekness, patience, wisdom, forgiveness, strength, purity, and love.

When believers focus on the realities of heaven, they can then truly enjoy the world their heavenly Father has created. As the writer of the hymn "I Am His, and He Is Mine" expressed it,

Heav'n above is softer blue
Earth around is sweeter green!
Something lives in every hue
Christless eyes have never seen:
Birds with gladder songs o'erflow
Flow'rs with deeper beauties shine,
Since I know, as now I know,
I am His, and He is mine.

When Christians begin to live in the heavenlies, when they commit themselves to the riches of "the Jerusalem above" (Gal. 4:26), they will live out their heavenly values in this world to the glory of God.

In 3:2, Paul gives instruction on how to seek the things above. He says, **Set your mind on the things above, not on the things that are on earth. Set your mind** is from *phroneō* and could simply be translated, "think," or more thoroughly, "have this inner disposition." Once again, the present tense indicates continuous action. Lightfoot paraphrases Paul's thought: "You must not only *seek* heaven, you must also *think* heaven" (*St. Paul's Epistles to the Colossians and to Philemon* [1879; reprint, Grand Rapids: Zondervan, 1959], p. 209; italics in the original). The believer's whole disposition should orient itself toward heaven, **where Christ is,** just as a compass needle orients itself toward the north.

Obviously, the thoughts of heaven that are to fill the believer's mind must derive from Scripture. The Bible is the only reliable source of knowledge about the character of God and the values of heaven. Paul describes that preoccupation as being "transformed by the renewing of [your] mind" (Rom. 12:2). In it we learn the true, honorable, right, pure, lovely, of good repute, excellent, and praiseworthy things our minds are to dwell on (cf. Phil. 4:8).

Such heavenly values dominating the mind produce godly behavior. Sin will be conquered and humility, a sacrificial spirit, and assurance will result.

THE RESOURCE

where Christ is, seated at the right hand of God. (3:1c)

The believer's resource is none other than the One in whom are hidden all the treasures of wisdom and knowledge: the risen and glorified Christ, **seated at the right hand of God** in the place of honor and majesty. The Bible speaks often of Christ's exalted position. Psalm 110:1 says, "The Lord says to my Lord: 'Sit at My right hand, until I make Thine enemies a footstool for Thy feet.'" Jesus told the accusers at His trial that "from now on the Son of Man will be seated at the right hand of the power of God" (Luke 22:69). In his sermon on the day of Pentecost, Peter told the crowd that Jesus had been "exalted to the right hand of God" (Acts 2:33). Peter and the other apostles described Jesus to the Sanhedrin as "the one whom God exalted to His right hand as a Prince and a Savior" (Acts 5:31). As he was being martyred, Stephen cried out, "Behold, I see the heavens opened up and the Son of Man standing at the right hand of God" (Acts 7:56). Paul describes Jesus as He "who is at the right hand of God, who also intercedes for us" (Rom. 8:34), because God "raised Him from the dead, and seated Him at His right hand in the heavenly places" (Eph. 1:20). The writer of Hebrews says of Christ, "When He had made purification of sins, He sat down at the right hand of the Majesty on high" (Heb. 1:3). Because of that, "we have such a high priest, who has taken His seat at the right hand of the throne of the Majesty in the heavens" (Heb. 8:1). He is the One "who is at the right hand of God, having gone into heaven, after angels and authorities and powers had been subjected to Him" (1 Pet. 3:22).

Because of Christ's coronation and exaltation to the Father's right hand, He is the fountain of blessing for His people. Jesus told the disciples, "Whatever you ask in My name, that will I do, that the Father may be glorified in the Son. If you ask Me anything in My name, I will do it" (John 14:13-14; cf. 15:16; 16:23-24, 26). Believers can be assured that what they seek is there, "for as many as may be the promises of God, in Him they are yes" (2 Cor. 1:20).

THE REASON

For you have died and your life is hidden with Christ in God. (3:3)

Paul stresses the reason that living in the heavenlies is to be the norm for the believer. Believers have died to the world system, through their faith union with Christ in His death and resurrection. Paul wrote in Galatians 6:14, "May it never be that I should boast, except in the cross of our Lord Jesus Christ, through which the world has been crucified to me, and I to the world." The past tense of *apothnēskō* (**you have died**) indicates that a death took place at salvation. "If any man is in Christ,"

Paul writes to the Corinthians, "he is a new creature; the old things passed away; behold, new things have come" (2 Cor. 5:17).

In what sense has the believer died? In the sense that the penalty for sin has been paid. The wages of sin is death, so we must die. By union with Jesus Christ, we die the required death in Him, thus the penalty is paid and sin can never claim us again. We have thus died to sin in the sense of paying its penalty. Its presence and power still affect us —but it cannot condemn us.

Not only have believers died to sin, but also their lives are **hidden with Christ in God.** What does **with Christ in God** mean? First, believers share a common life with the Father and Son. Paul writes in 1 Corinthians 6:17 that "the one who joins himself to the Lord is one spirit with Him." Believers are "partakers of the divine nature" (2 Pet. 1:4).

Second, that new life is concealed from the world. Unbelievers are unable to grasp the full import of the believer's new life, since "a natural man does not accept the things of the Spirit of God; for they are foolishness to him, and he cannot understand them, because they are spiritually appraised" (1 Cor. 2:14). Paul pointed out that the true manifestation of the sons of God is yet to come in the next world, so that people cannot see what believers really are like (Rom. 8:19). The apostle John implied as much about our true identity when he wrote: "Beloved, now we are children of God, and it has not yet appeared what we shall be" (1 John 3:2). The false teachers troubling the Colossians could not grasp the truth that the Colossians had already gained transcendent spiritual knowledge and life, and thus had no need of their false teaching.

Third, believers are eternally secure, hidden protectively from all spiritual foes. The blessings of salvation are "an inheritance which is imperishable and undefiled and will not fade away, reserved in heaven for you" (1 Pet. 1:4). Our great high priest "is able to save forever those who draw near to God through Him, since He always lives to make intercession for them" (Heb. 7:25). Those to whom the Son gives eternal life "shall never perish; and no one shall snatch them out of My hand" (John 10:28). They are hidden away deep in the shelter of their God.

No passage states that glorious truth more eloquently than Romans 8:31-39:

> If God is for us, who is against us? He who did not spare His own Son, but delivered Him up for us all, how will He not also with Him freely give us all things? Who will bring a charge against God's elect? God is the one who justifies; who is the one who condemns? Christ Jesus is He who died, yes, rather who was raised, who is at the right hand of God, who also intercedes for us. Who shall separate us from the love of Christ? Shall tribulation, or distress, or persecution, or famine, or na-

kedness, or peril, or sword? Just as it is written, "For Thy sake we are being put to death all day long; We were considered as sheep to be slaughtered." But in all these things we overwhelmingly conquer through Him who loved us. For I am convinced that neither death, nor life, nor angels, nor principalities, nor things present, nor things to come, nor powers, nor height, nor depth, nor any other created thing, shall be able to separate us from the love of God, which is in Christ Jesus our Lord.

All the riches of the eternal God are available to those whose lives are hidden with Him through His Son.

THE REVELATION

When Christ, who is our life, is revealed, then you also will be revealed with Him in glory. (3:4)

Although the world may not now recognize those whose lives are hidden with Christ in God, that will not always be the case. **When Christ . . . is revealed** at His second coming, we also will be revealed with Him in glory. The apostle John describes that scene in Revelation 19:11-13, 15-16:

> I saw heaven opened; and behold, a white horse, and He who sat upon it is called Faithful and True; and in righteousness He judges and wages war. And His eyes are a flame of fire, and upon His head are many diadems; and He has a name written upon Him which no one knows except Himself. And He is clothed with a robe dipped in blood; and His name is called The Word of God. . . . And from His mouth comes a sharp sword, so that with it He may smite the nations; and He will rule them with a rod of iron; and He treads the wine press of the fierce wrath of God, the Almighty. And on His robe and on His thigh He has a name written, "KING OF KINGS, AND LORD OF LORDS."

To this description of our Lord at His return in judgment, the vision adds that He will be accompanied by saints. John also wrote, "The armies which are in heaven, clothed in fine linen, white and clean, were following Him on white horses" (v. 14).

The verdict of eternity will reverse the verdicts of time. On that day, it will become apparent who really belongs to the Lord. "The Lord knows those who are His" (2 Tim. 2:19), and He will reveal them to the world. Lightfoot comments, "The veil which now shrouds your higher life from others, and even partly from yourselves, will then be withdrawn. The world which persecutes, despises, ignores now, will then be blinded with the dazzling glory of the revelation" (Lightfoot, p. 210). John wrote, "We know that, when He appears, we shall be like Him, because we shall see Him just as He is" (1 John 3:2).

Paul adds a wonderful parenthetical thought. He describes Christ as **our life.** Christ does not merely give life; He *is* life. Paul said, "I have been crucified with Christ; and it is no longer I who live, but Christ lives in me; and the life which I now live in the flesh I live by faith in the Son of God, who loved me, and delivered Himself up for me" (Gal. 2:20). He told the Corinthians that the life of Jesus was manifested in his body (2 Cor. 4:10). When facing possible martyrdom, he could say, "For to me, to live is Christ, and to die is gain" (Phil. 1:21).

The key to living the risen life is to have a life centered on Christ. The Son, not this present world, is the center of the believer's universe.

Putting Sin to Death 12

Therefore consider the members of your earthly body as dead to immorality, impurity, passion, evil desire, and greed, which amounts to idolatry. For it is on account of these things that the wrath of God will come, and in them you also once walked, when you were living in them. But now you also, put them all aside: anger, wrath, malice, slander, and abusive speech from your mouth. Do not lie to one another, (3:5-9*a*)

We might be surprised to read that living the risen life involves putting sin to death. Didn't Paul just say that that had already been done? At the moment of salvation, "our old self was crucified with [Christ], that our body of sin might be done away with, that we should no longer be slaves to sin" (Rom. 6:6). That positional reality, however, must be worked out in the believer's practical living. There can be no holiness or maturity in a life where sin runs unchecked.

We have died to sin's penalty, but sin's power still can be strong and our flesh is weak. That is why we must continually put sin to death by yielding to the Holy Spirit (Rom. 8:13).Sin is like a deposed monarch who no longer reigns, nor has the ability to condemn, but works hard to debilitate and devastate all his former subjects. Sin is still potent, and success against it demands the Spirit's power. The principle of Zechariah 4:6 applies in victory over Satan. It is "not by might nor by power, but by My Spirit." And the Spirit's weapon is the Word (Eph. 6:17). As the believer is strong in the Word, he "overcome[s] the evil one" (1 John 2:14). Being filled with the power of the Holy Spirit (Eph. 5:18) is the same as allowing the Word to dwell richly in you (Col. 3:16). So it is true that the believer has died in the sense of paying sin's penalty by being united with Christ in His death. But it is equally true that sin still attacks his unredeemed humanness (cf. Rom. 8:23) and must, as a deadly enemy, be killed by the power of the Spirit through the Word. So while we wait for "the redemption of [the] body" (Rom. 8:23), the redeemed spirit, empowered by the Holy Spirit, must kill the sin attacking the flesh.

Putting sin to death, then, is not optional in the Christian life. The Puritan Richard Baxter wrote, "Use sin as it will use you; spare it not, for it will not spare you; it is your murderer, and the murderer of the world: use it, therefore, as a murderer should be used. Kill it before it kills you; and though it bring you to the grave, as it did your Head, it shall not be able to keep you there" (cited in I. D. E. Thomas, *A Puritan Golden Treasury* [Edinburgh: Banner of Truth, 1977], p. 281). To be a Christian is to die to self, to ambition, to ego, and to pride. It is to bow in humble submission to Christ's lordship. It is to obey the Lord's command expressed in Luke 9:23: "If anyone wishes to come after Me, let him deny himself, and take up his cross daily, and follow Me." It is to follow the example of Paul himself, who told the Corinthians, "I die daily" (1 Cor. 15:31).

Consider . . . as dead is from *nekroō*, and literally means "kill," or "put to death." Believers are to make a decisive resolution to put sin to death, bringing the flesh under subjection to the Spirit-filled new disposition.

People have often misinterpreted Paul's words here, in much the same way as Jesus' words in Matthew 5:29-30 and 18:8 have been. Taking those passages literally, many have physically injured themselves. According to tradition, Origen, one of the great theologians of the early church, was voluntarily castrated (based on his misinterpretation of Matt. 19:12). A common sight in European cities during the Middle Ages was a group known as the Flagellants. Marching through the streets in solemn processions, they scourged themselves in penance for their sins. Nor are such misinterpretations a thing of the past. I once met a man who wore a belt studded with nails that constantly tore his flesh. He felt that by so doing he was killing the flesh as well as suffering to atone for his sins.

Paul, however, is not advocating the very asceticism he condemned in chapter 2. Rather, he is calling for the elimination of everything in the believer's life that is contrary to godliness. He told the Romans, "If you are living according to the flesh, you must die; but if by the Spirit you are putting to death the deeds of the body, you will live" (Rom. 8:13). Only then will the believer experience spiritual fullness as God intended.

The battle with sin is common to all believers, even Paul (cf. Rom. 7:14-25). The desire of the new inner man to live a life pleasing to God is held back by the old, sinful flesh with its fallen patterns. Although believers are new creatures on the inside (2 Cor. 5:17), the new creatures live in old bodies. Thus our bodies can either be instruments for righteousness, or for iniquity. For this reason Paul wrote in Romans 12:1-2, "I urge you therefore, brethren, by the mercies of God, to present your bodies a living and holy sacrifice, acceptable to God, which is your spiritual service of worship. And do not be conformed to this world, but be transformed by the renewing of your mind, that you may prove what the will of God is, that which is good and acceptable and perfect."

Therefore refers to the truths of 3:1-4. Paul constantly links doctrine and practice in his epistles. Since believers share in Christ's death and resurrection, have their lives hidden with Him, and will one day be revealed in glory with Him, they must kill sin. As heavenly citizens, believers need to cut the ties with the sinful patterns of their former life.

Theology is not an ivory tower academic exercise reserved for specialists. Sound theology is foundational to spiritual growth. As noted in the previous chapter, Romans 6 also shows the connection between doctrine and practice. In 6:1-10, Paul teaches the truth of the believer's union with Christ in His death, burial, and resurrection. On that basis he writes, "Even so consider yourselves to be dead to sin, but alive to God in Christ Jesus. Therefore do not let sin reign in your mortal body that you should obey its lusts, and do not go on presenting the members of your body to sin as instruments of unrighteousness; but present yourselves to God as those alive from the dead, and your members as instruments of righteousness to God" (Rom. 6:11-13).

Although obscured by the NASB translation, the Greek text says to kill the **members of your earthly body** (not just to consider them as dead). Paul uses a figure of speech known as metonymy. When he speaks of killing bodily parts or members, Paul is actually referring to the sins associated with those members. It should be noted that this hits at the Colossian dualism regarding body and spirit. Paul is saying that the body should be holy, under the control of the redeemed spirit. The body does what the inner disposition compels it to do—and a Spirit-controlled body must do what is good. This will happen until the day when the body will be redeemed (Rom. 8:23).

In 3:5-9a, Paul gives two sample lists of sins to kill. The lists include some of the most common and troubling sins believers face. They should not, however, be considered exhaustive. The first list, in 3:5, comprises sins of perverted love; the second, in 3:8-9a, contains those of wicked hate. The first list begins with acts and progresses to motives, whereas the second begins with motives and progresses to acts. The first list involves personal sins, the second social ones. The first list relates to feelings, the second to speech. In between the lists (3:6-7), Paul gives two reasons for putting sin to death.

SINS OF PERVERTED LOVE

immorality, impurity, passion, evil desire, and greed, which amounts to idolatry. (3:5b)

These are personal sins relate to our feelings. Paul progresses backward from the evil act to the underlying motive. Immorality, the evil act, takes place because of impurity. Impurity comes from perverted passion and evil desire, which in turn come from the root sin of greed.

Immorality translates *porneia* and refers to sexual sin. Our English word *pornography* derives from *porneia* and *graphē*, which means a writing. Pornography is thus a writing (or picture) about sexual sin. *Porneia* originally referred to prostitution (the related word *pornē* is the Greek word for "prostitute"). In the New Testament, however, its meaning broadens to include any form of illicit sex. In sharp contrast to the prevailing attitude in the ancient world, the Bible strictly forbids any sexual activity outside the marriage bond between a man and a woman. The Jerusalem Council ordered Gentile believers to avoid immorality (Acts 15:20, 29; 21:25). Paul was horrified to hear that it had surfaced in the Corinthian church (1 Cor. 5:1), and he told them to flee from it (1 Cor. 6:18). Immorality heads the list of the deeds of the flesh (Gal. 5:19) and is not proper behavior for the saints (Eph. 5:3). The biblical view of immorality is summarized in 1 Thessalonians 4:3: "This is the will of God, your sanctification; that is, that you abstain from sexual immorality."

Impurity translates *akatharsia*, from which the word *catharsis* or "cleansing" comes. The alpha privitive (*a*) makes it a negative, meaning "filthiness," or "uncleanness." It is a more general term than immorality, going beyond the act to the evil thoughts and intentions of the mind. Jesus said, "Everyone who looks on a woman to lust for her has committed adultery with her already in his heart" (Matt. 5:28), because "from within, out of the heart of men, proceed the evil thoughts, fornications, thefts, murders, adulteries, deeds of coveting and wickedness, as well as deceit, sensuality, envy, slander, pride and foolishness" (Mark 7:21-22). Impurity is also one of the deeds of the flesh (Gal. 5:19). It is not to be indulged in by believers (Eph. 5:3), because "God has not called us for the purpose of impurity, but in sanctification" (1 Thess. 4:7).

Evil behavior begins with evil thoughts. Therefore the battle against all sin, especially sexual sin, begins in the mind. Evil thoughts produce sinful behavior, and pure thoughts produce righteous behavior. That is why Paul counsels, "Whatever is true, whatever is honorable, whatever is right, whatever is pure, whatever is lovely, whatever is of good repute, if there is any excellence and if anything worthy of praise, let your mind dwell on these things" (Phil. 4:8), and "Let the word of Christ richly dwell within you" (Col. 3:16).

The distinction between **passion** and **evil desire** is not great. *Pathos* (**passion**) refers to the sexual passion set loose in the body, as its two other occurrences in the New Testament indicate (cf. Rom. 1:26; 1 Thess. 4:5). In this context, **evil desire** undoubtedly also refers to the sexual lust created in the mind (cf. James 1:15). Perhaps the difference between the two terms is that **passion** is the physical and **evil desire** the mental side of the same vice. The two terms appear together in 1 Thessalonians 4:5, where Paul commands Christians not to live "in lustful passion, like the Gentiles who do not know God." Such behavior is completely inappropriate for believers.

Paul mentions **greed,** or covetousness, last because it is the evil root from which all the previous sins spring. It is also mentioned last in the Ten Commandments (cf. Ex. 20:17; Deut. 5:21). *Pleonexia* (**greed**) comes from two Greek words: *pleon*, "more," and exō, "to have." It is the insatiable desire to have more, to have what is forbidden. As such, it is the source of fights and quarrels (James 4:2), as well as lusts, passion, and sin.

Because it places selfish desire above obedience to God, greed **amounts to idolatry.** Covetousness is the root cause of all sin. William Barclay wrote, "It is, therefore, a sin with a very wide range. If it is the desire for money, it leads to theft. If it is the desire for prestige, it leads to evil ambition. If it is the desire for power, it leads to sadistic tyranny. If it is the desire for a person, it leads to sexual sin" (*The Letters to the Philippians, Colossians, and Thessalonians* [Louisville, Ky.: Westminster, 1975], p. 152).

When people sin, it is at its basis their doing what they desire, rather than what God desires. That is, in essence, to worship themselves instead of God, and that is idolatry. The Puritan Stephen Charnock wrote,

All sin is founded in a secret atheism. . . . All the wicked inclinations in the heart . . . are sparks from this latent fire; the language of every one of these is, "I would be a Lord to myself, and would not have a God superior to me." . . . In sins of omission we own not God, in neglecting to perform what he enjoins; in sins of commission we set up some lust in the place of God, and pay to that the homage which is due to our Maker. . . . We deny his sovereignty when we violate his laws . . . Every sin invades the rights of God, and strips him of one or other of his perfections. . . . Every sin is a kind of cursing God in the heart; an aim at the destruction of the being of God; not actually, but virtually . . . A man in every sin aims to set up his own will as his rule, and his own glory as the end of his actions against the will and glory of God. (*The Existence and Attributes of God* [reprint, Grand Rapids: Baker, 1979], 1:93-94)

Paul links sexual immorality, covetousness, and idolatry in Ephesians 5:3-5: "Do not let immorality or any impurity or greed even be named among you, as is proper among saints; and there must be no filthiness and silly talk, or coarse jesting, which are not fitting, but rather giving of thanks. For this you know with certainty, that no immoral or impure person or covetous man, who is an idolater, has an inheritance in the kingdom of Christ and God."

The Old Testament also associates sexual sin with idolatry. People worshiped pagan deities because the sex orgies that were part of that worship legitimized and fulfilled their corrupt passions. Numbers 25:1-3 clearly associates Israel's sin of idolatry with sexual immorality: "While Israel remained at Shittim, the people began to play the harlot with the daughters of Moab. For they invited the people to the sacrifices of their gods, and the people ate and bowed down to their gods. So Israel joined themselves to Baal of Peor, and the Lord was angry against Israel."

The antidote for covetousness is contentment. A contented person will not desire to violate another person sexually, or covet anything that person owns. A person who can say with Paul, "I have learned to be content in whatever circumstances I am" (Phil. 4:11), is not likely to struggle with covetousness. Contentment comes from trusting God. The basis of that trust is our knowledge of Him and His purposes for His people as revealed in Scripture.

Contentment is the opposite of covetousness. Whereas the covetous, greedy person worships himself, the contented person worships God. The Puritan Jeremiah Burroughs wrote,

You worship God more by [contentment] than when you come to hear a sermon, or spend half an hour, or an hour, in prayer, or when you come to receive a sacrament. These are acts of God's worship, but they are only external acts of worship, to hear and pray and receive sacraments. But [contentment] is the soul's worship, to subject itself thus to God . . . in active obedience we worship God by doing what pleases God, but by passive obedience we do as well worship God by being pleased with what God does. (*The Rare Jewel of Christian Contentment* [reprint, Edinburgh: Banner of Truth, 1979], p. 120)

Attacking covetousness lays the axe to a root cause of sin. When contentment replaces covetousness, the latter cannot give rise to the process that culminates in an act of sin.

REASONS FOR PUTTING SIN TO DEATH

For it is on account of these things that the wrath of God will come, and in them you also once walked, when you were living in them. (3:5-6)

Having given one list of sins, Paul pauses before going on to the second and gives two strong, motivating reasons for putting sin to death.

SIN BRINGS GOD'S JUDGMENT

For it is on account of these things that the wrath of God will come, (3:6)

God's **wrath** is "His eternal detestation of all unrighteousness. It is the displeasure and indignation of Divine equity against evil. It is the holiness of God stirred into activity against sin" (Arthur W. Pink, *The Attributes of God* [Grand Rapids: Baker, 1975], p. 83). Wrath is God's constant, invariable reaction to sin.

Unbelievers will experience the full force of God's eternal wrath. Paul writes in Romans 1:18, "The wrath of God is revealed from heaven against all ungodliness and unrighteousness of men, who suppress the truth in unrighteousness." Because the unbeliever does not have faith in Christ, "the wrath of God abides on him" (John 3:36; cf. Rom. 2:8). Unbelievers are "storing up wrath for [themselves] in the day of wrath and revelation of the righteous judgment of God" (Rom. 2:5). Because wrath comes **on account of these things,** the sins Paul has just mentioned that typify sin in general, believers should have no part in them. Sin brings wrath, not blessing. It never brings true happiness. Because believers have been delivered "from the wrath to come" (1 Thess. 1:10), and will experience no wrath (1 Thess. 5:9), Paul is not warning us that if we sin we will feel the furious wrath of God. Rather he is saying that those who are Christ's, who have been made one with Him, who love Him and serve His glory, would certainly not wish to participate in those kinds of behaviors and thoughts that are characteristic of those who will feel His eternal wrath. The children of God would certainly not want to act like the children of wrath.

Although believers have been delivered from God's wrath (cf. Rom. 5:9), they are subject to His chastening. Hebrews 12:5-6 reminds us not to forget "the exhortation which is addressed to you as sons, 'My son, do not regard lightly the discipline of the Lord, nor faint when you are reproved by Him; for those whom the Lord loves He disciplines, and He scourges every son whom He receives.'" God will react against sin. The unbeliever will experience His eternal wrath, and the believer His loving chastening. Either way, all who pursue sin will suffer the consequences.

SIN IS A PART OF THE BELIEVER'S PAST

and in them you also once walked, when you were living in them. (3:7)

Paul gives a second reason for putting sin to death, saying in effect, "You know to some degree how it was to live in sin. You hated it and that is why you came to Christ—to be delivered from your manner of life." Similarly, Paul said to the Ephesian believers,

> You were dead in your trespasses and sins, in which you formerly walked according to the course of this world, according to the prince of the power of the air, of the spirit that is now working in the sons of disobedience. Among them we too all formerly lived in the lusts of our flesh, indulging the desires of the flesh and of the mind, and were by nature children of wrath, even as the rest. But God, being rich in mercy, because of His great love with which He loved us, even when we were dead in our transgressions, made us alive together with Christ (by grace you have been saved). (Eph. 2:1-5)

In light of that, Spurgeon asks,

> Christian, what hast thou to do with sin? *Hath it not cost thee enough already?* Burnt child, wilt thou play with the fire? What! when thou hast

already been between the jaws of the lion, wilt thou step a second time into his den? Hast thou not had enough of the old serpent? Did he not poison all thy veins once, and wilt thou play upon the hole of the asp, and put thy hand upon the cockatrice's den a second time? Oh, be not so mad! so foolish! Did sin ever yield thee real pleasure? Didst thou find solid satisfaction in it? If so, go back to thine old drudgery, and wear the chain again, if it delight thee. But inasmuch as sin did never give thee what it promised to bestow, but deluded thee with lies, be not a second time snared by the old fowler—be free, and let the remembrance of thy ancient bondage forbid thee to enter the net again! (*Evening by Evening* [reprint, Grand Rapids: Baker, 1979], p. 151; italics in the original)

Why would anyone who has been made rich return to the slums to live in poverty? How can a new creature act like an old one (cf. 2 Cor. 5:17)? "What shall we say then? Are we to continue in sin that grace might increase? May it never be! How shall we who died to sin still live in it?" (Rom. 6:1-2).

SINS OF WICKED HATE

But now you also, put them all aside: anger, wrath, malice, slander, and abusive speech from your mouth. Do not lie to one another, (3:8-9*a*)

The sins in this second list are not so much personal as social; they are committed directly against other people. Reversing the pattern of the first list, Paul begins with the motive and progresses to the evil act. **Put . . . aside** is from *apotithēmi*, a word that is used for taking off clothes (cf. Acts 7:58; 1 Pet. 2:1). As a person takes off his dirty clothes at the end of the day, so should believers discard the filthy, tattered rags of their old life. Paul may have in mind here the practice of baptism in the early church. Those being baptized would lay aside their old clothes before their baptism and be given a new white robe afterwards. Paul calls upon believers to put aside the remnants of their old life.

Orgē (**anger**) is a deep, smoldering, resentful bitterness. It is the settled heart attitude of the angry person. Provocations do not create his anger, but merely reveal that he is an angry person and give him a target for his fury. That has no place in a Christian's life (cf. Eph. 4:31). Rather, believers are to be "slow to anger; for the anger of man does not achieve the righteousness of God" (James 1:19-20).

In contrast to *orgē*, *thumos* (**wrath**) refers to a sudden outburst of anger. The Greeks likened it to a fire in straw, which flares up briefly and is gone. It is used to speak of those in the synagogue of Nazareth who exploded in anger upon hearing Jesus' teachings (Luke 4:28). It is used similarly of the Ephesian craftsmen's anger over Paul's preaching (Acts 19:28). It is one of the deeds of the flesh (Gal. 5:20), and it is not acceptable behavior for Christians (Eph. 4:31).

Anger and **wrath** are closely related. The churning, boiling anger that often lies just below the surface gives rise to eruptions of wrath. And many unbelievers live with a deep-seated resentment that feeds their anger. They do not understand why they are alive and enduring the pains of life. They did not ask for their circumstances, and they do not know how to handle them. All of that stokes the fires of their anger and makes them even more prone to explosions of wrath when exacerbated.

Malice translates *kakia*, a general term for moral evil. J. B. Lightfoot defines it as "the vicious nature which is bent on doing harm to others" (*St. Paul's Epistles to the Colossians and to Philemon* [1879; reprint, Grand Rapids: Zondervan, 1959], p. 214). In this context, it probably refers to the harm caused by evil speech.

Anger, wrath, and malice often result in **slander.** The Greek word translated "slander" is *blasphēmia,* from which our English word *blasphemy* derives. When used in relation to God, it is translated "blasphemy." When used in relation to people, as here, it is translated "slander." To slander people, however, is to blaspheme God, inasmuch as He created men and women (cf. James 3:9). Such foolish talk is not to be indulged in lightly. Our Lord solemnly warned in Matthew 5:22 that "whoever shall say to his brother, 'Raca,' shall be guilty before the supreme court; and whoever shall say, 'You fool,' shall be guilty enough to go into the fiery hell." People are to be treated with dignity because they are made in the image of God. The believer's speech must not be marred by insults or disparaging remarks directed at others. James laments that "from the same mouth come both blessing and cursing. My brethren, these things ought not to be this way" (James 3:10).

The result of anger, wrath, and malice is **abusive speech.** That term refers to obscene and derogatory speech intended to hurt and wound someone. It could be translated "foul-mouthed abuse" (Lightfoot, p. 214). Such talk is expressly forbidden in Scripture. "There must be no filthiness and silly talk, or coarse jesting, which are not fitting, but rather giving of thanks" (Eph. 5:4). Jesus said, "The good man out of his good treasure brings forth what is good; and the evil man out of his evil treasure brings forth what is evil" (Matt. 12:35). Our Lord further stressed the seriousness of watching what we say when He warned that "every careless word that men shall speak, they shall render account for it in the day of judgment" (Matt. 12:36).

Paul warns against a final sin by exhorting believers not to **lie to one another.** It would be a helpful (and time-consuming) study to begin in Genesis and find every lie in the Bible. Satan lied in deceiving Adam and Eve (Gen. 3:4-5). Cain lied to God after murdering Abel (Gen. 4:9). Abraham lied, claiming Sarah was his sister instead of his wife (Gen. 12:11-19; 20:2). Sarah lied to the three angelic visitors (Gen. 18:15), and to the king of Gerar (Gen. 20:5). Isaac lied by denying that Rebecca was his wife (Gen. 26:7-10). Rebecca and Issac lied in their conspiracy to defraud Esau of his birthright (Gen. 27:6-24). That list does not even get us out of Genesis.

Lying characterizes Satan (John 8:44), not God (Titus 1:2). When believers lie, they are imitating Satan, not their heavenly Father. They, of all people, should tell the truth.

So it is not unnecessary for Paul to urge those who are complete in Christ, and partakers of His risen life, to kill sin. That is because the battle for holiness is still being fought in the life of every Christian. It is because of that battle that Paul wrote, "We ourselves groan within ourselves, waiting eagerly for our adoption as sons, the redemption of our body" (Rom. 8:23). On that great day our flesh will be redeemed and we will no longer be temptable. We will have a new outer man acting in holiness that is a perfect match with the inner man who already loves holiness.

How can we be victorious in our struggle with sin? First, by starving it. Do not feed anger or resentment. Do not cater to sexual lust or covetousness. Second, by crowding it out with positive graces: "Whatever is true, whatever is honorable, whatever is right, whatever is pure, whatever is lovely, whatever is of good repute, if there is any excellence and if anything worthy of praise, let your mind dwell on these things" (Phil. 4:8). "Let the word of Christ richly dwell within you" (Col. 3:16).

Putting on the New Man

13

since you laid aside the old self with its evil practices, and have put on the new self who is being renewed to a true knowledge according to the image of the One who created him—a renewal in which there is no distinction between Greek and Jew, circumcised and uncircumcised, barbarian, Scythian, slave and freeman, but Christ is all, and in all. And so, as those who have been chosen of God, holy and beloved, put on a heart of compassion, kindness, humility, gentleness and patience; bearing with one another, and forgiving each other, whoever has a complaint against anyone; just as the Lord forgave you, so also should you. And beyond all these things put on love, which is the perfect bond of unity. And let the peace of Christ rule in your hearts, to which indeed you were called in one body; and be thankful. Let the word of Christ richly dwell within you, with all wisdom teaching and admonishing one another with psalms and hymns and spiritual songs, singing with thankfulness in your hearts to God. And whatever you do in word or deed, do all in the name of the Lord Jesus, giving thanks through Him to God the Father. (3:9b-17)

You can tell a lot about people in our society by the way they dress. From baseball players to bus drivers, from postal carriers to policemen, people wear the uniform of their profession. Who we are determines what we wear, and failing to "dress the part" can sometimes have embarrassing consequences. Many years ago a very wealthy man in a Southern California town was found wandering around the local country club wearing shabby clothes. He was promptly seized by security guards and charged with vagrancy—even though he owned the country club. He had failed to dress consistent with who he was.

That is precisely Paul's point in 3:9b-17. Christians must dress themselves spiritually in accordance with their new identity. They have died with Christ and risen to new life. Salvation thus produces a two-sided obligation for believers. Negatively, they must throw off the garment of the old, sinful lifestyle, as Paul pointed out in 3:5-9a. Positively, they must put on the lifestyle of the new man. To do that, they must understand the position, progress, partnership, performance, perfection, and priorities of the new man.

THE POSITION OF THE NEW MAN

since you laid aside the old self with its evil practices, and have put on the new self (3:9b-10a)

This section links 3:5-9a, which tells believers what to put off, and 3:12-17, which tells them what to put on. It bridges the chasm between the old self and the new self—a chasm that believers could never have crossed unless Jesus had made them new creatures. **Since** indicates that transition to be an accomplished fact. **The old self with its evil practices** has already been **laid aside.**

The relation of the **old self** and the **new self** has been much disputed. Many hold that at salvation believers receive a new self but also keep the old self. Salvation thus becomes addition, not transformation. They argue that the struggle in the Christian life comes from the battle between the two.

Such a view, however, is not precisely consistent with biblical teaching. At salvation the old self was done away with. Paul told the Corinthians, "If any man is in Christ, he is a new creature; the old things passed away; behold, new things have come" (2 Cor. 5:17). To the Romans he wrote, "Our old self was crucified with Him, that our body of sin might be done away with, that we should no longer be slaves to sin" (Rom. 6:6). Salvation is transformation—the old self is gone, replaced by the new self. R. C. H. Lenski writes, "The old man is not converted, he cannot be; he is not renewed, he cannot be. He can only be replaced by the new man" (*The Interpretation of St. Paul's Epistles to the Colossians, to the Thessalonians, to Timothy, to Titus and to Philemon* [Minneapolis: Augsburg, 1964], p. 162).

What is the **old self**? It is the unregenerate self, the former manner of existence in Adam. The old, wretched, depraved, sinful self is "being corrupted in accordance with the lusts of deceit" (Eph. 4:22). It is that which was replaced by the regenerate self. To argue that believers have both an old and a new self is to argue in effect that the believer's soul is half regenerate and half unregenerate. There is no support for such a spiritual half-breed in Scripture.

The **new self,** in contrast, is the regenerate self. It is what believers are in Christ. The new self is the new creature Paul refers to in 2 Corinthians 5:17. It walks differently from the world (Eph. 4:17), in divine love (Eph. 5:1), in the light of God's truth (Eph. 5:8), and in wisdom (Eph. 5:15), loving God's law and God's Son, hating sin and pursuing righteousness.

The Bible views all men as either in Christ, or in Adam. There is no middle ground. The Puritan Thomas Goodwin wrote, "There are but two men that are seen standing before God, Adam and Jesus Christ; and these two men have all other men hanging at their girdles" (cited in William Hendriksen, *Philippians, Colossians, and Philemon*, New Testament Commentary [Grand Rapids: Baker, 1981], p. 150).

Paul gives the contrast between Adam and Christ in Romans 5:12-21, one of the richest, most profound theological passages in the New Testament. Through Adam came sin and death (vv. 12-14); through Christ comes grace and righteousness (vv. 15-18). Through Adam's disobedience all people were made sinners; through Christ's obedience, people are made righteous (v. 19). Just as it is impossible to be in Adam and in Christ at the same time, so also is it impossible to be or to have an old and new self.

The question then arises as to why believers sin if the old self is gone. They do so because the new self lives in the old body and must contend with the flesh. Paul shows this in the conflict described in Romans 7:14-25. He makes it clear there that sin is not in the inner man, the "I" that loves what is holy, but is in the flesh. "'The flesh' does not mean the body in and of itself; but it does mean the body as it is being used and tyrannized over by sin. It means the body as it is possessed by sin and evil; it is the body as sin dwells in it during this earthly life" (D. Martyn Lloyd-Jones, *Romans: The New Man—Exposition of Chapter Six* [Grand Rapids: Zondervan, 1978], p. 76). The flesh includes all the sinful desires, drives, and passions associated with our humanness. The presence of the unredeemed flesh causes us to "groan within ourselves, waiting eagerly for our adoption as sons, the redemption of our body" (Rom. 8:23).

THE PROGRESS OF THE NEW MAN

who is being renewed to a true knowledge according to the image of the One who created him (3:10*b*)

Possession of the new self does bring the believer new life, but not instant spiritual maturity. The flesh will continually dangle the garments of the old self in front of the new man and urge him to put them on. The battle against the flesh will go on throughout this life. The new self is complete, yet has the capacity for growth, just as a baby is born complete and has the ability to grow. Paul wrote that "our inner man is being renewed day by day" (2 Cor. 4:16), so that it can cope with the decaying outer man.

The new self **is being renewed to a true knowledge. Being renewed** refers to being new in quality. The preposition on the front of the verb (*ana*) makes the verb (*kaioō*) have the sense of contrast to what was already there. This is a new quality of life that never before existed. Unlike the ever-decaying depraved nature, the new self is continually being renewed by God. *Epignōsis* (**true knowledge**) refers to a deep, thorough knowledge (cf. 1:9). The process of renewal brings increased knowledge. William Hendriksen writes, "When a man is led through the waters of salvation, these are ankle-deep at first, but as he progresses, they become knee-deep, then reach to the loins, and are finally impassable except by swimming (cf. Ezek. 47:3-6)" (*Philippians, Colossians, and Philemon* [Grand Rapids: Baker, 1981], p. 150). There is no growth in the Christian life apart from knowledge: "Do not be conformed to this world, but be transformed by the renewing of your mind, that you may prove what the will of God is, that which is good and acceptable and perfect" (Rom. 12:2). "Be renewed in the spirit of your mind" (Eph. 4:22). From mature knowledge flows holy living.

The source of knowledge is the Bible. Paul wrote to Timothy, "All Scripture is inspired by God and profitable for teaching, for reproof, for correction, for training in righteousness; that the man of God may be adequate, equipped for every good work" (2 Tim. 3:16-17). Peter exhorts believers, "Like newborn babes, long for the pure milk of the word, that by it you may grow in respect to salvation" (1 Pet. 2:2). The Word of God is the food that fuels the growth of the new self. How fast believers grow depends on how much knowledge they put into practice in their lives.

The goal of knowledge is to conform the believer to the image of the One who created him. The new self becomes progressively more and more like the Lord Jesus Christ who created him. First Corinthians 15:49 tells us, "Just as we have borne the image of the earthy, we shall also bear the image of the heavenly." It is God's plan to make believers like Jesus Christ. "For whom He foreknew, He also predestined to become conformed to the image of His Son, that He might be the first-born among many brethren" (Rom. 8:29). The new self will continue to progress toward Christlikeness until the Lord returns or the believer dies. The apostle John wrote, "Beloved, now we are children of God, and it has not appeared as yet what we shall be. We know that, when He appears, we shall be like Him, because we shall see Him just as He is" (1 John 3:2).

THE PARTNERSHIP OF THE NEW MAN

a renewal in which there is no distinction between Greek and Jew, circumcised and uncircumcised, barbarian, Scythian, slave and freeman, but Christ is all, and in all. (3:11)

The risen life also has implications for the church. Just as individual believers put off the habits of the old self, so also the church puts off the old barriers that separated people. There is no place for racial barriers or cultural snobbery. God has united all believers in Christ Jesus (cf. Gal. 3:28; Eph. 2:15). This was a startling, unbelievable revelation for the first-century world. The racial, religious, cultural, and social barriers separating people were as deep-seated and formidable as any in our day.

The **Greek and Jew,** one **circumcised** and the other **uncircumcised,** were separated by seemingly insurmountable racial and religious barriers. They had nothing to do with each other. Jewish people refused to enter a Gentile house. They would not eat a meal cooked by Gentiles, nor buy meat prepared by Gentile butchers. When they returned to Israel, they showed their disdain for Gentiles by shaking off the Gentile dust from their clothes and sandals. Even the apostles were reluctant to accept Gentiles as equal partners in the church (cf. Acts 10-11). Needless to say, the Gentiles returned those sentiments.

But the gospel broke down those barriers, and Jew and Gentile became one in Christ. Paul described that phenomenon in Ephesians 2:13-16:

> But now in Christ Jesus you who formerly were far off [Gentiles] have been brought near by the blood of Christ. For He Himself is our peace, who made both groups into one, and broke down the barrier of the dividing wall, by abolishing in His flesh the enmity, which is the Law of

commandments contained in ordinances, that in Himself He might make the two into one new man, thus establishing peace, and might reconcile them both in one body to God through the cross, by it having put to death the enmity.

Strong cultural barriers also pervaded the ancient world. The cultured, educated Greek or Jew looked with contempt on the **barbarian** or **Scythian.** Barbarian was an onomotopoetic word used to describe people who spoke an inarticulate and stammering speech. The Greeks intended it as a term of derision on those who were not among the elite (i.e., themselves). The Scythians, above all barbarians, were hated and feared. They were a nomadic, warlike people who invaded the Fertile Crescent in the seventh century before Christ. The Scythians were notorious for their savagery. William Hendriksen notes several historical references that help to describe these people (*Colossians*, p. 154). Herodotus, the Greek historian, wrote of them,

> They invaded Asia, after they had driven the Cimmerians out of Europe . . . and made themselves masters of all Asia. From there they marched against Egypt; and when they were in that part of Syria which is called Palestine, Psammethichus, king of Egypt, met them and with gifts and prayer persuaded them to come no farther. . . . They ruled Asia for twenty-eight years; and all the land was wasted by reason of their violence and their arrogance. . . . The greater number of them were entertained and made drunk and were slain by Cyaxares and the Medes. They drank the blood of the first enemy killed in battle, and made napkins of the scalps, and drinking bowls of the skulls of the slain. They had the most filthy habits and never washed with water. (4.64, 65, 75)

The Jewish historian Josephus added, "The Scythians delight in murdering people and are little better than wild beasts" (*Against Apion* 2.269). The early church Father Tertullian could think of no greater insult to the heretic Marcion than to describe him as "more filthy than any Scythian" (*Against Marcion* 1.1).

A fellowship including Greeks, Jews, and Scythians was unthinkable in the ancient world. Yet that is precisely what happened in the church. Christ demolished the cultural barriers separating men.

A social barrier existed between the slave and the freeman. The slave was viewed, in the words of Aristotle, as "a living tool." However, both slaves and freemen were saved and became brothers in Christ because they "were all baptized into one body, whether Jews or Greeks, whether slaves or free" (1 Cor. 12:13). Paul reminded the Galatians that "there is neither Jew nor Greek, there is neither slave nor free man, there is neither male nor female; for you are all one in Christ Jesus" (Gal. 3:28). He told Philemon to view Onesimus, his runaway slave, "no longer as a slave, but more than a slave, a beloved brother" (Philem. 16).

That unity of slave and freeman was dramatically demonstrated in the arena of Carthage in A.D. 202. Perpetua, a young woman from a noble family and Felicitas, a slave-girl, faced martyrdom for Christ. As they faced the wild beasts, they joined hands. Slave and freewoman died together for the love of the same Lord (M. A. Smith, *From Christ to Constantine* [Downers Grove, Ill: InterVarsity, 1973], p. 107).

There is no place for man-made barriers in the church since **Christ is all, and in all.** Because Christ indwells all believers, all are equal. He breaks down all racial, religious, cultural, and social barriers, and makes believers into one new man (Eph. 2:15).

The Performance of the New Man

And so, as those who have been chosen of God, holy and beloved, put on a heart of compassion, kindness, humility, gentleness and patience; bearing with one another, and forgiving each other, whoever has a complaint against anyone; just as the Lord forgave you, so also should you. (3:12-13)

In 3:5-9*a*, Paul told believers what to put off, while in 3:9*b*-11 he describes the believer's new identity in Christ. In 3:12, Paul begins to tell believers what to put on. In 3:9*b*-11, Paul describes what God has done for the believer. In 3:12-17 he describes what God expects of the believer in response. A righteous identity must issue in righteous behavior. Such behavior is the outward manifestation of the inward transformation, and it is the only sure proof that such transformation has taken place.

No one becomes a Christian solely by their own choice. Rather, believers are **those who have been chosen of God.** The truth of divine election is clearly taught in Scripture. Ephesians 1:4 says that God "chose us in Him [Christ] before the foundation of the world." Paul was confident of God's choice of the Thessalonians (1 Thess. 1:4) and thanked Him for it: "We should always give thanks to God for you, brethren beloved by the Lord, because God has chosen you from the beginning for salvation through sanctification by the Spirit and faith in the truth" (2 Thess. 2:13). God did not call us because of our good works, "but according to His own purpose and grace which was granted us in Christ Jesus from all eternity" (2 Tim. 1:9). Believers' names have been written in the book of life from before the foundation of the world (cf. Rev. 13:8; 17:8). Underlying our response to God's free, sovereign grace is His plan and initiative.

Because of God's election, believers are **holy and beloved.** *Hagios* (**holy**) means "set apart," or "separate." God chose believers out of the mainstream of mankind and drew them to Himself. They are different from the world. When believers fail to act differently from the world, they violate the very purpose of their calling.

That believers are **beloved** of God means they are objects of His special love. Election is not a cold, fatalistic doctrine. On the contrary, it is based in God's incomprehensible love for His elect: "In love He predestined us to adoption as sons through Jesus Christ to Himself, according to the kind intention of His will" (Eph. 1:4-5).

Chosen (Deut. 7:6; 14:2; 1 Chron. 16:13; Ps. 105:43; 135:4; Isa. 41:8; 44:1; 45:4), **holy** (Ex. 19:6; Lev. 19:2; Jer. 2:3), and **beloved** (1 Kings 10:9; 2 Chron. 9:8; Hos. 11:1) are all used of Israel in the Old Testament. A change has taken place in the economy of God. What was once true of the elect nation is now true of all who come to faith in Christ. Israel has been temporarily set aside and Gentiles grafted in (cf. Rom. 9-11). The saved in the church are chosen by God. We are called "the chosen" (cf. John 15:16; Rom. 8:33; 2 Tim. 2:10; Titus 1:1; 1 Pet. 1:1). Acts 13:46-48 speaks of those ordained by God to eternal life:

> Paul and Barnabas spoke out boldly and said, "It was necessary that the word of God should be spoken to you first; since you repudiate it, and judge yourselves unworthy of eternal life, behold, we are turning to the Gentiles. For thus the Lord has commanded us, 'I have placed You as a light for the Gentiles, that You should bring salvation to the end of the earth.'" And when the Gentiles heard this, they began rejoicing and glorifying the word of the Lord; and as many as had been appointed to eternal life believed.

Romans 9:13-16, 19-22 expresses God's sovereignty in choosing whom He will:

> Just as it is written, "Jacob I loved, but Esau I hated." What shall we say then? There is no injustice with God, is there? May it never be! For He says to Moses, "I will have mercy on whom I have mercy, and I will have compassion on whom I have compassion." So then it does not depend on the man who wills or the man who runs, but on God who has mercy.

> You will say to me then, "Why does He still find fault? For who resists His will?" On the contrary, who are you, O man, who answers back to

God? The thing molded will not say to the molder, "Why did you make me like this," will it? Or does not the potter have a right over the clay, to make from the same lump one vessel for honorable use, and another for common use? What if God, although willing to demonstrate His wrath and to make His power known, endured with much patience vessels of wrath prepared for destruction?

Romans 11:4-5 speaks of "God's gracious choice." Ephesians 1:4 affirms that believers were "[chosen] in Him before the foundation of the world." The Thessalonians were "chosen from the beginning for salvation" (2 Thess. 2:13). Perhaps 2 Timothy 1:8-9 sums it up as well as any text: "Therefore do not be ashamed of the testimony of our Lord, or of me His prisoner; but join with me in suffering for the gospel according to the power of God, who has saved us, and called us with a holy calling, not according to our works, but according to His own purpose and grace which was granted us in Christ Jesus from all eternity."

The doctrine of election crushes human pride, exalts God, produces joy and gratitude to the Lord, grants eternal privileges and assurance, promotes holiness, and makes one bold and courageous, for one who has been chosen by God for eternal life has no need to fear anything or anyone.

Put on is from *enduō*, which means "to put on clothes," or "envelope in." The qualities that follow are to cover the new man.

A heart of compassion is the first character trait that is to mark the new man. **Heart** translates *splanchna*, a Hebraism that literally refers to the inward parts of the human body (heart, lungs, liver, kidneys, etc.). As already noted in the discussion of 2:2, however, it is often used in the New Testament to speak figuratively of the seat of the emotions. That is its use here. *Oiktirmos* (**compassion**) means "pity," "mercy," "sympathy," or "compassion." Taken together, the phrase could be translated, "put on heartfelt compassion," or "have a deep, gut-level feeling of compassion." That divine quality (Luke 6:36; James 5:11), so perfectly exhibited by Jesus (Matt. 9:36), was sorely needed in the ancient world. For example, sick, injured, or elderly people were often left to fend for themselves. As a result, many died. Believers must not be indifferent to suffering, but should be concerned to meet people's needs.

Kindness is closely related to compassion. The Greek term refers to the grace that pervades the whole person, mellowing all that might be harsh. Jesus used the word when he said, "My yoke is easy" (Matt. 11:30), not harsh or hard to bear. The kind person is as concerned about his neighbor's good as he is about his own. God is kind, even to ungrateful and evil people (Luke 6:35). In fact, it was His kindness that led us to repentance (Rom. 2:4; cf. Titus 3:4). Jesus' kindness was expressed in His invitation to "take My yoke upon you, and learn from Me, for I am gentle and humble in heart; and you shall find rest for your souls. For My yoke is easy, and My load is light" (Matt. 11:29-30). Kindness was epitomized by the Good Samaritan (Luke 10:25-37), whose example we should follow.

Tapeinophrosunē (**humility**) and its related words always have a negative connotation in classical Greek (cf. H. H. Esser, *"tapeinos,"* in Colin Brown, ed., *The New International Dictionary of New Testament Theology* [Grand Rapids: Zondervan, 1977], 2:259). It took Christianity to elevate humility to a virtue. It is the antidote for the self-love that poisons relationships. Paul advocates genuine humility, in contrast to the false humility of the false teachers (cf. 2:18, 23). Humility characterized Jesus (Matt. 11:29), and it is the most cherished Christian virtue (Eph. 4:2; Phil. 2:3ff.; 1 Pet. 5:5).

Prautēs (**gentleness**) is closely related to humility. It is not weakness or spinelessness, but rather the willingness to suffer injury instead of inflicting it. The gentle person knows he is a sinner among sinners and is willing to suffer the burdens others' sin may impose on him. This gentleness can only be produced by the Holy Spirit (cf. Gal. 5:22-23) and should mark the Christian's behavior at all times, even when restoring a sinning brother (Gal. 6:1), or defending the faith against attacks from unbelievers (2 Tim. 2:25; 1 Pet. 3:15).

Patience translates *makrothumia.* The patient person does not get angry at others. William Barclay writes, "This is the spirit which never loses its patience with its fellow-men. Their foolishness and their unteachability never drive it to cynicism or despair; their insults and their ill-treatment never drive it to bitterness or wrath" (*The Letters to the Philippians, Colossians, and Thessalonians* [Louisville: Westminster, 1975], p. 158). Patience is the opposite of resentment and revenge. It was a characteristic of Jesus Christ. Paul wrote to Timothy, "For this reason I found mercy, in order that in me as the foremost, Jesus Christ might demonstrate His perfect patience, as an example for those who would believe in Him for eternal life" (1 Tim. 1:16). Were it not for God's patience, no one would ever be saved (2 Pet. 3:15).

Bearing with one another means "to endure, to hold out in spite of persecution, threats, injury, indifference, or complaints and not retaliate." It characterized Paul, who told the Corinthians, "when we are reviled, we bless; when we are persecuted, we endure" (1 Cor. 4:12). It did not characterize the Corinthians, who were actually taking each other to court. Paul exclaims, "Why not rather be wronged? Why not rather be defrauded?" (1 Cor. 6:7). Believers are to exhibit forbearance (Eph. 4:2). Such were the Thessalonians, of whom Paul wrote, "We ourselves speak proudly of you among the churches of God for your perseverance and faith in the midst of all your persecutions and afflictions which you endure [*anexomai*, the same term used here in 3:13]" (2 Thess. 1:4).

Believers are to be marked not only by endurance, but also by **forgiving each other.** The Greek *charizomenoi* literally means "to be gracious" and the text uses a reflexive pronoun, so it literally reads, "forgiving yourselves." The church as a whole is to be a gracious, mutually forgiving fellowship. By including the phrase **just as the Lord forgave you, so also should you** Paul makes Christ the model of forgiveness. Because He has forgiven us, so also must we forgive others (Eph. 4:32; cf. Matt. 18:21-35). The phrase **whoever has a complaint against anyone** refers to times when someone is at fault because of sin, error, or debt. The Lord Jesus is our pattern for forgiveness, because He forgave all our sins, errors, and debts. He is also the model for the rest of the virtues discussed in this section.

THE PERFECTION OF THE NEW MAN

And beyond all these things put on love, which is the perfect bond of unity. (3:14)

In keeping with the motif of putting on clothes, **love** is the belt or sash that pulls **all these things** just mentioned together (cf. Phil. 2:1-5). Love is the most important moral quality in the believer's life, for it is the very glue that produces unity in the church. Believers will never enjoy mutual fellowship through compassion, kindness, humility, gentleness, or patience; they will not bear with each other or forgive each other unless they love one another. In fact, the way to sum up the commands of 3:12-13 is to say, "Love one another." Paul said in Romans 13:10 that "love does no wrong to a neighbor; love therefore is the fulfillment of the law." To try to practice the virtues of 3:12-13 apart from love is legalism. They must flow from love, which in turn is a fruit of the Spirit-filled life (Gal. 5:22). Nothing is acceptable to God if not motivated by love (1 Cor. 13:1-3), including knowledge (Phil. 1:9), faith (Gal. 5:6), and obedience (John 14:15). Love is the beauty of the believer, dispelling the ugly sins of the flesh that destroy unity.

THE PRIORITIES OF THE NEW MAN

And let the peace of Christ rule in your hearts, to which indeed you were called in one body; and be thankful. Let the word of Christ richly dwell within you, with all wisdom teaching and admonishing one another with psalms and hymns and spiritual songs, singing with thankfulness in your hearts to God. And

whatever you do in word or deed, do all in the name of the Lord Jesus, giving thanks through Him to God the Father. (3:15-17)

Paul concludes his look at the qualities that should mark the lifestyle of the new man by giving three priorities. They are the outermost garments of the new man, those which cover all the others. The new man is concerned with the peace of Christ, the word of Christ, and the name of Christ.

THE PEACE OF CHRIST

And let the peace of Christ rule in your hearts, to which indeed you were called in one body; and be thankful. (3:15)

Eirēnē (**peace**) includes both the concept of an agreement, pact, treaty, or bond, and that of an attitude of rest or security. Both aspects are in view here. Objectively, believers are at peace with God: "Therefore having been justified by faith, we have peace with God through our Lord Jesus Christ" (Rom. 5:1). The war between the believer and God is over, and the treaty was paid for by the blood of Christ. Because of that, believers are at rest, and secure. Paul told the Philippians that the "peace of God . . . shall guard your hearts and your minds in Christ Jesus" (Phil. 4:7). Here he calls it the peace of Christ because it is the peace He brings (cf. John 14:27; Eph. 2:14).

Rule is from *brabeuō*, a word used only here in the New Testament (although a compound form appears in Col. 2:18). It was used to describe the activity of an umpire in deciding the outcome of an athletic contest. The peace of Christ guides believers in making decisions. When faced with a choice, the believer should consider two factors. First, is it consistent with the fact that he and Christ are now at peace and thus on the same side? Does it perpetuate that oneness with the Lord that is the believer's possession? First Corinthians 6:17-18 provides an excellent illustration of this point: "The one who joins himself to the Lord is one spirit with Him. Flee immorality." It is our union with the Lord that compels us to purity. Second, will it leave him with a deep and abiding peace in his heart? These two factors are also the two greatest deterrents to sin in the believer's life. Sin offends Christ, with whom he is at peace, and thereby shatters the rest and security in his heart.

Peace is not only objective and subjective, but also relational. Believers **were called** to live in peace **in one body.** Individuals who have peace with Christ and in their own hearts will live in unity and harmony with each other.

To maintain a peaceful heart one has to **be thankful.** Thankfulness is a constant theme in Colossians (cf. 1:3, 12; 2:7; 3:15, 16, 17; 4:2). Gratitude comes naturally to believers in response to all God has done (Eph. 5:20; Phil. 4:6; 1 Thess. 5:18; Heb. 13:15), whereas ingratitude marks unbelievers (Rom. 1:21). A spirit of humble gratitude toward God will inevitably affect our relations with others. Peace and gratitude are thus closely linked.

THE WORD OF CHRIST

Let the word of Christ richly dwell within you, with all wisdom teaching and admonishing one another with psalms and hymns and spiritual songs, singing with thankfulness in your hearts to God. (3:16)

The **word of Christ** refers to the revelation He brought into the world, which is Scripture. Peace and thankfulness, as well as unity, love, and all the required virtues, flow from a mind controlled by Scripture. **Dwell** is from *enoikeō* and means "to live in," or "to be at home." Paul calls upon believers to let the Word take up residence and be at home in their lives. *Plousiōs* (**richly**) could also be translated "abundantly or extravagantly rich." The truths of Scripture should permeate every aspect of the believer's life and govern every thought, word, and deed. The Word dwells in us when we hear it (Matt. 13:9), handle it (2 Tim. 2:15), hide it (Ps. 119:11), and hold it fast (Phil. 2:16). To do those things, the Christian must read, study, and live the Word. **To let the word of Christ richly dwell** is identical to being filled with the Spirit (cf. Eph. 5:18). The Word in the heart and mind is the handle by which the Spirit turns the will. It is clear that these two concepts are identical because the passages that follow each are so similar.

Colossians 3:18–4:1 is a more brief parallel to Ephesians 5:19– 6:9. The result of being filled with the Holy Spirit is the same as the result of letting the Word dwell in one's life richly. Therefore, the two are the same spiritual reality viewed from two sides. To be filled with the Spirit is to be controlled by His Word. To have the Word dwelling richly is to be controlled by His Spirit. Since the Holy Spirit is the author and the power of the Word, the expressions are interchangeable.

Paul then mentions two specific results of the Word of Christ dwelling in the believer, one positive and the other negative: **with all wisdom teaching and admonishing one another. Teaching** is the impartation of positive truth. **Admonishing** is the negative side of teaching. It means to warn people of the consequences of their behavior. Both are the result of a life overflowing with the Word of Christ.

Having the Word of Christ richly dwell in us produces not only information, but also emotion. It generates **psalms and hymns and spiritual songs,** and **singing with thankfulness in your hearts to God. Psalms** were taken from the Old Testament psalter, the book of Psalms. They sang psalms put to music, much as we do today. **Hymns** were expressions of praise to God. It is thought that some portions of the New Testament (such as Col. 1:15-20 and Phil. 2:6-11) were originally hymns sung in the early church. **Spiritual songs** emphasized testimony (cf. Rev. 5:9-10). They express in song what God has done for us. (For more details on this theme, see my commentary, *Ephesians*, MacArthur New Testament Commentary [Chicago: Moody, 1986].)

Commentators are divided on whether *chariti* (**thankfulness**) should be translated "thankfulness" (as in the NIV and NASB) or "grace" (as in the KJV). Perhaps its use here encompasses both ideas: believers sing out of thankfulness for God's grace. When Paul tells believers to sing **in your hearts** he does not mean not to sing with the voice. His concern is that the heart agree with the mouth (cf. Amos 5:23). Singing is to be directed to God as praise and worship offered to Him for His pleasure and glory. That it is edifying to believers is a by-product of its main purpose.

THE NAME OF CHRIST

And whatever you do in word or deed, do all in the name of the Lord Jesus, giving thanks through Him to God the Father. (3:17)

The simplest, most basic rule of thumb for living the Christian life is to do everything, whether **word** or **deed, in the name of the Lord Jesus.** To do everything in the name of Jesus is to act consistently with who He is and what He wants. Paul expressed the same thought in 1 Corinthians 10:31: "Whether, then, you eat or drink or whatever you do, do all to the glory of God." Again, Paul reminds that it is always to be done without reluctance or despair or legalistic duty, but with **giving thanks through Him to God the Father.**

To put on the new lifestyle is to put on Christ. That is the obligation of every believer: "Put on the Lord Jesus Christ, and make no provision for the flesh in regard to its lusts" (Rom. 13:14). The goal of the Christian life is Christlikeness.

Guy H. King relates the following story:

Years ago I was leading the Children's Special Service Mission at one of our South Coast holiday resorts. As I was approaching the beach one morning, this little fellow was going along there, too. As he caught sight of me, he said, "Mummie, here comes the JESUS man." He only meant that I was the man who spoke to the children about the Saviour; but his remark meant far more to my heart that day. What right had I— have I—to be called a JESUS man? What degree of resemblance is there about us?

I wonder if you have read that moving story of Jerome K. Jerome's called *The Passing of the Third Floor Back*? Roughly, the tale is of a poor-class lodging house, where lived a heterogeneous company of needy and seedy folk, and where there was a poor, ignorant little servant-girl, a good deal of a slut, and ready to sell her virtue for a worthless trinket. Into the place there came one day a lodger who at once seemed to be different, and who occupied the third floor back. He quickly revealed himself to have a very kind heart and way. He always had a kindly word for the little slavey, usually so ignored and downtrodden. She almost worshipped him. The other lodgers, too, owed him much for his many deeds of helpfulness. He was always doing something for somebody, in his kindly, sympathetic way. At last the day came for him to move elsewhere. The little maid watched him, open-eyed, as he walked with his bit of luggage to the front door; and as he turned to her with a smile and a gentle pat on the shoulder, she took her leave of him with the words, "Please, are you 'Im?" (*Crossing the Border* [Fort Washington, Pa.: Christian Literature Crusade, 1974], pp. 92-93)

Believers should so clothe themselves with Jesus Christ that when people look at them, they see Christ.

The New Man Makes a New Home

14

Wives, be subject to your husbands, as is fitting in the Lord. Husbands, love your wives, and do not be embittered against them. Children, be obedient to your parents in all things, for this is well-pleasing to the Lord. Fathers, do not exasperate your children, that they may not lose heart. Slaves, in all things obey those who are your masters on earth, not with external service, as those who merely please men, but with sincerity of heart, fearing the Lord. Whatever you do, do your work heartily, as for the Lord rather than for men; knowing that from the Lord you will receive the reward of the inheritance. It is the Lord Christ whom you serve. For he who does wrong will receive the consequences of the wrong which he has done, and that without partiality. Masters, grant to your slaves justice and fairness, knowing that you too have a Master in heaven. (3:18–4:1)

The major social problem facing human society is the inability of people to get along with each other. From sibling rivalry among children, to the break up of marriages, to crimes and battles, all the way to international confrontations between major powers, the problem is the same. Why it exists could be summed up in three words: amorality, anonymity, and alienation. Amorality means that man apart from God has no absolute moral or ethical standards to regulate his behavior. Man also struggles with anonymity. He does not know who he is or why he is here. Hence, his life has no meaning as far as he can see. Finally, people are alienated. As Francis Schaeffer points out in his book, *True Spirituality* (Wheaton, Ill.: Tyndale, 1973), the Fall alienated man not only from God, but also from himself and from other people.

All three problems are due to man's separation from God. People are characterized by amorality or immorality because apart from God there can be no absolute moral standards. They are then doomed to moral relativism and situational ethics.

Apart from God, man also faces anonymity, or emptiness. Trapped in an impersonal universe, he seems nothing more than a "chance configuration of atoms in the slip stream of meaningless chance history" (Francis A. Schaeffer, *Death in the City* [Downers Grove, Ill.: InterVarsity, 1972], p. 19).

Finally, man without God faces a terrible sense of alienation or loneliness. With no one home in the universe to give meaning to his aspirations, he feels isolated and alone.

A man without moral standards, facing emptiness and loneliness, will see others as threats to his pursuit of happiness. His negativism and despair will often cause him to retreat further into selfishness and alienation. That will create conflicts with others. James writes, "What is the source of quarrels and conflicts among you? Is not the source your pleasures that wage war in your members? You lust and do not have; so you commit murder. And you are envious and cannot obtain; so you fight and quarrel" (James 4:1-2).

When a person becomes a Christian, those three problems cease to exist. The Word of God contains an absolute moral standard that is rooted in the nature of God. No longer anonymous, the believer is a child of God and fellow heir with Jesus (Rom. 8:17). Nor do believers suffer from alienation or loneliness, since they are now beloved children of the heavenly Father and part of the family of believers.

Christianity is not just personal; it is relational. The life of the new man is a life lived among other new men. The new man is to have an impact also on the society in which he lives. That responsibility becomes Paul's theme in 3:18–4:1, where he discusses the new man's relationships to other people.

The teaching that Christians are to have relationships that affect society is not unique to Colossians. Jesus says in Matthew 5:13-14, "You are the salt of the earth; but if the salt has become tasteless, how will it be made salty again? It is good for nothing anymore, except to be thrown out and trampled under foot by men. You are the light of the world. A city set on a hill cannot be hidden." Paul urged the Philippians, saying, "Prove yourselves to be blameless and innocent, children of God above reproach in the midst of a crooked and perverse generation, among whom you appear as lights in the world" (Phil. 2:15). Peter counseled his readers: "Keep your behavior excellent among the Gentiles, so that in the thing in which they slander you as evildoers, they may on account of your good deeds, as they observe them, glorify God in the day of visitation" (1 Pet. 2:12; cf. Matt. 25:31-46; James 2:15-16). Christianity therefore is not the religion of monks and hermits. Believers are not called to withdraw from society, but to influence it for Christ—particularly through their relationsips.

Throughout history, Christianity has had a positive influence on society. J. C. Wenger wrote of the early church,

> Christianity burst into a corrupt world with a brilliantly new moral radiance. . . . The moral level of society was dismal, and sin prevailed in many forms. . . . Into this discouraged world came Christ and his Spirit-transformed disciples, filled with holy joy, motivated by a love which the pagans could not grasp, and proclaiming Good News—the message that God has provided a Saviour. . . . These Christians lived in tiny communities knit together in the power of the Holy Spirit, little colonies of heaven. They thought of themselves as pilgrims on their way to the celestial city, but they were very much concerned to manifest the love of Christ in all human relationships.
>
> These early Christians insisted on bringing all of life under the lordship of Christ. . . . It is men and women of this kind of moral purity who built into society a strong fabric of integrity and strength.
>
> Life was cheap in the pre-Christian world: murder, abortions, infant exposure, war: people died in great numbers without anyone being troubled in conscience. The early Christians brought a new concern into society on these points. ("Evangelical Social Concern," in *Baker's Dictionary of Christian Ethics*, ed. Carl F. H. Henry [Grand Rapids: Baker, 1973], pp. 223-24)

In more recent times, much of the social reform in Western society has been related to Christianity. Leaders of the eighteenth-century evangelical awakening, such as John Wesley, often spoke out against social evils. John Howard, a contemporary of John Wesley, worked tirelessly for prison reform. His work was continued by Elizabeth Gurney Fry. The Great Awakening of early eighteenth-century America, led by the preaching of such men as Jonathan Edwards and George Whitefield, resulted in the founding of several universities. Pressure from evangelicals, led by William Wilberforce, caused Britain to abolish the slave trade in 1807 and outlaw slavery in all her possessions in 1833. American evangelicals were also involved in the abolitionist movement that culminated in the Emancipation Proclamation of 1863. The nineteenth-century British evangelical, Lord Shaftesbury, was instrumental in getting Parliament to pass laws regulating child labor. He was also a champion of better treatment for the insane. Agencies like the YMCA, YWCA, and The Salvation Army were also active in social work during the nineteenth century. William Carey, missionary to India, worked for the abolition of widow burning and child sacrifice. Missionaries to Africa discouraged polygamy, fought the slave trade, and built schools and hospitals.

Nowhere should the social aspect of the new man be more evident than in the home—the single most important social institution in the world. Genuine Christianity consists of both doctrine and holy living. The New Testament reminds us in many places that an intellectual knowledge of our faith must be accompanied by a life that proves faith's reality. And such a life can only be lived by vital contact with God in Christ. It is difficult to see how Christianity can have any positive effect on society if it cannot transform its own homes.

The two basic principles Paul mentions, authority and submission, are not unique to Christianity. It has always been God's plan for homes to operate on that basis. Christianity did, however, introduce several new elements to the home. First, Christianity introduced a new presence into the home, the Lord Jesus Christ (cf. 3:18, 20, 23, 24; 4:1). That new presence brings a new power. Christ is there, and His Spirit provides the power to make the family what it ought to be. Second, there is a new purpose: "Whatever you do in word or deed, do all in the name of the Lord Jesus" (3:17). Finally, Christianity introduced a new pattern for the home: "Husbands, love your wives, just as Christ also loved the church" (Eph. 5:25). The new pattern is Christ. He is the model for us to follow.

In this passage Paul provides brief, direct instructions on Christian living in the home. He discusses the three relationships in ancient homes: Husbands and wives (3:18-19), parents and children (3:20-21), and masters and servants (3:22–4:1). He gives a word to wives, a word to husbands, a word to children, a word to parents, a word to servants, and a word to masters.

A WORD TO WIVES

Wives, be subject to your husbands, as is fitting in the Lord. (3:18)

The parallel exhortation in Ephesians expands this simple command: "Wives be subject to your own husbands, as to the Lord. For the husband is the head of the wife, as Christ also is the head of the church . . . But as the church is subject to Christ, so also the wives ought to be to their own husbands in everything" (Eph. 5:22-24). In spite of its straightforward clarity, Paul's simple statement has been widely challenged in our day, even by those claiming to be evangelicals. Many argue that Paul's teaching on this theme is not Spirit-inspired, but reflects his chauvinistic, rabbinic attitude toward women. Such people seek to usurp the role of God and decide for themselves which parts of Scripture are inspired. Still others insist that Paul is mistakenly commenting on Genesis 2 instead of Genesis 1. Genesis 1, they argue, teaches the equality of the sexes, and is divinely inspired. Genesis 2, which implies the headship of the man, is viewed as a later, uninspired rabbinic gloss. That argument, however, rests on the thoroughly discredited documentary hypothesis of the composition of the Pentateuch. Finally, some insist that Paul's teaching on authority and submission was cultural, and does not apply to our society. None of the critics, however, would argue that Paul's statement in 3:19 is cultural and that men are no longer required to love their wives. All the attacks on this straightforward principle for behavior deal devastating wounds to the marriage. When a woman submits to the loving leadership of her husband and follows God's intention for her, she is fulfilled and so is the husband. Efforts to reverse or confuse the duties of wife and husband destroy the blessing each is to be to the other.

The principle of authority and submission in the marriage relationship is found throughout the New Testament. Paul writes in 1 Corinthians 11:3, "Christ is the head of every man, and the man is the head of a woman." He also penned this principle in 1 Corinthians 14:34-35: "Let the women keep silent in the churches; for they are not permitted to speak, but let them subject themselves, just as the Law also says. And if they desire to learn anything, let them ask their own husbands at home; for it is improper for a woman to speak in church." To Timothy he wrote, "Let a woman quietly receive instruction with entire submissiveness. But I do not allow a woman to teach or exercise authority over a man, but to remain quiet. For it was Adam who was first created, and then Eve. And it was not Adam who was deceived, but the woman being quite deceived, fell into transgression" (1 Tim. 2:11-14).

Paul goes on to say that the woman is delivered from any stigma of inferiority to the man by the blessed achievement of raising up godly children (v. 15). Note also that Paul traces the woman's submission back to the order of creation, not the Fall. Titus 2:5 instructs women to "be sensible, pure, workers at home, kind, being subject to their own husbands, that the word of God may not be dishonored." Sarah's obedience to Abraham is a model for other women to follow (1 Pet. 3:6).

Be subject to is from *hupotassō*, and means "to subject oneself." It has the concept of putting oneself under (**hupo**), not by compulsion, but willingly. The term is used in Luke 2:51 to refer to Jesus' subjection to His parents, and in Luke 10:17, 20 to describe demons being subject to the disciples. In Romans 8:7, Paul employs the word to speak of being submissive to the commands of God's law. His use of it in Romans 13:1, 5 refers to the necessary submission of every person to governing authority, which is established by God. In both 1 Corinthians 15:27-28 and Ephesians 1:22, the verb looks to the time when all things in the universe are made subject to Christ and God in eternal glory.

Paul's word to wives is be submissive to **your** husbands. They do not submit to some detached, impersonal authority. Rather, they submit to the man with whom they have an intimate, personal, vital relationship. Ephesians 5:22 adds the word "own" ("your own husband") to demonstrate the uniqueness of this exclusive submission.

It is helpful to note several misconceptions about submission. First, submission does not imply inferiority. Galatians 3:28 clearly affirms that spiritually there is no difference between male and female. Jesus submitted to the Father during His life on earth, yet He was in no way inferior to Him. Second, submission is not absolute. Obedience in this passage is reserved for children and servants. There may be times when a wife must refuse to submit to her husband's desires (if they violate God's Word). Finally, the husband's authority is not to be exercised in an authoritative, overbearing manner. The wife's submission takes place in the context of a loving relationship.

That wives submit to their husbands is **fitting in the Lord.** The Greek form in this phrase expresses an obligation, a necessary duty. It is how He designed and commands the family to operate.

A WORD TO HUSBANDS

Husbands, love your wives, and do not be embittered against them. (3:19)

In Ephesians 5:25, Paul wrote, "Husbands, love your wives, just as Christ also loved the church." Obviously, in spite of the failings of the church, Christ has continually loved her with grace and forgiving mercy and thus has never become bitter because of the church's many sins. Paul addresses two commands to husbands. First, they must love their **wives.** The present tense of the imperative *agapate* (**love**) indicates continuous action. The verb itself seems best understood in the New

Testament to express a willing love, not the love of passion or emotion, but the love of choice—a covenant kind of love. It could be translated, "keep on loving." The love that existed from the start of the marriage is to continue throughout the marriage; it must not give way to bitterness. The willing, covenant love in view here is the activity of self-sacrifice. It is a deep affection that views the wife as a sister in the Lord and the object of a promise to be kept. The love that Paul commands sees the wife as a weaker vessel to be cared for while at the same time a fellow-heir to grace (cf. 1 Pet. 3:7), a best friend, and life-partner. Such love was expressed by Isaac for Rebekah. "Then Isaac brought her into his mother Sarah's tent, and he took Rebekah, and she became his wife; and he loved her" (Gen. 24:67).

The nature of this love is beautifully expressed in Ephesians 5:22-28:

> Wives, be subject to your own husbands, as to the Lord. For the husband is the head of the wife, as Christ also is the head of the church, He Himself being the Savior of the body. But as the church is subject to Christ, so also the wives ought to be to their husbands in everything. Husbands, love your wives, just as Christ also loved the church and gave Himself up for her; that He might sanctify her, having cleansed her by the washing of water with the word, that He might present to Himself the church in all her glory, having no spot or wrinkle or any such thing; but that she should be holy and blameless. So husbands ought also to love their own wives as their own bodies. He who loves his own wife loves himself. (For a fuller treatment of this passage see *Ephesians*, MacArthur New Testament Commentary [Chicago: Moody, 1986].)

God designed that a wife's submission operate within a context of love. In that way she is protected because a man who truly loves his wife would never force her to submit to something humiliating, degrading, or that violates her conscience. The godly husband loves his wife like Christ loves the church.

Husbands also must not be embittered against their wives. The imperative *pikrainesthe* (**embittered**) could be translated, "stop being bitter," or "do not have the habit of being bitter" (A. T. Robertson, *Word Pictures in the New Testament* [Grand Rapids: Baker, 1931], 4:506). In its only other uses in the New Testament (Rev. 8:11; 10:9, 10) it refers to something bitter in taste. Paul tells husbands not to call their wives "honey," and then act like vinegar. They must not display harshness of temper or resentment toward their wives. They are not to irritate or exasperate them, but rather to provide loving leadership in the home.

Paul adds another helpful note when, in 1 Corinthians 7:33-34, he calls for a mutual concern in marriage. The husband is to seek to find "how he may please his wife," and the wife to pursue "how she may please her husband." Though there is authority and submission by God's design, there is also spiritual equality and a mutual longing for each partner to please the other. The woman most pleases the man with loving submission, while he pleases her with loving authority.

A Word to Children

Children, be obedient to your parents in all things, for this is well-pleasing to the Lord. (3:20)

The parallel text in Ephesians is almost identical: "Children, obey your parents in the Lord, for this is right" (Eph. 6:1). Paul now turns to the second relationship in the ancient home, that of parents and children. This relationship category cannot be right unless the relationship between husband and wife is right. *Tekna* (**children**) is a general term for children and is not limited to a specific age group. It refers to any child still living in the home and under parental guidance. The present tense of the imperative *hupakouete* (**be obedient**) demands a continuous obedience.

That children are to honor and obey their parents is taught repeatedly in Scripture. It appears in the Ten Commandments: "Honor your father and your mother, that your days may be prolonged in the land which the Lord your God gives you" (Ex. 20:12). Striking or cursing one's parents was punishable by death in the Old Testament (Ex. 21:15-17; Lev. 20:9), as was continued disobedience (Deut. 21:18-21). Children are to listen to their parents' instruction and obey it (Prov. 1:8; 6:20). The consequences of disrespect for parents are graphically portrayed in Proverbs 30:17: "The eye that mocks a father, and scorns a mother, the ravens of the valley will pick it out, and the young eagles will eat it" (cf. Matt. 15:4-5; Mark 7:10-13).

Disobedience to parents marks the ungodly: "Men will be lovers of self, lovers of money, boastful, arrogant, revilers, disobedient to parents, ungrateful, unholy" (2 Tim. 3:2; cf. Rom. 1:30).

Children are to obey their **parents in all things.** The only limit placed on a child's obedience is when a parent demands something contrary to God's law. Jesus knew that some children would have to defy their parents to come to faith in Him. In Luke 12:51-53 our Lord says, "Do you suppose that I came to grant peace on earth? I tell you, no, but rather division; for from now on five members in one household will be divided, three against two, and two against three. They will be divided, father against son, and son against father; mother against daughter, and daughter against mother; mother-in-law against daughter-in-law, and daughter-in-law against mother-in-law." Later in Luke 14:26 He says, "If anyone comes to Me, and does not hate his own father and mother and wife and children and brothers and sisters, yes, and even his own life, he cannot be My disciple." Salvation can bring a breech in the family so that children may have to reject their parents' commands if they are contrary to Scripture.

The motive for obedience is that it **is well-pleasing to the Lord,** commendable before God Himself. As He was well-pleased with His own Son (Matt. 3:17), so He deserves to be with other children. Many young people struggle with knowing God's will for their lives. Obeying their parents is the right place to start.

A WORD TO PARENTS

Fathers, do not exasperate your children, that they may not lose heart. (3:21)

This verse also intersects with the apostle's teaching in Ephesians 6:4: "Fathers, do not provoke your children to anger; but bring them up in the discipline and instruction of the Lord." The duty in this relationship is not one-sided. Parents also have obligations to their children. *Pateres* (**fathers**) should be translated, "parents," as it is in Hebrews 11:23. Paul's word to parents is **do not exasperate your children. Exasperate** is from *erethizō* and means to stir up, provoke, irritate, or exasperate. Another way to phrase Paul's command is, "stop nagging your kids." Failure to obey this can cause children to **lose heart.** The idea of that term is "to be without courage, or spirit." It has the sense of being listless, sullen, discouraged, or despairing. Parents can take the heart out of their children by failing to discipline them lovingly and instruct them in the ways of the Lord with balance.

There are several ways parents can cause their children to lose heart.

First, parents can exasperate their children by overprotection. Overprotective parents never allow their children any liberty. They have strict rules about everything. No matter what their children do, overprotective parents do not trust them. Because nothing they do earns their parents' trust, children begin to despair and may believe that how they behave is irrelevant. That can lead to rebellion. Parents are to provide rules and guidelines for their children, but those rules should not become a noose that strangles them. Above all, parents must communicate to their children that they trust them.

Second, parents exasperate their children by showing favoritism. That is often done unwittingly by comparing a child unfavorably to siblings or classmates. By making a child feel like the black sheep of the family, parents can create a terrible sense of frustration.

Third, parents exasperate their children by depreciating their worth. Many children have been convinced that what they do and feel are not important. That is communicating to children that they are not significant. Many parents depreciate their children's worth by refusing to listen to them. Children who are not listened to may give up trying to communicate and become discouraged, shy, and withdrawn.

Fourth, parents exasperate their children by setting unrealistic goals. Parents can do that by never rewarding them, or never letting them feel they have succeeded. Nothing is enough, so the children never get full approval. Such parents are often trying to make their children into something they themselves were not. The results can be tragic. Some children become so frustrated that they commit suicide.

Fifth, parents exasperate their children by failing to show affection. Parents need to communicate love to their children both verbally and physically. Failing to do so will discourage and alienate a child.

Sixth, some parents exasperate their children by not providing for their needs. Children need things like privacy, a place to play, clean clothes, a place to study, their own possessions, and good meals. By providing those necessities, parents show their respect and concern for their children.

Seventh, parents exasperate their children by a lack of standards. This is the flip side of overprotection. When parents fail to discipline, or discipline inconsistently, children are left on their own. They cannot handle that kind of freedom and begin to feel insecure and unloved.

Eighth, parents exasperate their children by criticism. Haim Ginott wrote, "A child learns what he lives. If he lives with criticism he does not learn responsibility. He learns to condemn himself and to find fault with others. He learns to doubt his own judgment, to disparage his own ability, and to distrust the intentions of others. And above all, he learns to live with continual expectation of impending doom" (*Between Parent and Child* [New York: Macmillan, 1965], p. 72). Parents should seek to create in the home a positive, constructive environment.

Ninth, parents exasperate their children by neglect. The classic biblical example is Absalom. David was indifferent to him, and the result was rebellion, civil war, and Absalom's death. Parents need to be involved in their children's lives.

Finally, parents exasperate their children by excessive discipline. This is the parent who abuses his children, either verbally, emotionally, or physically. Parents often say things to their children that they would never say to anyone else. They should never discipline their children in anger. Rather, parents should lovingly correct their children, just as their heavenly Father does them.

The influence parents have in the lives of their children has been summed up in a perspective by Dorothy Law Nolte entitled "Children Learn What They Live":

> If a child lives with criticism,
> he learns to condemn.
>
> If a child lives with hostility,
> he learns to fight.
>
> If a child lives with ridicule,
> he learns to be shy.
>
> If a child lives with shame,
> he learns to feel guilty.
>
> If a child lives with tolerance,
> he learns to be patient.
>
> If a child lives with encouragement,
> he learns confidence.
>
> If a child lives with praise,
> he learns to appreciate.
>
> If a child lives with fairness,
> he learns justice.
>
> If a child lives with security,
> he learns to have faith.
>
> If a child lives with approval,
> he learns to like himself.
>
> If a child lives with acceptance and friendship,
> he learns to find love in the world.

(Copyright 1982 by Dorothy Law Nolte. Used by permission.)

Not exasperating their children is essential if parents are to "bring them up in the discipline and instruction of the Lord" (Eph. 6:4).

A Word to Servants

Slaves, in all things obey those who are your masters on earth, not with external service, as those who merely please men, but with sincerity of heart, fearing the Lord. Whatever you do, do your work heartily, as for the Lord rather than for men; knowing that from the Lord you will receive the reward of the inheritance. It is the Lord Christ whom you serve. For he who does wrong will receive the consequences of the wrong which he has done, and that without partiality. (3:22-25)

The final relationship in an ancient home was that of masters and slaves. Again Paul, in Ephesians 6:5-9, parallels this text. In our day, that relationship can largely be compared to that of employer and employee. It should be noted that although the Word of God never advocates slavery, it does recognize it as an element of society that could be beneficial if both slaves and masters treated each other as they should. Far from seeking to abolish slavery, the Lord and the apostles use it as a motif for spiritual instruction, by likening the believer, one who belongs to Christ and serves Him, to a slave. So New Testament literature accepts slavery as a social reality and seeks to instruct those in that system to behave in a godly manner. Certainly in the letter to Philemon (delivered at the same time as Colossians), Paul upholds the duties of slave and master. He was sending the runaway slave Onesimus back to his master, Philemon. Paul asked Philemon to treat his returned slave with kindness and forgiveness—restoring the relationship to its divine design.

Rather than commanding slaves to rebel and overthrow slavery, Paul says, **In all things obey those who are your masters on earth.** It really is irrelevant what the social form may be, slavery or freedom—if the relationship is godly. As in the relationships between husbands and wives and parents and children, the principle of authority and submission is central to Paul's thought. **In all things** is a comprehensive phrase referring to both enjoyable and distasteful duties. The obedience required of slaves is not **external service,** doing a duty with a reluctant attitude, **as those who merely please men.** Rather, Christian servants are to please the Lord by working **with sincerity of heart, fearing the Lord.** Holding God and His will in high regard is the right motive. They are to **work heartily** (putting their whole inner man into the effort), **as for the Lord rather than for men,** serving their master as they would the Lord Himself.

Paul stresses to Timothy that such obedience and honor given by slaves to their masters keeps "the name of God and our doctrine" from being evil-spoken of (1 Tim. 6:1).

Paul gives two reasons for slaves (or employees) to obey their masters. Positively, the Lord will repay them for their faithfulness. They can endure inequity now, **knowing that from the Lord** they **will receive the reward of the inheritance.** The earthly master or boss may not give the servant what he deserves, but the Lord will. He is the One who will assure the eternal compensation is what it should be (cf. Rev. 20:12-13). Christian slaves are also heirs of eternal reward. As an employee on the job, or a servant in the home, it is the Lord Christ whom believers serve. He will pay them back with grace and generosity.

Paul then gives a negative reason for obedience. The one **who does wrong will receive the consequences of the wrong which he has done, and that without partiality.** The warning is that the Lord will discipline without partiality in cases of disobedience (cf. Gal. 6:7). Paul acknowledged that the Christian slave Onesimus was responsible to repay Philemon (Philem. 18). The Christian servant is not to presume on his Christianity to justify disobedience. Even if we are God's children, we will reap what we sow, because God is impartial (cf. Acts 10:34).

A WORD TO MASTERS

Masters, grant to your slaves justice and fairness, knowing that you too have a Master in heaven. (4:1)

On the other side of the relationship, masters are to treat their slaves with the **justice and fairness** they expect to receive from their **Master in heaven.** God will judge masters who mistreat their slaves, as He will slaves who fail to serve their masters. As noted in the discussion of 3:11, slaves and masters are spiritually equal in Christ. Masters must accordingly treat their Christian servants as brothers in Christ, enacting toward them all the virtues required for holy fellowship. They should treat their employees like they desire the Lord Jesus to treat them.

If all Christians displayed the characteristics of relationships as embodied in the principles of this text, the results would be dramatic. Believers would indeed become lights shining in the darkness.

The Speech of the New Man

15

Devote yourselves to prayer, keeping alert in it with an attitude of thanksgiving; praying at the same time for us as well, that God may open up to us a door for the word, so that we may speak forth the mystery of Christ, for which I have also been imprisoned; in order that I may make it clear in the way I ought to speak. Conduct yourselves with wisdom toward outsiders, making the most of the opportunity. Let your speech always be with grace, seasoned, as it were, with salt, so that you may know how you should respond to each person. (4:2-6)

When our Lord told the Pharisees that "the mouth speaks out of that which fills the heart" (Matt. 12:34), He gave an important spiritual principle: Speech will reflect the kind of person one is. Because the tongue can speak so easily and is difficult to control, a person's speech becomes the truest indicator of his spiritual state (cf. Matt. 12:37).

The Bible has much to say about the speech of both the redeemed and the unredeemed mouth. The unredeemed mouth is characterized by evil (Prov. 15:28), sexual immorality (Prov. 5:3), deceit (Jer. 9:8), curses (Ps. 10:7), oppression (Ps. 10:7), lies (Prov. 12:22), destruction (Prov. 11:11), vanity (2 Pet. 2:18), flattery (Prov. 26:28), foolishness

(Prov. 15:2), madness (Eccles. 10:12-13), carelessness (Matt. 12:36), boasting (Rom. 1:30), false doctrine (Titus 1:11), evil plots (Ps. 37:12), hatred (Ps. 109:3), too many words (Eccles. 10:14), and gossip (Prov. 26:22).

In contrast, redeemed speech is characterized by confession of sin (1 John 1:9), confession of Christ (Rom. 10:9-10), edifying speech (Eph. 4:29), talk of God's law (Ex. 13:9), praise to God (Heb. 13:15), blessing of enemies (1 Pet. 3:9), talk about God (Ps. 66:16), wisdom and kindness (Prov. 31:26), and gentleness (Prov. 15:1). It takes as its model the Lord Jesus, who spoke instructively (Matt. 5:2), graciously (Luke 4:22), blamelessly (Luke 11:54), and without deceit (1 Pet. 2:22).

In 4:2-6 Paul continues the discussion of the new man in Christ that he began in 3:5. In 3:5-17 he discussed the personal characteristics of the new man. In 3:18–4:1, he discussed the home life of the new man. In this passage he broadens the scope of his discussion to include unbelievers (cf. 4:5). He focuses especially on the speech of the new man, because that is something the watching world will look at carefully when it evaluates Christianity. Next to the thoughts, attitudes, and motives, it is also the most difficult area for believers to control.

In an ancient story, it is said that Bios, a wise man of ancient Greece, was sent an animal to sacrifice. He was instructed to send back to the donor the best and worst parts of the animal. He sent the donor the tongue. The tongue is indeed the best and worst of man. James agrees with that evaluation:

> We all stumble in many ways. If anyone does not stumble in what he says, he is a perfect man, able to bridle the whole body as well. Now if we put the bits into the horses' mouths so that they may obey us, we direct their entire body as well. Behold, the ships also, though they are so great and are driven by strong winds, are still directed by a very small rudder, wherever the inclination of the pilot desires. So also the tongue is a small part of the body, and yet it boasts of great things. Behold, how great a forest is set aflame by such a small fire! And the tongue is a fire, the very world of iniquity; the tongue is set among our members as that which defiles the entire body, and sets on fire the course of our life, and is set on fire by hell. For every species of beasts and birds, of reptiles and creatures of the sea, is tamed, and has been tamed by the human race. But no one can tame the tongue; it is a restless evil and full of deadly poison. With it we bless our Lord and Father; and with it we curse men, who have been made in the likeness of God; from the same mouth come both blessing and cursing. My brethren, these things ought not to be this way. Does a fountain send out from the same opening both fresh and bitter water? Can a fig tree, my brethren, produce olives, or a vine produce figs? Neither can salt water produce fresh. (James 3:2-12)

In his discussion of the speech of the new man, Paul puts the emphasis on four areas: the speech of prayer, the speech of proclamation, the speech of performance, and the speech of perfection.

THE SPEECH OF PRAYER

Devote yourselves to prayer, keeping alert in it with an attitude of thanksgiving. (4:2)

It is fitting that Paul begins with prayer, because it is the most important speech the new man can utter. Prayer is the strength of the believer's fellowship with the Lord and the source of his power against Satan and his angels (cf. Eph. 6:18). Through prayer, believers confess their sin, offer praise to God, call on their sympathetic High Priest (Heb. 4:15-16), and intercede for each other. Prayer from a pure heart (Ps. 66:18) is to be directed to God (Matt. 6:9), consistent with the mind and will of the Holy Spirit (Eph. 6:18), in the name of Christ, and for the glory of the Father (John 14:13).

In 4:2, Paul touches on an often overlooked aspect of prayer, that of perseverance. **Devote yourselves** is from *proskartereō*, a compound word made up of *kartereō* ("to be steadfast," or "to endure") with an added preposition that intensifies the meaning. The verb means "to be courageously persistent," "to hold fast and not let go." Paul is calling strongly on believers to persist in prayer. They are to "pray at all times" (Eph. 6:18; cf. Luke 18:1), "pray without ceasing" (1 Thess. 5:17), and be devoted to prayer (Rom. 12:12). By so doing, they follow the example of Cornelius (Acts 10:2) and the apostles (Acts 6:4).

Praying at all times is not necessarily limited to constant vocalizing of prayers to God. Rather, it refers to a God consciousness that relates every experience in life to Him. That does not, however, obviate the need for persistence and earnestness in prayer. Such persistence is illustrated repeatedly in Scripture. The 120 disciples gathered in the Upper Room "were continually devoting themselves to prayer" (Acts 1:14). The early church followed their example (cf. Acts 2:42).

Our Lord told two parables illustrating the importance of persistent prayer:

> Now He was telling them a parable to show that at all times they ought to pray and not to lose heart, saying, "There was in a certain city a judge who did not fear God, and did not respect man. And there was a widow in that city, and she kept coming to him, saying, 'Give me legal protection from my opponent.' And for a while he was unwilling; but afterward he said to himself, 'Even though I do not fear God nor respect

man, yet because this widow bothers me, I will give her legal protection, lest by continually coming she wear me out.'" And the Lord said, "Hear what the unrighteous judge said; now shall not God bring about justice for His elect, who cry to Him day and night, and will He delay long over them? I tell you that He will bring about justice for them speedily." (Luke 18:1-8)

And He said to them, "Suppose one of you shall have a friend, and shall go to him at midnight, and say to him, 'Friend, lend me three loaves; for a friend of mine has come to me from a journey, and I have nothing to set before him '; and from inside he shall answer and say, 'Do not bother me; the door has already been shut and my children and I are in bed; I cannot get up and give you anything.' I tell you, even though he will not get up and give him anything because he is his friend, yet because of his persistence he will get up and give him as much as he needs. And I say to you, ask, and it shall be given to you; seek, and you shall find; knock, and it shall be opened to you. For everyone who asks, receives; and he who seeks, finds; and to him who knocks, it shall be opened." (Luke 11:5-10)

The point of both those parables is that if unwilling and sinful humans will honor persistence, how much more will our holy, loving heavenly Father?

Virginia Stem Owens wrote the following about wrestling with God in earnest prayer:

> Christians have always interpreted the splitting of the temple veil during the crucifixion as symbolic of their liberation from the *mediated* presence of God. Henceforth they were "free" to approach him directly—which is almost like telling someone he is "free" to stick his head in the lion's jaws. For once you start praying there is no guarantee that you won't find yourself before Pharaoh, shipwrecked on a desert island, or in a lion's den.

> This is no cosmic teddy bear we are cuddling up to. As one of the children describes him in C. S. Lewis's *Chronicles of Narnia*, "he's not a *tame* lion." [Jacques] Ellul is convinced that prayer for persons living in the technological age must be combat, and not just combat with the Evil One, with one's society, or even one's divided self, though it is also all of these; it is combat with God. We too must struggle with him just as Jacob did at Peniel where he earned his name Israel—"he who strives with God." We too must be prepared to say, "I will not let you go till you bless me."

> Consider Moses, again and again intervening between the Israelites and God's wrath; Abraham praying for Sodom; the widow demanding

justice of the unjust judge. But in this combat with God, Ellul cautions, we must be ready to bear the consequences: . . . "Jacob's thigh was put out of joint, and he went away lame. However, the most usual experience will be God's decision to put to work the person who cried out to him. . . . Whoever wrestles with God in prayer puts his whole life at stake."

Awful things happen to people who pray. Their plans are frequently disrupted. They end up in strange places. Abraham "went out, not knowing where he was to go". . . . After Mary's magnificent prayer at the annunciation, she finds herself the pariah of Nazareth society. . . . How tempting to up the stakes, making prayer merely another consumer product. How embarrassing to have to admit not only that prayer may get you into a prison, as it did Jeremiah, but also that while you're moldering away in a miry pit there, you may have a long list of lamentations and unanswered questions to present to your Lord. How are we going to tell them they may end up lame and vagrant if they grasp hold of this God? ("Prayer—Into the Lion's Jaws," *Christianity Today*, November 19, 1976, pp. 222-23; italics in the original)

That stands in marked contrast to the glib, self-centered prayers of our day. Much of the contemporary church has lost its reverence for God. He is too often viewed as a sort of cosmic automatic teller machine. If we punch in the right code, He's obligated to deliver what we want. The Lord might well ask the twentieth-century church what He asked the rebellious priests of Malachi's day: "'A son honors his father, and a servant his master. Then if I am a father, where is My honor? And if I am a master, where is My respect?' says the Lord of hosts" (Mal. 1:6).

True prayer often involves struggling and grappling with God, proving to Him the deepest concern of one's heart. Prayer is to be a persistent, courageous struggle from which the believer may come away limping.

Such prayer gives the believer a holy boldness to pray forcefully when convinced of God's will, as the following example shows.

In 1540 Luther's great friend and assistant, Friedrich Myconius, became sick and was expected to die within a short time. On his bed he wrote a loving farewell note to Luther with a trembling hand. Luther received the letter and sent back a reply: "I command thee in the name of God to live because I still have need of thee in the work of reforming the church. . . . The Lord will never let me hear that thou art dead, but will permit thee to survive me. For this I am praying, this is my will, and may my will be done, because I seek only to glorify the name of God."

Those words are shocking to us, but they were certainly heartfelt. Although Myconius had already lost the ability to speak when

Luther's letter came, he recovered completely and lived six more years to survive Luther himself by two months.

There is a tension between boldness and waiting on God's will. That tension is resolved by being persistent, yet accepting God's answer when it finally comes.

True prayer also involves **keeping alert.** In its most basic sense, that means to stay awake and not fall asleep during prayer. While in Gethsamane, Jesus "came to the disciples and found them sleeping, and said to Peter, 'So, you men could not keep watch with Me for one hour? Keep watching and praying, that you may not enter into temptation; the spirit is willing, but the flesh is weak'" (Matt. 26:40-41). It is impossible to pray while sleeping. Christians should choose times when they are awake and alert to pray.

Paul's thought here, however, is broader than mere physical alertness. He also means that believers should look for those things about which they ought to be praying. Christians sometimes pray vague, general prayers that are difficult for God to answer because they do not really ask anything specific. To be devoted to prayer requires something specific to pray for. We will never persistently pray for something we are not concerned about. And to be concerned, we must be alert to specific needs.

A third element in prayer is **an attitude of thanksgiving.** This is the fifth time that Paul has mentioned gratitude in this epistle. Believers are to be grateful for salvation (1:12), for growth (2:6), for fellowship with Christ and His church (3:15), for the opportunity to serve (3:17), and, here, for the guarantee that God will answer prayer in accordance with His purpose. That, of course, is what is best for our good in time and our glory in eternity.

When believers pray, they can begin by being thankful for the following spiritual blessings and privileges. First, believers are to be thankful for God's presence. In Psalm 75:1, the psalmist writes, "We give thanks to Thee, O God, we give thanks, for Thy name is near." Second, believers are to be thankful for God's provision. Adrift at sea in the midst of a raging storm, Paul nevertheless was grateful to God for the food He provided: "He took bread and gave thanks to God in the presence of all" (Acts 27:35). Third, believers are to be thankful for God's pardon. Paul said in Romans 6:17, "Thanks be to God that though you were slaves of sin, you became obedient from the heart to that form of teaching to which you were committed." Christians should be grateful for their salvation. Fourth, believers are to be thankful for God's promise: "Thanks be to God, who gives us the victory through our Lord Jesus Christ" (1 Cor. 15:57; cf. 2 Cor. 2:14). "For as many as may be the promises of God, in Him they are yes; wherefore also by Him is our Amen to the glory of God through us" (2 Cor. 1:20). Finally, believers are to be thankful for God's purpose: "We know that God causes all things to work together for good to those who love God, to those who are called according to His purpose" (Rom. 8:28).

THE SPEECH OF PROCLAMATION

praying at the same time for us as well, that God may open up to us a door for the word, so that we may speak forth the mystery of Christ, for which I have also been imprisoned; in order that I may make it clear in the way I ought to speak. (4:3-4)

Paul turns from prayer, which is speech directed to God, to the proclamation of the gospel, which is speech directed to people. Having exhorted the Colossians to pray, he gives them a specific request, to pray **at the same time for us as well.** The plural pronoun **us** probably includes the list of Paul's friends and co-workers that begins in 4:7. The content of Paul's request was **that God may open up to us a door for the word, so that we may speak forth the mystery of Christ.** A *door* in the New Testament usually refers to an opportunity. In 1 Corinthians 16:8-9, Paul writes, "I shall remain in Ephesus until Pentecost; for a wide door for effective service has opened to me, and there are many adversaries." He later wrote to the Corinthians of the door that had opened for him at Troas (2 Cor. 2:12).

Believers are to pray for open doors because it is God who opens them. At the end of Paul's first missionary journey, he and Barnabas reported to the church "all things that God had done with them and how He had opened a door of faith to the Gentiles" (Acts 14:27). In Acts 16, after several doors had been shut, "a vision appeared to Paul in the night: a certain man of Macedonia was standing and appealing to him, and saying, 'Come over to Macedonia and help us'" (v. 9). Upon seeing the vision, Luke writes, "immediately we sought to go into Macedonia, concluding that God had called us to preach the gospel to them" (Acts 16:10). Revelation 3:7 describes Jesus as the One "who opens and no one will shut, and who shuts and no one opens." That was literally the case when God opened locked prison doors and freed Peter to preach the gospel (Acts 12:1-11).

Paul desired an open door so he could **speak forth the mystery of Christ.** As already noted in the discussion of 1:26-27, the term *mystery* refers to something hidden in the Old Testament but manifest in the New. In the present context, it refers to the content of the gospel. Paul asks the Colossians to pray that he would have an open door to speak the full truth of the gospel.

It was for the sake of the gospel that Paul was **imprisoned.** In Jerusalem, at the end of his third missionary journey, he was falsely accused of bringing a Gentile into the area of the Temple forbidden to them. He was rescued from the angry crowd by the Romans and eventually sent by them to Felix, the governor of Judea. After languishing in custody for two years, Paul exercised his right as a Roman citizen and appealed his case to Caesar (Acts 25:11). Following a harrowing voyage, during which he was shipwrecked following a violent storm, he reached Rome. The book of Acts closes with Paul under house arrest there (Acts 28:16, 30).

Paul's imprisonment did not spell the end of his ministry. It was during this period that he wrote Colossians, Ephesians, Philippians, and Philemon. He also evangelized those he came into contact with, whether the mob in Jerusalem (Acts 22:1ff.), Felix (Acts 24:10ff.), Herod Agrippa (Acts 26:1ff.), Roman soldiers (Phil. 1:13), members of Caesar's household (Phil. 4:22), or members of Rome's Jewish community (Acts 28:17ff.). Paul's activity during his imprisonment in Rome is summed up in Acts 28:30-31: "He stayed two full years in his own rented quarters, and was welcoming all who came to him, preaching the kingdom of God, and teaching concerning the Lord Jesus Christ with all openness, unhindered." For Paul, there were no devastating circumstances, only unique opportunities.

Paul further asked the Colossians to pray that when God opened a door for the gospel, **I may make it clear in the way I ought to speak. Ought** can be understood in two ways. First, it refers to the compulsion Paul felt to preach the gospel. That was a constant burden in his life. To the Romans he wrote, "I am not ashamed of the gospel, for it is the power of God for salvation to everyone who believes, to the Jew first and also to the Greek" (Rom. 1:16). In 1 Corinthians 9:16 he said, "If I preach the gospel, I have nothing to boast of, for I am under compulsion; for woe is me if I do not preach the gospel."

Second, **ought to speak** refers to the mandate for using the God-ordained method of presenting the gospel. Paul preached the gospel by "solemnly testifying to both Jews and Greeks of repentance toward God and faith in our Lord Jesus Christ" (Acts 20:21). "Solemnly testifying" is from *diamarturomai*, which means to give a thorough and complete testimony. The gospel should be proclaimed clearly, boldly (Eph. 6:19), wisely (Prov. 25:11), and graciously (Eph. 4:15).

There are three popular kinds of evangelism that this instruction precludes. First, experience-centered evangelism is inappropriate. It focuses not on delineating the gospel message from Scripture passages, but on a person's testimony of personal feelings and experiences. The obvious danger in this method is that people may not really understand the gospel at all, yet respond to what was said emotionally and think they are saved.

A second kind of evangelism to be avoided is ego-focused evangelism. This evangelism sells Jesus as the panacea for all of life's problems and as the source of earthly comfort, well-being, and prosperity. It promises that continual happiness and freedom from struggle are available through Him in this life. In short, it is man-centered, not God-centered. Although salvation does bring joy and peace, the gospel does not guarantee a life without difficulty. Paul warned that "through many tribulations we must enter the kingdom of God" (Acts 14:22). Jesus told the disciples that "a slave is not greater than his master. If they persecuted Me, they will also persecute you" (John 15:20; cf. Matt. 5:11, 44; 10:23). In fact, Jesus promised, "In the world you have tribulation, but take courage; I have overcome the world" (John 16:33).

A final form of evangelism to be avoided is expedience evangelism. This wrong method of evangelism uses high-pressure tactics, manipulation, cleverness, emotional stimulation, or technique to force commitments. It, too, often results in false professions of faith (Matt. 13:19-22; cf. James 2:14-26).

Paul wanted people to pray that he would speak as he ought to speak, as God wanted him to speak. That should be our prayer for everyone who proclaims Christ.

THE SPEECH OF PERFORMANCE

Conduct yourselves with wisdom toward outsiders, making the most of the opportunity. (4:5)

What believers are gives credibility to what they say. As already noted in the discussion of 1:9, wisdom involves properly evaluating circumstances and making godly decisions. Believers are to exhibit a carefully planned, consistent, righteous Christian life.

If those who say they are believers live as fools, **outsiders** or unbelievers (cf. 1 Cor. 5:12-13; 1 Thess. 4:12; 1 Tim. 3:7), will denigrate the faith and shun the gospel. Only if believers live wisely will the watching world see the power of God at work in them. Be warned: believers can live like fools. One way is by living for money. Paul warns against that in 1 Timothy 6:9: "Those who want to get rich fall into temptation and a snare and many foolish and harmful desires which plunge men into ruin and destruction."

Another way to live foolishly is to live the Christian life legalistically. Paul said to the Galatians, "You foolish Galatians, who has bewitched you, before whose eyes Jesus Christ was publicly portrayed as crucified? Are you so foolish? Having begun by the Spirit, are you now being perfected by the flesh?" (Gal. 3:1, 3). Jealousy and selfish ambition, being the opposite of wisdom, are other ways even believers can express foolishness (James 3:16).

On the other hand, there are several sources for wisdom. First, worship: "The fear of the Lord is the beginning of wisdom, and the knowledge of the Holy One is understanding" (Prov. 9:10). Second, prayer: "If any of you lacks wisdom, let him ask of God, who gives to all men generously and without reproach, and it will be given to him" (James 1:5). Third, Bible study: "Let the word of Christ richly dwell within you, with all wisdom teaching and admonishing one another" (Col. 3:16). Fourth, godly instruction: "And we proclaim Him, admonishing every man and teaching every man with all wisdom, that we may present every man complete in Christ" (Col. 1:28). It is only through walking in wisdom that believers' words will mean anything. The early church had none of the modern means of advertising the gospel, such as TV, radio, tracts, books, magazines, or bumper stickers—and fewer of the scandals and hypocrites. Yet by living out the truth of the gospel in their personal and corporate lives, they turned their world upside down. May that be said of us.

Living a godly life also involves **making the most of the opportunity.** Moses prayed in Psalm 90:12, "So teach us to number our days, that we may present to Thee a heart of wisdom." Opportunity is fleeting. Life is short, and every day more people die without Christ. "Night is coming, when no man can work" (John 9:4). Our Lord may return at any moment. Paul expressed the urgency of redeeming the time in Romans 13:11-14:

> This do, knowing the time, that it is already the hour for you to awaken from sleep; for now salvation is nearer to us than when we believed. The night is almost gone, and the day is at hand. Let us therefore lay aside the deeds of darkness and put on the armor of light. Let us behave properly as in the day, not in carousing and drunkenness, not in sexual promiscuity and sensuality, not in strife and jealousy. But put on the Lord Jesus Christ, and make no provision for the flesh in regard to its lusts.

The time is now for believers to speak with their lives.

The Speech of Perfection

Let your speech always be with grace, seasoned, as it were, with salt, so that you may know how you should respond to each person. (4:6)

Consistency of life must be followed by consistency of speech. Paul is not speaking here of preaching the gospel, but general conversation. Believers' **speech** must **always be with grace,** as was Christ's (Luke 4:22). There is no place for those things that characterize the unredeemed mouth. Whether undergoing persecution, stress, difficulty, or injustice, whether with your spouse, children, believers, or unbelievers—in all circumstances believers are to make gracious speech a habit. To speak with **grace** means to say what is spiritual, wholesome, fitting, kind, sensitive, purposeful, complementary, gentle, truthful, loving, and thoughtful. Paul wrote in Ephesians 4:29, "Let no unwholesome word proceed from your mouth, but only such a word as is good for edification according to the need of the moment, that it may give grace to those who hear."

The speech of the new man must also be **seasoned . . . with salt.** It is not only to be gracious, but also to have an effect. Salt can sting when rubbed into a wound (cf. Prov. 27:6). It also prevents corruption. Believers' speech should act as a purifying influence, rescuing conversation from the filth that so often engulfs it. Salt also adds flavor, and the speech of the new man should add charm and wit to conversation.

Believers must also know how to **respond to each person.** They must know how to say the right thing at the right time. In Peter's words, they must be "ready to make a defense to everyone who asks you to give an account for the hope that is in you, yet with gentleness and reverence" (1 Pet. 3:15).

The speech of the new man is vitally important: "If anyone does not stumble in what he says, he is a perfect man, able to bridle the whole body as well" (James 3:2). Unlike the ungodly, who say "Our lips are our own; who is lord over us?" (Ps. 12:4), we as believers should echo the prayer of the psalmist in Psalm 141:3: "Set a guard, O Lord, over my mouth; keep watch over the door of my lips."

With a Little Help from My Friends

16

As to all my affairs, Tychicus, our beloved brother and faithful servant and fellow bond-servant in the Lord, will bring you information. For I have sent him to you for this very purpose, that you may know about our circumstances and that he may encourage your hearts; and with him Onesimus, our faithful and beloved brother, who is one of your number. They will inform you about the whole situation here. Aristarchus, my fellow prisoner, sends you his greetings; and also Barnabas' cousin Mark (about whom you received instructions: if he comes to you, welcome him); and also Jesus who is called Justus; these are the only fellow workers for the kingdom of God who are from the circumcision; and they have proved to be an encouragement to me. Epaphras, who is one of your number, a bondslave of Jesus Christ, sends you his greetings, always laboring earnestly for you in his prayers, that you may stand perfect and fully assured in all the will of God. For I bear him witness that he has a deep concern for you and for those who are in Laodicea and Hierapolis. Luke, the beloved physician, sends you his greetings, and also Demas. Greet the brethren who are in Laodicea and also Nympha and the church that is in her house. And when this letter

**is read among you, have it also read in the church of the Laodi-
ceans; and you, for your part read my letter that is coming from
Laodicea. And say to Archippus, "Take heed to the ministry
which you have received in the Lord, that you may fulfill it." I,
Paul, write this greeting with my own hand. Remember my imprisonment. Grace be with you.** (4:7-18)

As Paul closes Colossians, he encloses with his letter a verbal
group photograph. He includes in it a number of those who helped him
in his ministry while he was imprisoned at Rome. He gives recognition
to some of the unsung heroes of the New Testament, and by so doing
uses them as an encouragement to those who read this letter. This section adds a warm, personal touch to what has been largely a doctrinal
letter. It is similar to the personals he adds in chapter 16 of Romans.
That many of those mentioned had stuck with Paul for years indicates
the tremendous loyalty he inspired.

To Paul, these people were indispensable assets to his ministry.
He knew well that he could not do it alone; no one can. God's leaders
have always depended on others to support them in their work. Exodus
17:8-13 illustrates that truth:

> Then Amalek came and fought against Israel at Rephidim. So Moses
> said to Joshua, "Choose men for us, and go out, fight against Amalek.
> Tomorrow I will station myself on the top of the hill with the staff of
> God in my hand." And Joshua did as Moses told him, and fought
> against Amalek; and Moses, Aaron, and Hur went up to the top of the
> hill. So it came about when Moses held his hand up, that Israel pre-
> vailed, and when he let his hand down, Amalek prevailed. But Moses'
> hands were heavy. Then they took a stone and put it under him, and he
> sat on it; and Aaron and Hur supported his hands, one on one side and
> one on the other. Thus his hands were steady until the sun set. So
> Joshua overwhelmed Amalek and his people with the edge of the
> sword.

With help from Aaron and Hur, Moses was able to lead Israel to a great
victory.

Moses, like the apostle Paul, recognized that he could not carry
out his ministry alone. On another occasion, fed up with the grumbling
of the Israelites, he cried out to God,

> Why hast Thou been so hard on Thy servant? And why have I not found
> favor in Thy sight, that Thou hast laid the burden of all this people on
> me? Was it I who conceived all this people? Was it I who brought them

forth, that Thou shouldest say to me, "Carry them in your bosom as a nurse carries a nursing infant, to the land which Thou didst swear to their fathers?" Where am I to get meat to give to all this people? For they weep before me, saying, "Give us meat that we may eat!" I alone am not able to carry all this people, because it is too burdensome for me. So if Thou art going to deal thus with me, please kill me at once, if I have found favor in Thy sight, and do not let me see my wretchedness. (Num. 11:11-15)

The Lord answered by giving him some help:

The Lord therefore said to Moses, "Gather for Me seventy men from the elders of Israel, whom you know to be the elders of the people and their officers and bring them to the tent of meeting, and let them take their stand there with you. Then I will come down and speak with you there, and I will take of the Spirit who is upon you, and will put Him upon them; and they shall bear the burden of the people with you, so that you shall not bear it all alone." (Num. 11:16-17)

With their support, Moses was enabled by God to accomplish things he could never have accomplished alone.

Leaders are made more effective by those who help them. Proverbs 27:17 says, "Iron sharpens iron, so one man sharpens another." Ecclesiastes 4:9-12 adds, "Two are better than one because they have a good return for their labor. For if either of them falls, the one will lift up his companion. But woe to the one who falls when there is not another to lift him up. Furthermore, if two lie down together they keep warm, but how can one be warm alone? And if one can overpower him who is alone, two can resist him. A cord of three strands is not quickly torn apart."

Paul never ministered alone. He shared his first leadership opportunity in the church at Antioch with four other men, and throughout the following years of his missionary travels, he always had companions. The only time we find him alone in Acts is for a brief period in Athens (Acts 17). Although he is a prisoner as he writes Colossians, he still is not alone. The eight men he names are not all well-known figures. Each was, however, a special person to Paul. And each was willing to pay the price of associating with a prisoner. In this passage we meet the man with a servant's heart, the man with a sinful past, the man with a sympathetic heart, the man with a surprising future, the man with a strong commitment, the man with a single passion, the man with a specialized talent, and the man with a sad future.

THE MAN WITH A SERVANT'S HEART

As to all my affairs, Tychicus, our beloved brother and faithful servant and fellow bond-servant in the Lord, will bring you information. For I have sent him to you for this very purpose, that you may know about our circumstances and that he may encourage your hearts; (4:7-8)

Tychicus means "fortuitous," or "fortunate." Indeed, he was fortunate to have ministered with Paul for so many years. He is mentioned five times in the New Testament. Although the references are brief, they give us a rich profile of the man.

We first meet Tychicus in Acts 20:4. Paul was in Ephesus near the end of his third missionary journey. He planned to return to Jerusalem via Macedonia, where he intended to collect an offering. With the offerings from Galatia and Achaia, he would present it to the needy believers at Jerusalem (cf. 1 Cor. 16:1-9). By so doing, he hoped to cement the bond between the predominantly Gentile churches outside of Palestine, and the predominantly Jewish church at Jerusalem. He also planned to take some Gentile believers from Greece and Asia Minor as representatives of their churches to the Jerusalem church. Among them was Tychicus.

Tychicus's willingness to travel with Paul to Jerusalem shows his servant's heart. Such a journey was not to be undertaken lightly. Travel in the ancient world was far more difficult and dangerous than in our day. The trip to Jerusalem would be very arduous, and it would take Tychicus away from his family, friends, and church for a long time. Along the way, Paul was repeatedly warned that trouble awaited him in Jerusalem. Although Tychicus must certainly have heard those warnings, he remained with Paul.

As Paul wrote Colossians, it had been more than two years since his arrest at Jerusalem. Since then he had survived a plot by the Jewish leaders to murder him, trials before Felix, Festus, and Agrippa, and a harrowing voyage to Rome. Tychicus may have been with Paul through that entire time. He definitely was with him during his imprisonment at Rome. After Paul's release, Tychicus remained with him. When Paul needed a temporary replacement for Titus as pastor of the church on Crete, Tychicus was one of the ones considered (Titus 3:12). Tychicus, who had begun as a messenger, was now a candidate to fill in for as great a man as Titus.

At the very end of Paul's life, during his second Roman imprisonment, Tychicus was still with him. Facing imminent execution, Paul desired to see Timothy one last time. Because Timothy could not leave his congregation at Ephesus without a replacement, Paul sent Tychicus (2 Tim. 4:12). Once again, Tychicus's name comes up as a replacement for one of Paul's prominent associates. That speaks highly of his character.

The writing of Colossians finds Tychicus in Rome with Paul during his first imprisonment. By this time about four years have passed since Tychicus joined Paul in Ephesus. Because he is a man of proven loyalty, Paul has an important task for him: He is to deliver the letter to the Colossians. Not only does he carry Colossians, but Ephesians (cf. Eph. 6:21) and probably Philemon as well (cf. 4:9). The trip from Rome to Colossae was a difficult one. Tychicus would first have to cross much of Italy on foot, then sail across the Adriatic Sea. After traversing Greece on foot, he would sail across the Aegean Sea to the coast of Asia Minor. After all that, he still faced a journey of nearly one hundred miles on foot to reach Colossae. That he was entrusted with delivering three inspired books of Scripture once again indicates Paul's trust in him.

Not only will Tychicus deliver the letter of Colossians, he will also **bring** the Colossians **information** about Paul's **affairs** and update them on his **circumstances.** That would include bringing them information on Paul's health, his hopes, and his future prospects. He would also **encourage** their **hearts** by adding a personal word of encouragement to what was written in the letter and answering their queries about Paul's condition.

Paul next lists three credentials Tychicus possessed that qualified him to act as Paul's personal envoy. First, he was a **beloved brother** in the Lord. That Paul calls him a **brother** shows he was one of the family of believers. His personal character had earned him the designation **beloved** from no less than the apostle Paul himself. Second, Paul describes him as a **faithful servant.** He never achieved prominence, but he served in an important capacity as Paul's liaison to the churches. He was a **faithful** steward of his ministry—the highest commendation Paul could give (cf. 1 Cor. 4:2). Finally, Paul calls him a **fellow bond-servant in the Lord.** He was a *diakonos* (**servant**) in relationship to Paul, but a *sundoulos* (**fellow bond-servant**) with Paul in relationship to **the Lord.**

THE MAN WITH A SINFUL PAST

and with him Onesimus, our faithful and beloved brother, who is one of your number. They will inform you about the whole situation here. (4:9)

Onesimus, the man with the sinful past, is the runaway slave whose return to his master was the occasion for the book of Philemon. Philemon was one of the leaders of the Colossian church, and it is likely that the church met in his home. Onesimus had been a slave in Philemon's household until he ran away and made his way to Rome. There he met the apostle Paul, who led him to Christ. Now he was returning to Colossae and his master. Paul wrote to urge Philemon to forgive Onesimus for running away and defrauding him and to welcome Onesimus as a brother in Christ.

Although Onesimus was a runaway slave, Paul describes him as **our faithful and beloved brother.** When a person comes to faith in Christ, the past is no longer an issue. "Therefore if any man is in Christ, he is a new creature; the old things passed away; behold, new things have come" (2 Cor. 5:17). Onesimus was a testimony to the power of God to transform a life. Paul tells the Colossians that the man who left Colossae as a runaway slave now returns as **one of your number.** He was to be treated as a member of the church, because in Christ there was neither slave nor freeman (Gal. 3:28). Paul shows his regard for him by having him, along with Tychicus, **inform** the Colossians **about** Paul's **whole situation.** More detailed information about Onesimus is presented in my commentary on Philemon.

THE MAN WITH A SYMPATHETIC HEART

Aristarchus, my fellow prisoner, sends you his greetings; (4:10*a*)

Aristarchus was a Jewish believer (cf. 4:11), though like many Jews of the Diaspora, he had a Greek name. He was a native of Thessalonica (Acts 20:4; 27:2). Aristarchus first appeared during Paul's three-year ministry at Ephesus. He was seized by the rioting mob, who recognized him as one of Paul's companions (Acts 19:29). He accompanied Paul on his return trip to Jerusalem (Acts 20:4), and on his voyage to Rome (Acts 27:4). It is possible he stayed with Paul throughout his imprisonment in Palestine as well. As Paul writes Colossians, Aristarchus is still beside the apostle.

Fellow prisoner is from *aichmalōtos,* which literally means "one caught with a spear." It refers to war captives, or prisoners. It is unlikely that Aristarchus was actually a prisoner; Paul refers to him as such because he shared Paul's prison existence. That he chose to make Paul's lifestyle his own speaks of his sympathetic, caring heart. He gave up his own freedom to minister to Paul's needs. Any leader would be enriched to have a faithful Aristarchus at his side through all his trials.

The Lord's work would not be done if it were not for people like Aristarchus, who humbly bear hardships without the fame of those they serve.

THE MAN WITH A SURPRISING FUTURE

and also Barnabas' cousin Mark (about whom you received instructions: if he comes to you, welcome him); (4:10*b*)

John **Mark** had a very different career in the ministry than either Tychicus or Aristarchus. A companion of Paul and Barnabas on their first missionary journey (Acts 13:5), he deserted them when the going got tough. Acts 13:13 relates the story: "Paul and his companions put out to sea from Paphos and came to Perga in Pamphylia; and John left them and returned to Jerusalem." Mark's desertion was later to become a source of friction between Paul and Barnabas. Barnabas wanted to take his cousin along on the second missionary journey, but Paul, not trusting Mark to be loyal, refused. That led to such a sharp disagreement between Paul and Barnabas that they separated from each other (Acts 15:37-39).

Fortunately, the story does not end there. By the time Paul wrote Colossians, Mark had become a changed man. He had been restored to usefulness, probably through the ministry of Peter (himself no stranger to failure) in his life (cf. 1 Pet. 5:13). In Philemon 24, Paul names him among his fellow workers. The man whom Paul once rejected became one of his greatest helpers. In 2 Timothy 4:11, Paul tells Timothy to "pick up Mark and bring him with you, for he is useful to me for service."

Paul told the Colossians that if Mark came to them, they were to obey their **instructions** (which may have come from Paul, Peter, or Barnabas) and **welcome him.** They were not to shun him because of his previous failure.

We might also call Mark the man with a second chance. His life was a testimony to God's ability to use failures. In fact, he later received a privilege shared by only three other men in history: writing one of the gospels.

THE MAN WITH A STRONG COMMITMENT

and also Jesus who is called Justus; these are the only fellow workers for the kingdom of God who are from the circumcision; and they have proved to be an encouragement to me. (4:11)

Nothing is known of **Jesus who is called Justus** apart from this verse. It is possible that he was one of the Roman Jews who believed Paul's message (Acts 28:24). **Jesus** is the Greek form of Joshua, which means "savior." That certainly was a difficult name to live up to, but his Latin surname, **Justus** ("righteous"), indicates that he in some measure did. Jesus Justus, Mark, and Aristarchus were Paul's **only fellow workers for the kingdom of God who are from the circumcision.** The lack of response from his fellow Jews must have grieved Paul's heart. The Jewish leaders in Jerusalem rejected his message, plotted to kill him, and denounced him to the Roman authorities. Much of the opposition he received on his missionary journeys was from his fellow countrymen (cf. 2 Cor. 11:26). Even those who believed his message (cf. Acts 28:24) apparently did not commit themselves to him. (Many Gentiles who appeared to receive his message soon deserted him, according to 2 Tim. 1:15.) Only these three **proved to be an encouragement** to him. *Parēgoria* (**encouragement**) appears only here in the New Testament. It could also be translated "comfort." Jesus Justus, along with Aristarchus and Mark, was a source of comfort and encouragement to Paul.

That Jesus Justus was willing to leave his people to identify with Paul demonstrates his strong commitment. He was willing to take a stand alongside Paul for Jesus Christ no matter what the cost.

THE MAN WITH A SINGLE PASSION

Epaphras, who is one of your number, a bondslave of Jesus Christ, sends you his greetings, always laboring earnestly for you in his prayers, that you may stand perfect and fully assured in all the will of God. For I bear him witness that he has a deep concern for you and for those who are in Laodicea and Hierapolis. (4:12-13)

As noted in the introduction, **Epaphras** was the founder of the Colossian church, and he most likely was its current pastor. He had journeyed to Rome bringing Paul news of the dangerous heresy threatening the churches of the Lycus Valley. Like Tychicus, and Paul himself, Epaphras is designated a *doulos* (**bondslave**) of Jesus Christ. Because he was **one of** their **number,** he sends along **his greetings.**

Although separated from them, Epaphras still ministered to the Lycus Valley churches. He did so by **always laboring earnestly for** them **in his prayers. Laboring earnestly** is from *agōnizomai*, from which our English word *agonize* is derived. It is used in 1 Corinthians 9:25 to speak of the grueling competition endured by athletes in the games. In John 18:36 it is translated, "fight." Related words appear in Romans 15:30, to speak of fighting in prayer, and Luke 22:44, in reference to Jesus' agony in Gethsemane. Epaphras was a living example of Paul's command to the Colossians in 4:2 to "devote yourselves to prayer."

The goal of Epaphras's prayers was that the Colossians **stand perfect and fully assured in all the will of God. Perfect** is from *teleios* and means "complete," "mature," or "fully developed." **Fully assured** is from *plērophoreō* and could be translated, "persuaded," or "satisfied fully." Epaphras, like Paul (cf. 2:2 where a related word is used) wanted the Colossians to be mature and satisfied **in all the will of God.** Only those who live in obedience to God's will can grow to the fullness of Christ and be content (cf. Eph. 4:13-14).

Having observed Epaphras firsthand, Paul could **bear witness** to his **deep concern** for the Colossians, and those at nearby **Laodicea and Hierapolis.** His fervent, agonizing prayers and his single-minded passion for his people's maturity, must have greatly encouraged Paul and his other co-workers.

The Man with a Specialized Talent

Luke, the beloved physician, sends you his greetings, (4:14*a*)

Luke was Paul's personal **physician,** as well as his close friend. He was a Gentile believer (cf. 4:11) who traveled frequently with Paul on his missionary voyages. It may, in fact, have been Paul's recurring illnesses on the first missionary journey that prompted him to take Luke along on the second. Like Paul, he was an educated, cultured man, as evidenced by the literary quality of his Greek in his gospel and the book of Acts. His conversations with Paul were undoubtedly stimulating.

Luke is mentioned by name only two other times in the New Testament. All three times his name appears, it does so in Paul's writings from prison (cf. Philem. 24; 2 Tim. 4:11). After joining Paul on his second missionary journey, he was with him for most of the remainder of Paul's life.

Nothing definite is known about Luke's background. According to the church Fathers Eusebius and Jerome, he was born in Syrian Antioch. Some have speculated that he was Titus's brother, that he knew Paul when Paul was a student at Tarsus, and that he was a freed slave from the household of Theophilus (mentioned in the prologue to Acts). Those speculations, however, cannot be proved.

Luke was the prototype of the medical missionary. Not everyone in the Lord's service has to have a seminary degree. God's work needs specialists too. Luke surrendered his special talent to God, giving up what might have been a lucrative private practice. In return, God gave him the privilege of writing a sizeable portion of the New Testament, and of being the beloved companion of the apostle Paul.

THE MAN WITH A SAD FUTURE

and also Demas. (4:14*b*)

Demas is the last man in Paul's group photograph, and the one fly in the ointment. He had made a substantial commitment to the Lord's work, and was with Paul in both his imprisonments. Unlike Paul's other companions, however, his future was sad. Paul records the tragedy of Demas's desertion in 2 Timothy 4:9-10: "Make every effort to come to me soon; for Demas, having loved this present world, has deserted me and gone to Thessalonica." The pull of the world system eventually became irresistible to Demas, and he abandoned both Paul and the ministry. Jesus had His Judas, and Paul had his Demas. Anyone who has been in the ministry long enough has shared in that heartbreaking experience. That is not necessarily a reflection on one's own ministry, however. It is comforting to note that even the two greatest leaders the world has ever known had those who failed them.

CONCLUDING REMARKS

Greet the brethren who are in Laodicea and also Nympha and the church that is in her house. And when this letter is read among you, have it also read in the church of the Laodiceans; and you, for your part read my letter that is coming from Laodicea. And say to Archippus, "Take heed to the ministry which you have received in the Lord, that you may fulfill it." I, Paul, write this greeting with my own hand. Remember my imprisonment. Grace be with you. (4:15-18)

Paul closes by asking the Colossians to **greet the brethren** in nearby **Laodicea** for him. The manuscripts vary between **Nympha** (feminine) and Nymphas (masculine), and in the corresponding pronoun ("her," or "his"). **The church that is in her house** may have been the church at Laodicea, or that of Hierapolis, which would otherwise go unnamed. **The church of the Laodiceans** was to read the letter to the Colossians, and they were to read the **letter that is coming from Laodicea.** There has been much debate over the identity of the Laodicean letter. It has been variously identified as a letter from the Laodiceans to Paul, a letter written by Paul from Laodicea, the apocryphal Epistle to the Laodiceans, and a genuine letter of Paul to the Laodiceans that is now lost. In all likelihood, however, Paul here refers to the book of Ephesians. The oldest manuscripts of Ephesians do not contain the words "in Ephesus" in Ephesians 1:1, indicating that it was a circular letter intended for several churches. Tychicus probably delivered Ephesians to the Laodiceans, so Paul commands the Colossians and Laodiceans to exchange letters.

Archippus appears only here and in Philemon 2. He is commanded to **take heed** to his **ministry** that he might **fulfill** it. The examples of Paul's co-workers in the preceding verses would be a powerful incentive for him to do that. To fulfill our ministry is what the Lord expects of all of us.

Paul customarily used an amanuensis (recording secretary) when writing his letters, but frequently added a **greeting with** his **own hand** (cf. 1 Cor. 16:21; 2 Thess. 3:17; Philem. 19). He asks them to **remember** his **imprisonment** in their prayers, and closes with the common salutation, **Grace be with you** (cf. Rom. 16:24; 1 Cor. 16:23; 2 Cor. 13:14; 1 Thess. 5:28; 2 Thess. 3:18; 1 Tim. 6:21; 2 Tim. 4:22; Titus 3:15).

That sums up the message of Colossians: salvation is by grace through faith in the all-sufficient Christ, not through human works advocated by false teachers.

Introduction
to Philemon

The book of Philemon is unique in many respects. The shortest of Paul's inspired writings, it is the only one of the prison epistles addressed to an individual. Although it does not reach the lofty doctrinal heights of the others (Colossians, Philippians, and Ephesians), it does deal with a vitally important practical issue. Paul takes the truth that Christians are to forgive each other (cf. Eph. 4:32; Col. 3:13), first taught in the New Testament by our Lord Himself in the gospel of Matthew, and applies it to a specific situation.

The Bible clearly teaches the wonderful truth that God is a forgiving God. In Exodus 34:6-7, God described Himself to Moses as "the Lord, the Lord God, compassionate and gracious, slow to anger, and abounding in lovingkindness and truth; who keeps lovingkindness for thousands, who forgives iniquity, transgression and sin."

That theme runs throughout Scripture (cf. Pss. 32:1; 85:23; 130:3-4; Isa. 43:25; 55:7; Jer. 33:8; Eph. 1:7; Col. 1:14; 1 John 1:9; 2:12), but it is perhaps nowhere better illustrated than in the story of the prodigal son (Luke 15:11-32). A father had two sons, one of whom took his share of the inheritance and left home (vv. 11-12). After living a debauched life until his money ran out, the one son was forced to take a menial job (vv. 13-16). He finally came to his senses and exclaimed,

"How many of my father's hired men have more than enough bread, but I am dying here with hunger!" (v. 17). He decided to return to his father (v. 18), but apparently did not expect forgiveness. He hoped merely to be tolerated (v. 19). But the father did not wait for his sinning son to reach him. While his son was still a long ways away, he ran to him and embraced him (v. 20). Later, he threw a party to celebrate his son's return (vv. 22-24).

That story illustrates how God, represented in the story by the father, forgives: eagerly, totally, lavishly. We could say, in a sense, that God is never more like Himself than when He forgives.

There are two extremely important corollaries to that truth. If God is never more like Himself than when He forgives, man is never more like God than when he forgives. Proverbs 19:11 says, "A man's discretion makes him slow to anger, and it is his glory to overlook a transgression."

The second corollary is that God's forgiveness of us is based on our forgiveness of others. James wrote, "Judgment will be merciless to one who has shown no mercy" (James 2:13). Our Lord stated that truth positively in Matthew 5:7: "Blessed are the merciful, for they shall receive mercy." He taught His disciples to pray, "Forgive us our debts, as we also have forgiven our debtors" (Matt. 6:12). Then He warned, "If you forgive men for their transgressions, your heavenly Father will also forgive you. But if you do not forgive men, then your Father will not forgive your transgressions" (Matt. 6:14-15).

The forgiveness envisioned in the above-mentioned passages is not the complete and comprehensive forgiveness that accompanies the event of salvation, because that already is done. It is rather God's relational, continual forgiveness that accompanies the process of sanctification of believers. Paradoxically, Christians are already fully forgiven (cf. Eph. 1:7), but still need ongoing forgiveness (cf. 1 John 1:9). It is a sobering truth that believers will forfeit God's blessing and invite His chastening in their lives if they fail to forgive others. That Christians are to forgive each other, as God has forgiven them, is the underlying theme of Philemon.

AUTHORSHIP

At only two periods of church history has the Pauline authorship of Philemon been seriously questioned. Some, embroiled in the theological disputes of the fourth century, questioned its authorship because it contains no doctrine. They were countered by Jerome, Chrysostom, and Theodore of Mopseustia. Some of the radical nineteenth-century critics, having rejected the Pauline authorship of the other prison epistles, felt compelled to reject Philemon as well. Their reasoning, however, is entirely subjective and has no factual basis. In fact, the very lack of doctrinal content makes it difficult to imagine a motive for forgery. If someone were going to create a forgery, they would certainly be motivated by a desire to corrupt some doctrine of importance to the faith.

The late second-century Muratorian Fragment, the earliest extant list of New Testament books, includes Philemon. The church Fathers Tertullian and Eusebius accepted Philemon as genuine. Even the heretic Marcion, who rejected the pastoral epistles, accepted the Pauline authorship of Philemon. The book itself claims Paul as its author in three places (vv. 1, 9, 19). Not surprisingly, the Pauline authorship of Philemon is almost universally accepted today.

DATE AND PLACE OF WRITING

Philemon was written at the same time as Colossians, from Rome during Paul's first imprisonment. For a defense of the view that the prison epistles were written from Rome, not Caesarea or Ephesus, see the introduction to Colossians.

OCCASION

Philemon had been led to saving faith in Jesus Christ several years earlier by Paul, probably during the apostle's ministry in Ephesus. He had become a prominent member in the church at Colossae. Philemon was wealthy, owning a house large enough for the Colossian church to meet in (Philem. 2). He was obviously active in serving the cause of Christ, because Paul refers to him as a "fellow worker" (Philem. 1). He also owned at least one slave, a man named Onesimus (cf. Col. 4:9, which associates Onesimus with Colossae). Onesimus, who was not a Christian, ran away from his master to Rome. He no doubt hoped to lose himself in the multitudes that thronged the imperial city. While in Rome, through circumstances unknown to us, he met the apostle Paul. Perhaps he ran into Epaphras, who was also from Colossae. He may also have sought out Paul on his own. It is possible that he traveled to Ephesus with his master and met Paul during the apostle's ministry in that city. He certainly would have heard Philemon and his household speak lovingly of the great apostle. Whatever the circumstances by which he met Paul, his life was forever changed, for through that great preacher he met Jesus Christ.

Onesimus quickly endeared himself to the apostle (cf. Philem. 12, 16). He then began to live up to his name (Onesimus means "useful") by assisting Paul (Philem. 11, 13). Paul would have gladly kept him at his side to continue to minister to him. There was, however, a matter that needed to be settled. As a runaway slave, Onesimus was a criminal. In running away he had defrauded his master, Philemon, by depriving him of his services. He may even have stolen money from Philemon when he fled (Philem. 18). Paul knew that the relationship between Onesimus and Philemon needed to be restored. Onesimus had to return to his master and seek forgiveness and restoration.

To send Onesimus back alone would have exposed him to the danger of being caught by the ever-vigilant slave catchers. The opportunity to send him back with someone came when Paul finished his letters to the Colossians and Ephesians. Because Tychicus would be delivering those letters, Onesimus could return to Colossae with him in relative safety.

If returning Onesimus to his master was a sacrifice for Paul, it was a grave risk for Onesimus. "Roman law . . . practically imposed no limits to the power of the master over his slave. The alternative of life or death rested solely with Philemon, and slaves were constantly crucified for far lighter offenses than his. A thief and a runaway, he had no claim to forgiveness" (J. B. Lightfoot, *St. Paul's Epistles to the Colossians and to Philemon* [1879; reprint, Grand Rapids: Zondervan, 1959], p. 314). Runaway slaves could also be branded with an "F" (for *fugitivus*) on their heads, or beaten. A large percentage of the Empire's population was slaves, and the Romans lived in constant fear of a slave uprising. Although the last such uprising (the one led by Spartacus) had taken place over a century earlier, the Romans took no chances—they dealt harshly with runaway slaves. That Onesimus was willing to risk such punishment speaks of the genuineness of his faith.

Not content merely to send Onesimus back under the protection of Tychicus, Paul sends along a letter to Philemon. In that letter, he urges Philemon to forgive Onesimus and receive him as a new brother in Christ. Paul implores Philemon to put into practice the principle taught in Ephesians 4:32 and Colossians 3:13 and treat Onesimus as Christ treated him.

CHRISTIANITY AND SLAVERY

Slavery forms the backdrop to Philemon, and it is impossible to fully appreciate the book without some understanding of slavery in the Roman Empire.

Slavery was taken for granted as a normal part of life in the ancient world. Indeed, the whole structure of Roman society was based on it. "Slavery grew with the growth of the Roman state until it changed the economic basis of society, doing away with free labor, and transferring nearly all industries to the hands of slaves" (Marvin R. Vincent, *The Epistles to the Philippians and to Philemon*, International Critical Commentary [Edinburgh: T. & T. Clark, 1979], p. 162). During the period of the wars of conquest, most slaves were war captives. By the time of the New Testament, however, most slaves were born into slavery. The number of slaves was enormous, making up as much as one third of the population of the Empire.

Slaves were not actually considered persons under the law, but the chattel property of their owners. They could be sold, exchanged, given away, or seized to pay their master's debt. A slave had no legal right to marriage, and slave cohabitation was regulated by their masters. As already noted, masters had almost unlimited power to punish their slaves. The Roman writer Juvenal told of a wealthy woman who ordered the crucifixion of a slave and refused to give any reason except her own good pleasure.

By the New Testament era, however, slavery was changing. Treatment of slaves was improving, in part because masters came to realize that contented slaves worked better. Although not legally recognized as persons, slaves began to acquire some legal rights. In A.D. 20, the Roman senate decreed that slaves accused of crimes were to be tried in the same manner as free men (A. Rupprecht, "Slave, Slavery," in *The Zondervan Pictorial Encyclopedia of the Bible*, ed. Merrill C. Tenney [Grand Rapids: Zondervan, 1977], 5:459). In some cases, their wills were recognized as valid. They were often permitted to own property.

Slaves were often better off than freemen. They were assured of food, clothing, and shelter, while poor freemen often slept in the streets, or in cheap housing. Freemen had no job security and could lose their livelihood in times of economic duress. Many slaves ate and dressed as well as freemen.

Slaves could be doctors, musicians, teachers, artists, librarians, and accountants. It was not uncommon for a Roman to train a slave at his own trade. They had opportunities for education and training in almost all disciplines.

By the first century, freedom was a real possibility for many slaves. Owners often held out the hope of freedom to inspire their slaves to work better. Many shared deep friendships with their masters and were loved and cared for with generosity. Many slaves would not have taken their freedom if it had been offered because their employment was happy and beneficial. Slaves could also purchase their own freedom. Masters often designated in their wills that their slaves were to be freed or receive part of their estate after the master's death. Manumission was thus widespread. One study indicated that in the period 81-49 B.C., five hundred thousand slaves were freed (Rupprecht, 5:458). By the time of Augustus Caesar, so many slaves were being freed upon the death of their owners that a law had to be passed restricting that practice (Rupprecht, 5:459). Estimates of the average length of time a slave had to wait for his freedom range from seven to twenty years.

It is significant that the New Testament nowhere attacks slavery directly. Had Jesus and the apostles done so, the result would have been chaos. Any slave insurrection would have been brutally crushed, and the slaves massacred. The gospel would have been swallowed up by the message of social reform. Further, right relations between slaves and masters made it a workable social institution, if not an ideal one.

Christianity, however, sowed the seeds of the destruction of slavery. It would be destroyed not by social upheaval, but by changed hearts. The book of Philemon illustrates that principle. Paul does not order Philemon to free Onesimus, or teach that slavery is evil. But by ordering Philemon to treat Onesimus as a brother (Philem. 16; cf. Eph. 6:9; Col. 4:1), Paul eliminated the abuses of slavery. Marvin Vincent comments, "The principles of the gospel not only curtailed [slavery's] abuses, but destroyed the thing itself; for it could not exist without its abuses. To destroy its abuses was to destroy it" (Vincent, *Philemon*, p. 167).

One writer summed up the importance of Philemon in relation to slavery in these words:

> The Epistle brings into vivid focus the whole problem of slavery in the Christian Church. There is no thought of denunciation even in principle. The apostle deals with the situation as it then exists. He takes it for granted that Philemon has a claim of ownership on Onesimus and leaves the position unchallenged. Yet in one significant phrase Paul transforms the character of the master-slave relationship. Onesimus is returning no longer as a slave but as a brother beloved (verse 16). It is clearly incongruous for a Christian master to "own" a brother in Christ in the contemporary sense of the word, and although the existing order of society could not be immediately changed by Christianity without a political revolution (which was clearly contrary to Christian principles), the Christian master-slave relationship was so transformed from within that it was bound to lead ultimately to the abolition of the system. (Donald Guthrie, *New Testament Introduction* [Downers Grove, Ill.: InterVarsity, 1970], p. 640)

OUTLINE

Introduction (vv. 1-3)
The Spiritual Character of One Who Forgives (vv. 4-7)
The Spiritual Action of One Who Forgives (vv. 8-18)
The Spiritual Motivation of One Who Forgives (vv. 19-25)

The Spiritual Character of One Who Forgives

17

Paul, a prisoner of Christ Jesus, and Timothy our brother, to Philemon our beloved brother and fellow worker, and to Apphia our sister, and to Archippus our fellow soldier, and to the church in your house: Grace to you and peace from God our Father and the Lord Jesus Christ. I thank my God always, making mention of you in my prayers, because I hear of your love, and of the faith which you have toward the Lord Jesus, and toward all the saints; and I pray that the fellowship of your faith may become effective through the knowledge of every good thing which is in you for Christ's sake. For I have come to have much joy and comfort in your love, because the hearts of the saints have been refreshed through you, brother. (1-7)

We live in an ego-centered, selfish society that knows and cares little about forgiveness. We have become so decadent and non-Christian as to see forgiving people as weak, and unforgiving ones as strong. Our culture celebrates and exalts those TV and movie heroes who take vengeance on others. Pop psychologists write books extolling the virtues of blameshifting, unforgiveness, and making those who offend us pay. The result is a society filled with bitterness, vengeance, anger, hate, and hostility. Retaliatory crimes and lawsuits are rampantly common-place as people seek vengeance either outside or inside the bounds of the law. Further, lack of forgiveness is perhaps the leading cause of the breakups in family relationships.

For a Christian, unwillingness to forgive is unthinkable. It is a re-bellious, blatant, open act of disobedience to God. We are to forgive others as God has forgiven us (Eph. 4:32; Col. 3:13). Failure to do so will bring at least four unpleasant results. First, failure to forgive will impris-on believers in their past. Unforgiveness keeps the pain alive. Unforgive-ness keeps the sore open; it never allows the wound to heal. Dwelling on the wrong done feeds anger and resentment and robs one of the joy of living. Forgiveness, on the other hand, opens the prison doors and sets the believer free from the past.

Second, unforgiveness produces bitterness. The longer believ-ers dwell on offenses committed against them, the more bitter they be-come. Bitterness is not just a sin; it is an infection. The writer of Hebrews warns, "See to it that no one comes short of the grace of God; that no root of bitterness springing up causes trouble, and by it many be defiled" (Heb. 12:15). A bitter person's speech is cutting, sarcastic, even slanderous. Bitterness distorts a person's whole outlook on life, produc-ing violent emotions, intolerance, and thoughts of revenge. It is espe-cially devastating to the marriage relationship. Bitterness shuts off the affection and kindness that should exist between the partners. The root of bitterness and unforgiveness all too often produces the weed of di-vorce. Forgiveness, on the other hand, replaces bitterness with love, joy, peace, and the other fruits of the Spirit (cf. Gal. 5:22-23).

Third, unforgiveness gives Satan an open door. Paul warns be-lievers in Ephesians 4:26-27, "Be angry, and yet do not sin; do not let the sun go down on your anger, and do not give the devil an opportunity." To the Corinthians he wrote, "Whom you forgive anything, I forgive also; for indeed what I have forgiven, if I have forgiven anything, I did it for your sakes in the presence of Christ, in order that no advantage be taken of us by Satan; for we are not ignorant of his schemes" (2 Cor. 2:10-11). It is no exaggeration to say that most of the ground Satan gains in our lives is due to unforgiveness. (If love fulfills the law toward others [Rom. 13:8], lack of love violates it. Unforgiveness is lack of love.) Forgiveness bars that avenue of demonic attack.

Fourth, unforgiveness hinders fellowship with God. Our Lord solemnly warned, "If you forgive men for their transgressions, your heavenly Father will also forgive you. But if you do not forgive men, then your Father will not forgive your transgressions" (Matt. 6:14-15). As not-ed in the introduction, that passage speaks not of the completed, past forgiveness of salvation, but of ongoing relational forgiveness between believers and the Father. It is a serious matter nonetheless to know that one cannot be right with God if he is unforgiving of others. Forgiveness restores the believer to the place of maximum blessing from God. It restores the purity and joy of fellowship with God.

The importance of forgiveness is a constant theme of Scripture. There are no less than seventy-five different word pictures about forgiveness in the Bible. They help us grasp the importance, the nature, and the effects of forgiveness.

- To forgive is to turn the key, open the cell door, and let the prisoner walk free.
- To forgive is to write in large letters across a debt, "Nothing owed."
- To forgive is to pound the gavel in a courtroom and declare, "Not guilty!"
- To forgive is to shoot an arrow so high and so far that it can never be found again.
- To forgive is to bundle up all the garbage and trash and dispose of it, leaving the house clean and fresh.
- To forgive is to loose the moorings of a ship and release it to the open sea.
- To forgive is to grant a full pardon to a condemned criminal.
- To forgive is to relax a stranglehold on a wrestling opponent.
- To forgive is to sandblast a wall of graffiti, leaving it looking like new.
- To forgive is to smash a clay pot into a thousand pieces so it can never be pieced together again. (John Nieder and Thomas Thompson, *Forgive and Love Again* [Eugene, Oreg.: Harvest House, 1991], p. 48)

Forgiveness is so important that the Holy Spirit devoted an entire book of the Bible to it. In the brief book of Philemon, the spiritual duty to forgive is emphasized, but not in principle, parable, or word picture. Through a real life situation involving two people dear to him, Paul teaches the importance of forgiving others. Following the introduction in verses 1-3, Paul describes the spiritual character of one who forgives in verses 4-7. Such a person has a concern for the Lord, a concern for people, a concern for fellowship, a concern for knowledge, a concern for glory, and a concern to be a blessing.

INTRODUCTION

Paul, a prisoner of Christ Jesus, and Timothy our brother, to Philemon our beloved brother and fellow worker, and to Apphia our sister, and to Archippus our fellow soldier, and to the church in your house: Grace to you and peace from God our Father and the Lord Jesus Christ. (1-3)

Paul starts the letter with his name, following the customary practice in the ancient world. Philemon's heart must have skipped a beat as soon as he saw who the letter was from. Paul was the noble apostle largely responsible for the spread of Christianity throughout the Greco-Roman world. He was also the one who had led Philemon to Christ (v. 19). So, from the view of both his vast influence and his personal touch in Philemon's life, the name would compel Philemon to read on eagerly. What a privilege—to have a letter from Paul, an inspired letter. Only Timothy and Titus were also so privileged.

Paul describes himself as **a prisoner of Christ Jesus.** He does not begin any of his other letters with that description. Paul usually begins by stressing his apostleship and thus emphasizing his authority. That is true even of the pastoral epistles. Although they, like Philemon, were addressed to individuals, they dealt with issues relating to the church, and so carried a tone of authority. In this letter, however, Paul chooses not to use his authority (cf. vv. 8-9), but rather to appeal gently and singularly to a friend.

Although imprisoned by Rome, Paul viewed himself as a prisoner of **Christ Jesus** (cf. Eph. 3:1; 4:1; 6:19-20; Phil. 1:13; Col. 4:3). It was for the sake of Christ and through the will of Christ that he was a prisoner. By mentioning his imprisonment, Paul makes a subtle appeal to Philemon. He sets up his case by saying in effect, "If I can face the harder task of being in prison, can you not do the easier one that I'm going to ask of you?" Philemon knew all that Paul had suffered for the cause of Christ. That knowledge was bound to have an effect on his willingness to do what Paul asked of him.

Timothy was not the coauthor of Philemon, but was with Paul when he wrote the letter. Paul describes him as **our brother** because Philemon knew him. Timothy had been with Paul in Ephesus, where Philemon probably met him. Unlike the rest of his companions, Paul mentions Timothy at the beginning of the letter. The frequent mention of Timothy at the beginning of his letters (cf. 2 Cor. 1:1; Phil. 1:1; Col. 1:1; 1 Thess. 1:1; 2 Thess. 1:1) identifies him more closely with Paul in ministry. Paul knew that someday he would even pass the baton of spiritual leadership to him. He wanted Timothy to be recognized as a leader and his heir apparent.

As noted in the introduction, **Philemon** was a wealthy member of the Colossian church. The Colossian church met in his house, and he was active in Christian service. *Agapētos* (**beloved**) is a familiar description, used by Paul of both individuals and groups (cf. Rom. 1:7; 16:5, 8-9, 12; 1 Cor. 10:14; Phil. 2:12). **Fellow worker** is from *sunergos*, a term used by Paul for those who had worked alongside him in the cause of Christ (cf. Rom. 16:3; 2 Cor. 8:23; Phil. 2:25; Col. 4:11). Because Paul had never visited Colossae (Col. 2:1), their friendship probably developed during Paul's ministry in Ephesus. In this letter, Paul puts that friendship on the line for the sake of the spiritual principle of forgiveness and reconciling Philemon and Onesimus.

The letter is also addressed to **Apphia,** no doubt Philemon's wife, and **Archippus,** who was most likely their son. Paul describes Archippus as a **fellow soldier** (cf. 2 Tim. 2:3), which shows he was also actively involved in the ministry (cf. Col. 4:17). He may have served both the Laodicean and Colossian churches.

Also named in the address is **the church** that met **in** Philemon's **house.** First-century churches met in homes, church buildings being unknown until the third century. The oldest known church was found at Dura Europos, on the bank of the Euphrates River in the Syrian desert. It dates from the first half of the third century, and had been made by joining two rooms of a house and building a platform (E. M. Blaiklock, "Dura Europos," in *The New International Dictionary of Biblical Archaeology*, ed. E. M. Blaiklock and R. K. Harrison [Grand Rapids: Zondervan, 1983], p. 165). Although Philemon was a private letter, Paul wanted it read to the church. They would then understand the importance of forgiveness and could hold Philemon accountable.

Grace to you and peace from God our Father and the Lord Jesus Christ is Paul's standard greeting. It appears in all thirteen of his epistles (cf. Rom. 1:7; 1 Cor. 1:3; 2 Cor. 1:2; Gal. 1:3; Eph. 1:2; Phil. 1:2; Col. 1:2; 1 Thess. 1:1; 2 Thess. 1:2; 1 Tim. 1:2; 2 Tim. 1:2; Titus 1:4). **Grace** is the means of salvation, **peace** its result. The linking of **God our Father** and **the Lord Jesus Christ** as joint sources of grace and peace would be blasphemous if Jesus were a mere man or angel. That phrase is to be understood as an affirmation of the deity of Christ, His equality with God.

A CONCERN FOR THE LORD

I thank my God always, making mention of you in my prayers, because I hear of . . . the faith which you have toward the Lord Jesus, (4-5*a*)

Paul begins the main body of his letter by praising Philemon. It was not Paul's intent to flatter him. Rather, the apostle knew that legitimate praise feeds virtue and provides an antidote for sin. The virtuous character of Philemon becomes the foundation upon which Paul bases his appeal for him to forgive Onesimus.

Paul knew firsthand of Philemon's character, having been God's chosen tool to bring him to Christ and having worked with him. Epaphras, Philemon's pastor at Colossae, was with Paul in Rome (v. 23). He, too, could testify about Philemon, as could Onesimus. That combined testimony to Philemon caused Paul to say to him, **I thank my God always, making mention of you in my prayers.** Paul was always able to give thanks to God when he prayed for Philemon; he knew nothing negative about him. The book of Philemon bears that out. Paul does not correct Philemon, and there is no suggestion that anything was amiss in his life. Everything Paul heard about Philemon was good. There is no threatening language that might assume Paul felt forgiving Onesimus would be difficult for Philemon, but rather a spirit that expected he would.

The first characteristic of one who forgives is a concern for the Lord. Paul had heard of **the faith which** Philemon had **toward the Lord Jesus.** As a genuine believer, Philemon was concerned about the Lord and desired to please Him. Because the Lord had forgiven him, Philemon could forgive others. Conviction from the indwelling Holy Spirit and from the Word of God would also provide the impetus for Philemon to do what was right. The present tense of *echō* (**you have**) demonstrates the continuous nature of Philemon's concern for the Lord. His unwavering faith gave Paul confidence in his willingness to forgive.

Christians forgive because they are reconciled to Jesus Christ. Unbelievers do not have that capacity. Paul points that out in Romans 3:10-16:

> As it is written, "There is none righteous, not even one; there is none who understands, there is none who seeks for God; all have turned aside, together they have become useless; there is none who does good, there is not even one. Their throat is an open grave, with their tongues they keep deceiving, the poison of asps is under their lips; whose mouth is full of cursing and bitterness; their feet are swift to shed blood, destruction and misery are in their paths."

Those controlled by bitterness will find it difficult to forgive.

A CONCERN FOR PEOPLE

because I hear of your love . . . toward all the saints; (5b)

This verse exhibits a chiastic construction in the Greek text. The first part of the verse, **love,** goes with the last phrase, **toward all the saints.**

Agapē **(love)** is the love of will and choice, of self-sacrifice and humility. Love is a fruit of the Spirit (Gal. 5:22) and a manifestation of genuine saving faith (Gal. 5:6; 1 John 3:14). Believers should not need to be taught this love (1 Thess. 4:9) because its source is already in them in the indwelling Holy Spirit (Rom. 5:5).

Because Philemon's faith was real, it manifested itself in true biblical love. That love expressed itself in a concern for people. Philemon's concern for people gave him the ability to forgive.

A CONCERN FOR FELLOWSHIP

and I pray that the fellowship of your faith may become effective (6a)

Real faith and love will inevitably result in a concern for fellowship. There is no place in the Body of Christ for an individualism that does not care about others. That concern for fellowship was also motivation for Philemon to forgive Onesimus. Failing to do so would lead to a rift in the fellowship since Onesimus was now also a believer. By forgiving Onesimus, Philemon would maintain the harmony, peace, and unity of the Colossian church.

Koinōnia **(fellowship)** is difficult to render precisely in English. It is usually translated "fellowship," but it means much more than merely enjoying each other's company. It refers to a mutual sharing of all life, and could be translated "belonging." Believers belong to each other in a mutual partnership, produced by their **faith** in Christ. By forgiving him, Philemon would acknowledge that he belonged to Onesimus as a brother in Christ. **Effective** translates *energēs*, which literally means "powerful." Such an act of forgiveness would send a powerful message to the church about the importance of fellowship, even among slaves and masters (cf. Gal. 3:28). Forgiving a fellow believer, no matter what their offense, makes a strong statement of concern for fellowship.

A Concern for Knowledge

through the knowledge of every good thing which is in you (6*b*)

Christians have been blessed "with every spiritual blessing in the heavenly places in Christ" (Eph. 1:3). They have a new nature within them (2 Cor. 5:17). How was Philemon to discover **every good thing which** was in him? *Epignōsis* (**knowledge**) refers to deep, rich, full, experiential knowledge. It is the knowledge that comes through personal acquaintance with the truth. Philemon could read of forgiveness, or hear a sermon about it. But until he forgave, he could have no experiential knowledge of it. By forgiving Onesimus, Philemon would experience that good thing in him known as forgiveness. By walking in obedience to God's will, believers experience the good things God has placed within them.

There is a vast difference between reading a book on skiing and actually skiing. There is a certain flat, one-dimensional knowledge to be gained from a book, but it cannot compare to experiencing the exhilaration of a downhill run. The same thing is true in the spiritual realm. It is thrilling to grasp a truth from Scripture intellectually. But it is far more exciting to live that truth out in practice. Practicing the truths of Scripture leads to the *epignōsis* that brings spiritual maturity (cf. Eph. 4:12-13). It is wonderful to understand what it means to trust God, but more wonderful to experience His power in the times when we trusted Him with no strength of our own.

Paul is confident that Philemon will want to experience a true knowledge of forgiveness by forgiving Onesimus. He gives both Philemon and us a gentle reminder of the importance of a concern for knowledge.

A Concern for Glory

for Christ's sake. (6*c*)

The Christian life, with all its joys, duties, and responsibilities, is **for Christ's sake.** The Greek text literally reads, "unto Christ." The goal of everything believers do should be the glory of Christ (cf. 1 Cor. 10:31). Someone devoted to Christ's glory would certainly forgive another, as an unforgiving spirit does not glorify Christ. Paul was confident that Philemon would forgive Onesimus because he knew of Philemon's great concern to glorify Christ.

A Concern to Be a Blessing

For I have come to have much joy and comfort in your love, because the hearts of the saints have been refreshed through you, brother. (7)

Philemon had a reputation for **love,** a fact that brought Paul **much joy and comfort.** Through Philemon, **the hearts of the saints** had **been refreshed. Hearts** translates *splanchna*, which literally means "bowels." It refers to the seat of the feelings. People struggling, suffering, and hurting emotionally, had been **refreshed** by Philemon. **Refreshed** is from *anapauō*, a military term that speaks of an army resting from a march. Philemon brought troubled people rest and renewal; he was a peacemaker.

Philemon, as far as we know, was not an elder, deacon, or teacher in the church. Most likely, he was a businessman. But he was a man of instinctive kindness, a source of blessing to everyone. That kind of person, Paul knew, could be counted on to forgive.

The following poem, entitled "The Toys," by Coventry Patmore, a nineteenth-century English poet (cited in *Masterpieces of Religious Verse*, ed. James Dalton Morrison [New York: Harper & Bros., 1948], p. 342), is a reminder of the simple qualities of forgiveness:

> My little Son, who look'd from thoughtful eyes
> And moved and spoke in quiet grown-up wise,
> Having my law the seventh time disobey'd,
> I struck him, and dismiss'd
> With hard words and unkiss'd,
> —His Mother, who was patient, being dead.
> Then, fearing lest his grief should hinder sleep,
> I visited his bed,
> But found him slumbering deep,
> With darken'd eyelids, and their lashes yet
> From his late sobbing wet.
> And I, with moan,
> Kissing away his tears, left others of my own;
> For, on a table drawn beside his head,
> He had put, within his reach,
> A box of [tokens] and a red-vein'd stone,
> A piece of glass abraded by the beach
> And six or seven shells,
> A bottle with bluebells,
> And two French copper coins, ranged there
>   with careful art,
> To comfort his sad heart.

So when that night I pray'd
To God, I wept and said:
Ah, when at last we lie with [tranquil] breath,
Not vexing Thee in death,
And Thou rememberest of what toys
We made our joys,
How weakly understood
Thy great commanded good,
Then, fatherly not less
Than I whom Thou hast moulded from the
    clay,
Thou'lt leave Thy wrath, and say,
"I [forgive] their childishness."

If God can so tenderly forgive us, can we not, like Philemon, have the character that forgives others?

The Actions of
One Who Forgives

18

Therefore, though I have enough confidence in Christ to order you to do that which is proper, yet for love's sake I rather appeal to you—since I am such a person as Paul, the aged, and now also a prisoner of Christ Jesus—I appeal to you for my child, whom I have begotten in my imprisonment, Onesimus, who formerly was useless to you, but now is useful both to you and to me. And I have sent him back to you in person, that is, sending my very heart, whom I wished to keep with me, that in your behalf he might minister to me in my imprisonment for the gospel; but without your consent I did not want to do anything, that your goodness should not be as it were by compulsion, but of your own free will. For perhaps he was for this reason parted from you for a while, that you should have him back forever, no longer as a slave, but more than a slave, a beloved brother, especially to me, but how much more to you, both in the flesh and in the Lord. If then you regard me a partner, accept him as you would me. But if he has wronged you in any way, or owes you anything, charge that to my account; (8-18)

Although it is the theme of the letter to Philemon, the word *forgiveness* does not appear in the book. Neither does the articulation of any doctrinal principles that would provide the theological foundation for forgiveness. Paul does not appeal to law or principle but to love (v. 9). He could do that since he knew Philemon to be a godly, spiritually mature man whose heart was right with God.

Paul surely assumed that Philemon knew the biblical principles that lead Christians to forgive. Unfortunately, I cannot assume that all Christians have that knowledge, so it is important to note eight foundational elements of a biblical doctrine of forgiveness.

First, it is not merely murder that is forbidden by the sixth commandment, "You shall not murder" (Ex. 20:13), but also anger and lack of forgiveness. Jesus gave the deeper meaning of that command in Matthew 5:21-22: "You have heard that the ancients were told, 'You shall not commit murder' and 'Whoever commits murder shall be liable to the court.' But I say to you that everyone who is angry with his brother shall be guilty before the court; and whoever shall say to his brother, 'Raca,' shall be guilty before the supreme court; and whoever shall say, 'You fool,' shall be guilty enough to go into the fiery hell." When God gave the commandment not to murder, He also forbad hate, malice, anger, vengeance, and lack of forgiveness toward anyone. How are those negative attitudes to be dealt with? One must first remember that those who need forgiveness are created by God. Believers have the life of God indwelling them, while even unbelievers are at least created in His image. We are to love and forgive people for that image of God that is in them. Seeing people as created in God's image should replace lack of forgiveness with reverence.

Another way to deal with negative attitudes is to remember Jesus' words in Matthew 22:39: "You shall love your neighbor as yourself." We find ourselves eminently worthy of forgiveness, and have a hard time understanding why others would not forgive us. We are quick to forgive and excuse ourselves. It is utter selfishness to fail to extend that same forgiveness to others. Selfishness also causes us to exaggerate the faults of those who offend us. Humble, unselfish people, in contrast, do not see offenses against themselves as significant.

Second, whoever offends us gives greater offense to God. All sin is ultimately against God. When David committed adultery with Bathsheba, he sinned against her, her husband, his own family, and the nation. Yet in Psalm 51:4 he cried out to God, "Against Thee, Thee only, I have sinned, and done what is evil in Thy sight." Whatever his offense against men, he gave a greater offense to God. God has forgiven those who wrong us of the greater offense of sinning against Him. Can we not forgive them of the lesser one of offending us? We are not more just, holy, or deserving than God, nor are we a higher court with a higher law.

No one could ever offend us the way we have offended God. Yet He graciously, mercifully forgives us. Believers who fail to forgive others are like the wicked slave of Jesus' parable in Matthew 18. Although forgiven a huge, unpayable debt by the king, that evil man refused to forgive another slave of a small, insignificant debt. There is no comparison between other people's offenses against us and our offenses against God.

Third, Christians who fail to forgive others will not enjoy forgiveness from God. Jesus said in Matthew 6:14-15, "If you forgive men for their transgressions, your heavenly Father will also forgive you. But if you do not forgive men, then your Father will not forgive your transgressions." Failing to forgive others hinders our fellowship with God and puts us in danger of His chastening. That is too high a price to pay for wickedly enjoying a lack of forgiveness.

Fourth, believers who manifest an unforgiving spirit will not enjoy the fellowship, communion, and love of other saints. In the parable of Matthew 18, it was the unforgiving slave's fellow slaves who reported him to his lord (Matt. 18:31). That is a picture of church discipline. An unforgiving attitude will destroy a believer's relationships with his fellow believers. They will then, through church discipline, ask God to bring chastening into his life. Unforgiveness not only hinders our relationship with God, but also with other Christians.

Fifth, by refusing to forgive others and seeking our own revenge, we usurp the authority of God. Paul urged believers to "bless those who persecute you; bless and curse not. Never take your own revenge, beloved, but leave room for the wrath of God, for it is written, 'Vengeance is Mine, I will repay,' says the Lord" (Rom. 12:14, 19). By failing to forgive, believers presume to take the sword of divine judgment out of God's hand and wield it themselves. Such an attitude implies that God is unjust, indifferent, or unable to judge, all of which is blasphemous.

God is far more able to deal with offenses against us than we are. He has a complete understanding of the situation, while our understanding is limited. He has the supreme authority; we have none. He is impartial and just; we are partial to our own selfish interests. He is omniscient and eternal, seeing how everything will turn out. We are shortsighted and ignorant, seeing nothing beyond the moment. He is wise and good, and does everything for righteous purposes. We are often blinded by our anger, and our purposes may be evil. We must, then, leave vengeance to God.

Sixth, an unforgiving spirit makes believers unfit for worship. In the Sermon on the Mount, our Lord said, "If therefore you are presenting your offering at the altar, and there remember that your brother has something against you, leave your offering there before the altar, and go your way; first be reconciled to your brother, and then come and present your offering" (Matt. 5:23-24).

It should be noted that reconciliation, forgiveness, and restoration can and should be initiated by either party. Maybe the one who has something against you has not asked for forgiveness and is enjoying his bitterness. Go and offer forgiveness anyway. Seek reconciliation. Maybe you have offended him and never asked forgiveness. Go and ask.

Unforgiveness makes Christians unfit for fellowship not only with other believers, but also with God. Worshiping God, though living in an unrestored relationship with another believer, is hypocrisy.

Seventh, the injuries and offenses believers suffer are their trials and temptations. Jesus said, "Love your enemies, and pray for those who persecute you in order that you may be sons of your Father who is in heaven" (Matt. 5:44-45). If we obey that command and forgive those who offend us, their offense becomes a trial. It will produce growth and strength in our lives. If we disobey and refuse to forgive, it becomes a temptation resulting in sin. We should be little concerned about the actions of others against us. We should be greatly concerned that our response makes them a trial and not a temptation.

Eighth, forgiveness should be given even if it is not sought. Our Lord said, "Father, forgive them," asking forgiveness for those who did not even seek it. Stephen asked the Lord to forgive those who were murdering him, though they had not asked for it. Though the relationship will never be restored until the offending person desires forgiveness, still we are not to hold a grudge, but forgive from the heart and be free from any bitterness—showing only love and mercy.

Therefore links the introduction with the main body of the letter. Because Philemon understood the doctrinal foundation of forgiveness, Paul does not reiterate it. And though Paul had **enough confidence** in his apostolic authority **in Christ to order** Philemon **to do that which is proper,** he did not. Instead, he appealed to him to do what is right **for love's sake.**

Paul loved Philemon. In verse 1, he called him *agapētos*, "beloved." In verse 7 he wrote, "I have come to have much joy and comfort in your love." Such was the bond of love between the two men that Paul did not need to command Philemon. Paul knew that he was motivated by love (cf. vv. 4-7). Such love, being the fulfillment of the law (Rom. 13:10), compels one to do **that which is proper.** Hence it was unnecessary for Paul to use his apostolic authority.

Despite Philemon's spiritual maturity and deep love for Paul, the apostle knew it would be humanly difficult for him to forgive Onesimus. As Philemon read this letter, Onesimus was no doubt standing there in front of him. As he viewed his runaway slave, who had caused him so much trouble, he may have struggled to control his emotions. To help

Philemon overcome any feelings of anger and hostility, Paul includes two statements about himself. He thereby hopes to persuade Philemon to grant his appeal for Onesimus. That appeal comes from **such a person as Paul, the aged, and now also a prisoner of Jesus Christ.** *Presbutēs* (**aged**) differs in only one letter from *presbeutēs* ("ambassador"), which was sometimes spelled *presbutēs.* Because of that, some commentators have argued that *presbutēs* here should be translated "ambassador" (cf. Eph. 6:20). Such a translation, however, seems out of place in this context. Paul has just declined to use his apostolic authority. It is difficult to see why he would then reverse himself and allude to it.

Though Paul was now about sixty—an old man in that era of shorter life spans—he may not have been much older than Philemon, who had a grown son in the ministry. But **aged** in relation to Paul meant more than chronological age. Paul was older than his years. In his case the aging process had been accelerated by all that he had suffered (cf. 2 Cor. 11:23-30). The years of imprisonments, beatings, poor food, illnesses, difficult journeys, persecution, and concern for the churches had taken their toll. He had packed five lifetimes into his threescore years. All that was bound up in Paul's description of himself as **the aged.** It should cause Philemon to respond in sympathy and love for the valiant old warrior who had led him to Christ.

If that were not enough to elicit Philemon's sympathy, Paul rattles his chains again. He reminds Philemon that he is **a prisoner of Christ Jesus.** Philemon could not possibly turn down a request from a man in such honorable suffering.

Beginning in verse 10, Paul moves into the specifics of his request. In verses 10-18 he describes three actions that one who forgives must take. Forgiveness involves reception, restoration, and restitution.

RECEPTION

I appeal to you for my child, whom I have begotten in my imprisonment, Onesimus, who formerly was useless to you, but now is useful both to you and to me. And I have sent him back to you in person, that is, sending my very heart, whom I wished to keep with me, that in your behalf he might minister to me in my imprisonment for the gospel; but without your consent I did not want to do anything, that your goodness should not be as it were by compulsion, but of your own free will. (10-14)

Reception is the first step in the process of forgiveness. It entails opening up one's life and taking back the person who offended. Philemon needed to receive this slave back into his life, because Onesimus did seek forgiveness, as shown by three things that were true of him.

First, he was repentant. The very fact that Onesimus was standing there as Philemon read the letter proved his repentant attitude. He returned to face the master he had wronged and who had the power to punish him severely. Before he ever verbally repented, Onesimus demonstrated the fruit of genuine repentance (cf. Matt. 3:8). Paul appeals for his **child** in the faith, **begotten** in his **imprisonment,** who now seeks restoration with the one he had wronged. The former fugitive is now Paul's spiritual offspring, like Timothy, Titus, and Philemon himself. His repentance shows the genuineness of his faith.

Second, Onesimus was transformed. Philemon was not getting back the same man he had lost. He who **formerly was useless** had been radically changed by the grace of God. He **now is useful** both to Paul and Philemon. He was ready to serve Philemon "with sincerity of heart, fearing the Lord" (Col. 3:22). In verse 11, Paul engages in a play on words. Onesimus was a common slave name meaning "useful." Paul says, in effect, "Useful formerly was useless, but now is useful." He was a different man, as Paul had already found out and Philemon would shortly.

Third, Onesimus was proven faithful. So useful had he become to Paul that sending him **back to** Philemon was like **sending** Paul's **very heart.** As in verse 7, **heart** translates *splanchna*, which literally means "bowels," the location of feelings. Paul's feelings ran deep for this fugitive Phrygian slave. He had taken him in and found him to be a great man to know and love. Paul knew Philemon would find him the same, if he would take him back.

So helpful had Onesimus become to Paul that the apostle **wished to keep** him at his side. In Rome, Onesimus could on Philemon's **behalf . . . minister to** Paul **in** his **imprisonment for the gospel.** Paul affirms once again the gracious, loving character of Philemon. He knew Philemon would have loved to have been there in person to minister to him. Having his slave Onesimus there would have been the next best thing. Paul assumes that is what Philemon would want, but would not presume on that nor leave the relationship between the two men unresolved for some personal gain of his own. **Without** Philemon's **consent,** Paul **did not want to do anything.** Paul did not wish to presume on their friendship, and Onesimus and Philemon needed to meet. Further, he did not want Philemon's **goodness** to be **by compulsion,** but of his **own free will.** Paul did not want to force Philemon to do anything. He wanted him to make the choice to do good by his own will. More than that, Paul wanted Philemon to observe the transformation and value of Onesimus first hand.

RESTORATION

For perhaps he was for this reason parted from you for a while, that you should have him back forever, no longer as a slave, but more than a slave, a beloved brother, especially to me, but how much more to you, both in the flesh and in the Lord. (15-16)

Paul asks Philemon not only to welcome Onesimus back, but to restore him to service. While not intending to mitigate the guilt of Onesimus, Paul suggests that God's providence was at work. He tells Philemon that **perhaps he was for this reason parted from you for a while that you should have him back forever,** as a believer sharing the same eternal life. He says **perhaps** because no man can see the secret providence of God at work. But it is surely reasonable to assume that God had this in mind when Onesimus left. Paul suggests to Philemon that God was using this evil to produce good (cf. Gen. 50:20; Rom. 8:28). God triumphs over sin through His providential power and grace. He takes the myriad contingencies of human actions and uses them to accomplish His own purposes. Onesimus's being **parted** from Philemon **for a while** resulted in his having **him back forever.**

Onesimus left a slave, but returned **no longer as a slave, but more than a slave, a beloved brother.** Paul does not call here for Onesimus's emancipation (cf. 1 Cor. 7:20-22). He urges Philemon to receive Onesimus not merely as a slave, but as **a beloved brother.** He had already become that to Paul. **How much more** could Philemon now enjoy fellowship with Onesimus **both in the flesh,** as they worked together, **and in the Lord,** as they worshiped and ministered together. Paul enjoyed a relationship with Onesimus as a partner in Christ. Philemon enjoyed that relationship as well as one in the flesh, that of master and slave. He was doubly blessed. He received Onesimus's physical service as a slave, and his spiritual service as a fellow believer in Christ.

RESTITUTION

If then you regard me a partner, accept him as you would me. But if he has wronged you in any way, or owes you anything, charge that to my account; (17-18)

Philemon had been wronged by Onesimus's flight. Not knowing if Onesimus would return, Philemon may have had to purchase a replacement for him. Further, it seems likely that Onesimus took money or possessions from Philemon to finance his flight. The Bible teaches clearly that restitution needs to be made in such cases (cf. Num. 5:6-8).

Onesimus could not possibly pay back all he owed Philemon. He probably had not found a job in Rome and Colossians implies he spent most of his time serving Paul. Paul deals with the issue of restitution by asking Philemon to **accept him as you would me.** Philemon undoubtedly regarded Paul as a *koinōnon* (**partner**), and Paul urges him to welcome back Onesimus as he would the apostle himself.

Restitution is an essential component of forgiveness, and it would have been right for Philemon to demand it of Onesimus. It is not wrong, however, to be gracious. It would have been a wonderful, loving, gracious act on Philemon's part to forgive the debt altogether. But once again, Paul desires that Philemon be under no compulsion to do that. Accordingly, he writes, **but if he has wronged you in any way, or owes you anything, charge that to my account.** By offering to make good Onesimus's debt, Paul removes any pressure Philemon may have felt.

Paul's willingness to meet Onesimus's debt to restore his relationship with Philemon is a marvelous picture of Christ's work. Philemon, like God, had been wronged. Onesimus, like the sinner, stood in need of reconciliation. Paul offered to pay the price to bring about that reconciliation. That is the same role Jesus plays in the relationship between the sinner and God. Paul, like Christ, was willing to pay the price of reconciliation.

Never are we more like God than when we forgive. Never are we more like Christ than when we pay someone else's debt so that reconciliation can take place. Paul's willingness to suffer the temporal consequences of Onesimus's sin mirrors Christ's willingness to suffer the eternal consequences of our sin.

Although the Bible does not record what Philemon did, he no doubt freely forgave Onesimus and charged nothing to Paul. In light of Christ's forgiveness of him, and Paul's appeal, he could do no less.

The Motives of One Who Forgives

19

I, Paul, am writing this with my own hand, I will repay it (lest I should mention to you that you owe to me even your own self as well). Yes, brother, let me benefit from you in the Lord; refresh my heart in Christ. Having confidence in your obedience, I write to you, since I know that you will do even more than what I say. And at the same time also prepare me a lodging; for I hope that through your prayers I shall be given to you. Epaphras, my fellow prisoner in Christ Jesus, greets you, as do Mark, Aristarchus, Demas, Luke, my fellow workers. The grace of the Lord Jesus Christ be with your spirit. (19-25)

Sir Thomas More, Lord Chancellor of England under Henry VIII, spoke the following words to the judges who had unjustly condemned him to death: "As the blessed apostle St. Paul . . .consented to the death of St. Stephen, and kept their clothes that stoned him to death, and yet be they now both twain holy saints in Heaven, and shall continue there friends for ever, so I verily trust, and shall therefore right heartily pray, that though your Lordships have now here in earth been judges to my condemnation, we may yet hereafter in Heaven merrily all meet together, to our everlasting salvation" (cited in R. W. Chambers, *Thomas More*

225

[London: Bedford Historical Series, 1938], p. 342). More's statement exhibits the beauty of forgiveness. So also do the words of Stephen, "Lord, do not hold this sin against them!" (Acts 7:60), and of our Lord, "Father, forgive them; for they do not know what they are doing" (Luke 23:34).

As he closes his letter to Philemon, Paul gives insight into the motives for forgiveness. His gracious but pregnant words are meant to be the final push to move the heart of Philemon to forgive Onesimus. Each of his remarks contains the embryo of a truth that should motivate us to forgive as well. In this passage, we can discern six motives for forgiving others: the recognition of an unpayable debt, the possibility of being a blessing, the necessity of obedience, the acknowledgment of accountability, the importance of maintaining fellowship, and the requirement of grace.

THE RECOGNITION OF AN UNPAYABLE DEBT

I, Paul, am writing this with my own hand, I will repay it (lest I should mention to you that you owe to me even your own self as well). (19)

It was Paul's custom to dictate his letters to an amanuensis. In many of his letters, however, he wrote a closing greeting **with** his **own hand** (cf. Col. 4:18; 2 Thess. 3:17). That is not unlike a businessman dictating a letter and then signing it and adding a postscript in his own handwriting. Verses 19-25, if not the whole letter, are a handwritten note from Paul himself.

In verse 18, Paul offered to make good Onesimus's debt. As noted earlier, it is likely that Onesimus stole property or money from Philemon when he fled. Paul knew that restitution was an essential part of forgiveness, and that Onesimus did not have the means to repay Philemon. By offering in his own writing to **repay** Onesimus's debt, Paul is in effect personally signing an I.O.U. Although he was in prison, Paul probably had the financial resources to pay Onesimus's debt (cf. Phil. 4:14-18).

Then, in a parenthetical statement, Paul reminds Philemon, **you owe to me even your own self as well.** Paul's plan is to put Onesimus's debt on his account and then cancel it because Philemon owes Paul an even greater debt. Onesimus owes Philemon a material debt; Philemon owes Paul a spiritual debt. Onesimus owes Philemon a temporal debt; Philemon owes Paul an eternal one. Paul had shared the gospel with him and led him to a saving knowledge of Jesus Christ. That is a debt Philemon could never repay.

That principle applies to us as well. When someone offends us and incurs a debt, we should remember that we owe debts to others. All of us have people in our lives who have benefited us spiritually in ways we could never repay. We are in debt to them.

I am indebted to many people. I am in debt to my godly parents for leading me to Christ, teaching me the Scriptures, and encouraging me to go into the ministry. I owe them a debt for supporting me, supplying my needs, and educating me. I am in debt to them for disciplining me and holding me spiritually accountable for my behavior while growing up.

I am in debt to my wife for her friendship, love, support, wisdom and input into my life. I owe my children a debt for their kindness, concern, and care for me, and for responding to the things I have asked of them.

I am in debt to the many friends who have ministered to me. I am in debt to my teachers in college and seminary, and to the many men whose books have instructed me. I owe a debt to my co-workers and co-pastors, who share the ministry with me. I am indebted to my congregation for their support, encouragement, and fellowship.

We who owe so much to so many should be quick to forgive others who owe us a debt. Having received so many unpayable spiritual riches from so many who ask nothing in return, can I not forgive a temporal debt?

THE POSSIBILITY OF BEING A BLESSING

Yes, brother, let me benefit from you in the Lord; refresh my heart in Christ. (20)

Me and **my** are emphatic in the Greek text. Philemon has been a blessing to many people (cf. v. 7). Paul now asks to receive that blessing. **Benefit** is from *oninēmi*, the verb from which the name Onesimus derives. Paul is probably making another word play on his name (cf. v. 11). By forgiving Onesimus, Philemon would **benefit** Paul **in the Lord** by bringing him joy because of his example of obedience and love to the church. Paul urged the Philippians to "make my joy complete by being of the same mind, maintaining the same love, united in spirit, intent on one purpose" (Phil. 2:2). By forgiving Onesimus, Philemon would maintain the unity in the Colossian fellowship, and that would bring great joy to Paul. It would **refresh** his **heart in Christ;** he would be spiritually blessed. Failing to forgive Onesimus would sadden the heart of the apostle, because he dearly loved both men. It would also mar the testimony of the Colossian church before the watching world. Believers should be motivated to forgive by the knowledge that forgiveness brings joy and blessing to other believers.

THE NECESSITY OF OBEDIENCE

Having confidence in your obedience, I write to you, since I know that you will do even more than what I say. (21)

Paul had **confidence** in Philemon's **obedience** to Christ. He did not doubt Philemon's willingness to obey him (cf. v. 8), but here reminds him of the necessity of obeying Christ. Knowing Philemon's godly character (cf. vv. 4-7), Paul was confident of his response.

As already noted, we can assume Philemon was well instructed in the theology of forgiveness. He knew the principle taught in Matthew 6, that the believer's relational forgiveness from God depends on his willingness to forgive others. He knew that our Lord had taught that there must be no limits to forgiveness (Matt. 18:21-22; Luke 17:3-4). He no doubt was familiar with Paul's teaching on forgiveness (cf. 2 Cor. 2:7; Eph. 4:32; Col. 3:13). Because Philemon was aware of the commands to forgive, Paul does not repeat them.

Some have found in Paul's words **I know that you will do even more than what I say** a call for Onesimus's emancipation. Such an assumption is unwarranted (cf. v. 16). There are several other possibilities. Paul may be calling upon Philemon to welcome Onesimus back not grudgingly, but with open arms (cf. Luke 15:22-24). He may also be requesting Philemon to permit Onesimus to minister alongside him, as well as to perform menial service. Paul may also be urging Philemon to forgive others who have wronged him.

Voluntarily, not because of law, nor out of fear, but because of love, Philemon is to obey the God who commanded him to forgive.

THE ACKNOWLEDGMENT OF ACCOUNTABILITY

And at the same time also prepare me a lodging; for I hope that through your prayers I shall be given to you. (22)

Because he knew the case against him was very weak, Paul expected to be released from this first imprisonment (cf. Phil. 2:23-24). He now believes his release to be imminent, perhaps because a date for his hearing before the imperial court had been set. Accordingly, he asks Philemon to **prepare me a lodging** where he can stay when he visits

Colossae. Some years earlier, Paul had written to the Romans of his desire to go to Spain (Rom. 15:24, 28). In the intervening years, however, his plans had changed. He now intended to revisit the churches to the east before heading west.

Of all Paul's appeals to Philemon, this is the least subtle. He does not threaten Philemon, as he did the Corinthians (cf. 1 Cor. 4:21). Nevertheless, "there is a gentle compulsion in this mention of a personal visit to Colossae. The Apostle would thus be able to see for himself that Philemon had not disappointed his expectations" (J. B. Lightfoot, *St. Paul's Epistles to the Colossians and to Philemon* [1879; reprint, Grand Rapids: Zondervan, 1959], p. 345).

Paul then mentions the means by which his release will be effected. He writes to Philemon, **I hope that through your prayers I shall be given to you.** Prayers are the nerves that move the muscles of omnipotence. Prayer is not an exercise in futility because God's will will be done in any case; prayer is the means by which God's will is carried out. "The effective prayer of a righteous man," wrote James, "can accomplish much" (James 5:16). Paul understood that the sovereignty of God works its purposes through prayer.

Paul's request would certainly affect Philemon's treatment of Onesimus. Philemon could hardly pray for God to bring Paul to Colossae if he had not forgiven Onesimus. Yet if he fails to pray for Paul's release, Paul might remain in prison. The apostle deftly maneuvers Philemon into a corner from which he can extricate himself only by forgiving Onesimus. That is spiritual accountability at work.

All believers are to be accountable to those over them in the Lord. Hebrews 13:17 says, "Obey your leaders, and submit to them; for they keep watch over your souls, as those who will give an account." Because leaders are responsible for watching over those in their charge, they have the right to expect accountability from them. Acknowledgment of that accountability is a powerful motive for forgiveness.

THE IMPORTANCE OF MAINTAINING FELLOWSHIP

Epaphras, my fellow prisoner in Christ Jesus, greets you, as do Mark, Aristarchus, Demas, Luke, my fellow workers. (23-24)

The Christian life is not lived in a vacuum. Believers do not act alone, independent of the fellowship. By sending greetings from five men known to him, Paul reminds Philemon of his accountability to all of them. Failing to forgive Onesimus would disappoint their high expectations of him and bring him under their discipline.

These five are also mentioned in Colossians 4:10-14. Tychicus, who is mentioned in Colossians, is not mentioned here. As the bearer of the letters to Philemon and to the Colossians, he was able to deliver his own greetings. That Jesus Justus was mentioned in Colossians but not here implies he was unknown to Philemon. He may have been a native of Rome.

Epaphras was probably converted under the ministry of Paul. He was most likely the founder of the churches at Colossae and its neighboring cities of Laodicea and Hierapolis. He was a native of Colossae (Col. 4:12), and hence well known to Philemon. He was probably the pastor of the church that met in Philemon's home. He is described in Colossians 1:7 as "our beloved fellow bond-servant, who is a faithful servant of Christ on our behalf." From Colossians 4:12-13 we learn that he was a man devoted to prayer, with a deep pastoral concern for his people. Paul describes him as **my fellow prisoner in Christ Jesus.** It is not known whether he, too, was a prisoner, or whether he simply identified closely with Paul in the apostle's imprisonment.

Mark was John Mark, the cousin of Barnabas and author of the gospel that bears his name. His defection during the first missionary journey (Acts 13:13) led to a falling out between Paul and Barnabas (Acts 15:36-39). By now, though, Mark was a changed man. Through the discipline imposed on him by Paul, and through the tutelage of Peter (cf. 1 Pet. 5:13) and Barnabas, he had come to spiritual maturity. So valuable had he become to Paul that the apostle asked for him shortly before his death (2 Tim. 4:11).

Aristarchus was a Jewish believer (Col. 4:11), a native of Thessalonica (Acts 20:4; 27:2). He had a long association with Paul, and had been through some rough times with him. He was with Paul during the riot at Ephesus (Acts 19:29), and on the ill-fated sea voyage to Rome that ended in shipwreck (Acts 27:4). He was Paul's beloved fellow-worker, and was with him in his imprisonment (Col. 4:10). According to tradition, he was martyred in Rome during the persecutions under Nero.

Not much is known of **Demas,** but what we do know is sad. In 2 Timothy 4:10 Paul writes of him, "Demas, having loved this present world, has deserted me." He most likely was an apostate, since John wrote, "If anyone loves the world, the love of the Father is not in him" (1 John 2:15). Here, though, he was still Paul's fellow-worker.

Luke, "the beloved physician" (Col. 4:14), was a Gentile Christian doctor and the author of the third gospel. He was a frequent traveling companion of Paul, and no doubt he helped care for the apostle's frequent physical ailments. He was a faithful and loyal friend to Paul, and he alone was with him in his final days (2 Tim. 4:11).

These five men were well known to Philemon. He had the opportunity to set a good example for them by forgiving Onesimus. On the other hand, failing to forgive would fracture the bond of fellowship Philemon enjoyed with them.

THE REQUIREMENT OF GRACE

The grace of the Lord Jesus Christ be with your spirit. (25)

By now Philemon was undoubtedly convicted of his need to forgive Onesimus. In case he wondered where he would find the strength to do so, Paul adds these final words. This familiar benediction is really a prayer that Philemon, his household, and the Colossian assembly would receive the grace needed to forgive Onesimus.

Paul realizes that what he asks is not possible in the flesh, because the flesh seeks vengeance. Nor is it possible through the law, because the law demands justice. Although Philemon could not forgive Onesimus in his own strength, through **the grace of the Lord Jesus Christ,** working with his spirit, he could. Paul's prayer is that Philemon would have the same grace that allowed Christ to forgive.

CONCLUSION

The book of Philemon ends here, but not the story. How did things turn out? No doubt Philemon forgave Onesimus. It is extremely unlikely that the book would have found its way into the New Testament canon if he had not. If Philemon had not forgiven Onesimus, including the book in the canon would have left a false impression for all history. If he were not the godly, virtuous man Paul describes in this letter, there would have been no purpose in the Holy Spirit's adding it to the New Testament. Further, as a part of the canon, this book would have circulated widely in the early church. If Philemon had not forgiven Onesimus, it is inconceivable that someone would not have objected to including it in the canon. (This circulation would also confirm its authenticity.)

As to the further histories of Paul and Onesimus, Paul was released from prison, as he anticipated (cf. v. 22), and traveled extensively. One of his trips was no doubt to Colossae, where he saw for himself how Philemon had treated Onesimus.

Half a century later the church Father Ignatius, in Smyrna on his way to martyrdom in Rome, wrote a letter to the Ephesian church. In that letter he writes, "I received your large congregation in the person of Onesimus, your bishop [pastor] in this world, a man whose love is beyond words" (cited in Cyril C. Richardson, ed., *Early Christian Fathers* [New York: Macmillan, 1978], p. 88). Could this be the same man? Perhaps not, because Onesimus would have had to be very old. But if so, it would be a fitting conclusion to one of the great stories of the apostolic age.

There is a story in our own century that also illustrates the power of forgiveness. It begins at 7:55 A.M. on Sunday, December 7, 1941. In a daring surprise air raid, the Japanese attacked the United States naval base at Pearl Harbor, Hawaii. In less than two hours, 2,403 American soldiers, sailors, and civilians were killed, and another 1,178 wounded. Aircraft losses totalled 188 planes, and much of the United States Pacific Fleet was destroyed or damaged.

The raid was led by a brilliant thirty-nine year old Japanese Navy pilot named Mitsuo Fuchida, whose idol was Adolf Hitler. Although his plane was hit several times by ground fire, he survived the raid. The attack on Pearl Harbor led to the United States's entry into World War II, and ultimately to the devastation of the Japanese homeland by American conventional and atomic bombs.

After the war, Fuchida was haunted by memories of all the death he had witnessed. In an attempt to find solace, he took up farming near Osaka. His thoughts turned more and more to the problem of peace, and he decided to write a book on the subject. In his book, which he intended to call *No More Pearl Harbors*, he would urge the world to pursue peace. Fuchida struggled in vain, however, to find a principle upon which peace could be based. His story is picked up by Donald A. Rosenberger, an American naval yeoman who survived the Pearl Harbor attack. He writes,

> [Fuchida] heard two stories about prisoners of war that filled him with excitement. They seemed to illustrate the principle for which he was searching.
>
> The first report came from a friend—a lieutenant who had been captured by the Americans and incarcerated in a prisoner of war camp in America. Fuchida saw his name in a newspaper, in a list of POWs who were returning to Japan. He determined to visit him. When they met, they spoke of many things. Then Fuchida asked the question uppermost in his mind. "How did they treat you in the POW camp?" His friend said they were treated fairly well, although they suffered much mentally and spiritually. But then he told Fuchida a story which, he said, had made a great impression upon him and upon every prisoner in the camp. "Something happened at the camp where I was interred," he said, "which has made it possible for us who were in that camp to

forego all our resentment and hatred and to return with a forgiving spirit and a feeling of lightheartedness instead."

There was a young American girl, named Margaret "Peggy" Covell, whom they judged to be about twenty, who came to the camp on a regular basis doing all she could for the prisoners. She brought things to them they might enjoy, such as magazines and newspapers. She looked after their sick, and she was constantly solicitous to help them in every way. They received a great shock, however, when they asked her why she was so concerned to help them. She answered, "Because my parents were killed by the Japanese Army!"

Such a statement might shock a person from any culture, but it was incomprehensible to the Japanese. In their society, no offense could be greater than the murder of one's parents. Peggy tried to explain her motives. She said her parents had been missionaries in the Philippines. When the Japanese invaded the islands, her parents escaped to the mountains in North Luzon for safety. In due time, however, they were discovered. The Japanese charged them with being spies and told them they were to be put to death. They earnestly denied that they were spies, but the Japanese would not be convinced, and they were executed.

Peggy didn't hear about her parents' fate until the end of the war. When the report of their death reached her, her first reaction was intense anger and bitter hatred. She was furious with grief and indignation. Thoughts of her parents' last hours of life filled her with great sorrow. She envisioned them trapped, wholly at the mercy of their captors, with no way out. She saw the merciless brutality of the soldiers. She saw them facing the Japanese executioners and falling lifeless to the ground on that far-off Philippine mountain.

Then Peggy began to consider her parents' selfless love for the Japanese people. Gradually, she became convinced that they had forgiven the people God had called them to love and serve. Then it occurred to her that if her parents had died without bitterness or rancor toward their executioners, why should her attitude be different? Should she be filled with hatred and vengefulness when they had been filled with love and forgiveness? Her answer could only be, "Definitely not." Therefore she chose the path of love and forgiveness. She decided to minister to the Japanese prisoners in the nearby POW camp as a proof of her sincerity.

Fuchida was touched by this story, but he was especially impressed with the possibility that it was exactly what he had been searching for: a principle sufficient to be a basis for peace. Could it be that the answer for which he was seeking was a forgiving love, flowing from God to man, and then from man to man? Could that be principle upon which the message of his projected book, *No More Pearl Harbors* should be based?

Shortly after this, Fuchida was summoned by General Douglas MacArthur to Tokyo. As he got off the train at Shibuya station, he was handed a pamphlet entitled, "I Was a Prisoner of Japan." It told about an American sergeant, Jacob DeShazer, who had spent forty months in a Japanese prison cell and who, after the war, had come back to Japan to love and serve the Japanese people by helping them to come to know Jesus Christ.

Fuchida read the story with interest. DeShazer had been a bombardier on one of the sixteen Army B-25 airplanes which, under the leadership of General Jimmy Doolittle, had been launched on 18 April 1942 from the deck of the USS Hornet to bomb Tokyo. None of the planes were shot down, but all of them ran out of gasoline before they could be landed properly. The crew of five in the plane in which DeShazer was flying bailed out over occupied China. The next morning, they were captured and incarcerated for the duration of the war.

DeShazer notes that all prisoners were treated badly. He said that at one point he almost went insane from his violent hatred of the Japanese guards. Then one day a guard brought them a Bible. They were all in solitary confinement, so they took turns reading it. When it was De-Shazer's turn, he had it for three weeks. He read it eagerly and intensely, both Old and New Testaments. Finally, he writes, "the miracle of conversion took place June 8, 1944."

DeShazer determined that if he lived until the war was over, and if he were released, he would return the United States, devote a period of time to serious Bible study, and then return to Japan to share the message of Christ with the Japanese people. That is exactly what he did-. . . . Great crowds came to hear his story, and many responded to his invitation to receive Christ.

Fuchida was deeply impressed. Here it was again: a second example of love overcoming hatred. He sensed the power of forgiveness to actually change the hearts and lives of people. . . . Excitedly, he sensed that it could be a principle strong enough to be the basis for his projected book. He determined to learn all he could about DeShazer and his beliefs.

At the train station on his way home, he obtained a copy of the New Testament in Japanese. A few months later, he began to read two or three chapters a day in the Scriptures. . . . Then in September 1949, Fuchida read Luke 23. This was the first time he had read the story of the crucifixion.

The Calvary scene pierced Fuchida's spirit. It all came alive in St. Luke's starkly beautiful prose. In the midst of the horror of His death, Christ said, "Father, forgive them for they know not what they do." Tears sprang to Fuchida's eyes; he had reached the end of his "long, long wondering." Surely these words were the source of the love that DeShazer and Peggy Covell had shown. . . . As Jesus hung there, on the cross, He prayed not only for His persecutors but for all humanity. That meant He had prayed and died for Fuchida, a Japanese man living in the twentieth century. ("What Happened to the Man Who Led the Attack on Pearl Harbor?" *Command*, Fall/Winter 1991, pp. 6-8. Used by permission.)

By the time Fuchida finished reading Luke, he had received the Lord Jesus Christ. He did end up writing his book and entitled it *From Pearl Harbor to Golgotha*. His life verse, which he signed under his every signature, was Luke 23:34: "Father, forgive them for they know not what they do."

Forgiveness has a tremendous power to affect the world. God knew it, Paul knew it, and Philemon needed to know it. The Holy Spirit knew that all men and women needed to know it, and that's why this wonderful little letter was included in Scripture. May we take its message to heart.

Bibliography

Abbott, T. K. *A Critical and Exegetical Commentary on the Epistles to the Ephesians and to the Colossians.* Edinburgh: T & T Clark, 1985.

Barclay, William. *The Letters to the Philippians, Colossians, and Thessalonians.* Rev. ed. Philadelphia: Westminster, 1975.

_____. *The Letters to Timothy, Titus, and Philemon.* Rev. ed. Philadelphia: Westminster, 1975.

Barnes, Albert. *Barnes' Notes on the Old & New Testaments: Ephesians, Philippians, and Colossians.* Grand Rapids: Baker, 1974.

_____. *Barnes' Notes on the Old & New Testaments: Thessalonians, Timothy, Titus and Philemon.* Grand Rapids: Baker, 1975.

Barrett, William. *Irrational Man.* Garden City, N. Y.: Doubleday, 1962.

Bruce, F. F. *The Epistles to the Colossians, to Philemon, and to the Ephesians.* Grand Rapids: Eerdmans, 1984.

Carson, Herbert M. *The Epistles of Paul to the Colossians and Philemon.* Grand Rapids: Eerdmans, 1982.

Chesnut, D. Lee. *The Atom Speaks.* San Diego: Creation-Science Research Center, 1973.

Dana, H. E., and Julius R. Mantey. *A Manual Grammar of the Greek New Testament.* New York: Macmillan, 1927.

DeYoung, Donald B. "Design in Nature: The Anthropic Principle." *Impact* 149 (November 1985).

Eadie, John. *A Commentary on the Greek Text of the Epistle of Paul to the Colossians*. Reprint. Grand Rapids: Baker, 1979.

Erdman, Charles R. *The Epistles of Paul to the Colossians and to Philemon*. Philadelphia: Westminster, 1966.

Gromacki, Robert G. *Stand Perfect in Wisdom: An Exposition of Colossians and Philemon*. Grand Rapids: Baker, 1981.

Guiness, Os. *The Dust of Death*. Downers Grove, Ill.: InterVarsity, 1973.

Guthrie, Donald. *New Testament Introduction*. Downers Grove, Ill.: InterVarsity, 1970.

Harrison, Everett F. *Colossians: Christ All-Sufficient*. Chicago: Moody, 1971.

Hendriksen, William. *Philippians, Colossians and Philemon*. Grand Rapids: Baker, 1964.

Henry, Matthew. *Matthew Henry's Commentary on the Whole Bible*. Vol. 6. Old Tappan, N.J. Revell, n.d.

Ironside, H. A. *Lectures on the Epistle to the Colossians*. New York: Loizeaux, 1928.

Jastrow, Robert, and Malcolm H. Thompson. *Astronomy: Fundamentals and Frontiers*. New York: John Wiley & Sons, 1977.

Kent, Homer A. *Treasures of Wisdom: Studies in Colossians & Philemon*. Grand Rapids: Baker, 1978.

Lenski, R. C. H. *The Interpretation of St. Paul's Epistles to the Colossians, to the Thessalonians, to Timothy, to Titus and to Philemon*. Minneapolis: Augsburg, 1946.

Lightfoot, J. B. *St. Paul's Epistles to the Colossians and to Philemon*. 1879. Reprint. Grand Rapids: Zondervan, 1959.

Maclaren, Alexander. *The Epistles of St. Paul to the Colossians and Philemon*. New York: A. C. Armstrong and Son, 1903.

Morris, Henry M. *The Biblical Basis for Modern Science*. Grand Rapids: Baker, 1984.

Moule, H. C. G. *Colossian Studies*. New York: Hodder and Stoughton, n.d.

Nieder, John, and Thomas Thompson. *Forgive and Love Again*. Eugene, Oreg.: Harvest House, 1991.

Richardson, Cyril C. *Early Christian Fathers*. New York: Macmillan, 1978.

Rienecker, Fritz, and Cleon Rogers. *Linguistic Key to the Greek New Testament*. Grand Rapids: Zondervan, 1982.

Robertson, A. T. *Word Pictures in the New Testament*. Vol. 4, *The Epistles of Paul*. Nashville: Broadman, 1931.

Rosenberger, Donald A. "What Happened to the Man Who Led the Attack on Pearl Harbor?" *Command*, Fall/Winter, 1991.

Rupprecht, Arthur A. "Philemon." In *The Expositor's Bible Commentary*, vol. 11. Grand Rapids: Zondervan, 1978.

Schaeffer, Francis. *Escape from Reason*. Downer's Grove, Ill.: InterVarsity, 1972.

_____. *He Is There and He Is Not Silent*. Wheaton, Ill.: Tyndale, 1972.

_____. *The God Who Is There*. Downers Grove, Ill.: InterVarsity, 1968.

Schlatter, Adolf. *The Church in the New Testament Period*. London: SPCK, 1955.

Smith, M. A. *From Christ to Constantine*. Downer's Grove, Ill.: InterVarsity, 1973.

Vaughan, Curtis. "Colossians." In *The Expositor's Bible Commentary*, vol. 11. Grand Rapids: Zondervan, 1978.

Vincent, Marvin R. *Word Studies in the New Testament*. Vol. 3, *The Epistles of Paul*. New York: Scribner's, 1904.

Vine, W. E. *An Expository Dictionary of New Testament Words*. Old Tappan, N. J.: Revell, 1966.

Wuest, Kenneth S. *Wuest's Word Studies from the Greek New Testament*. Vol. 1. Grand Rapids: Eerdmans, 1973.

Indexes

Index of Greek Words

Index of Scripture

Index of Subjects